INTERWEAVING CURRICULUM AND CLASSROOM ASSESSMENT

INTERWEAVING CURRICULUM AND CLASSROOM ASSESSMENT

Engaging the 21st-Century Learner

Susan M. Drake
Joanne L. Reid
Wendy Kolohon

OXFORD
UNIVERSITY PRESS

OXFORD
UNIVERSITY PRESS

Oxford University Press is a department of the University of Oxford.
It furthers the University's objective of excellence in research, scholarship,
and education by publishing worldwide. Oxford is a registered trade mark of
Oxford University Press in the UK and in certain other countries.

Published in Canada by
Oxford University Press
8 Sampson Mews, Suite 204,
Don Mills, Ontario M3C 0H5 Canada

www.oupcanada.com

Library and Archives Canada Cataloguing in Publication
Drake, Susan M., 1944–, author
Interweaving curriculum and classroom assessment : engaging
the twenty-first-century learner / Susan M. Drake, Joanne L. Reid, and
Wendy Kolohon.

Includes bibliographical references and index.
ISBN 978–0–19–544748–4 (pbk.)

1. Curriculum planning. 2. Education—Curricula. 3. Interdisciplinary
approach in education. I. Reid, Joanne L., author II. Kolohon, Wendy, author
III. Title.

LB2806.15.D73 2013   375'.001   C2013-904619-4

Cover image: © Karmen Smolnikar/Flickr Open/Getty Images.com

Printed and bound in Canada

1 2 3 4 — 17 16 15 14

Contents

Preface

Writing this book as a collaborative endeavour has been a challenging learning experience. We live miles apart from each other, are extremely busy in our working lives, and our educational careers have gone in very different directions. But we have all spent many years in the field and share a passion about education.

Susan and Joanne had known each other previously and spent several years teaching in the same secondary school before Joanne moved to another school board. Wendy was the "newcomer" in that she worked at a different school board and was unknown to Joanne. She met Susan at an Ontario Ministry of Education conference, after which they worked together in various capacities—most often around developing and implementing integrated curriculum.

The three of us began our discussions about this book one summer at a cottage with our partners in tow. Over collaboratively cooked meals and an occasional glass of wine, we shared our educational philosophies and experiences. We turned the kitchen table into a makeshift workspace; a projector projected onto a white sheet tacked to the pine-panelled wall. Here we outlined what the book would look like and had our first conversations with twenty-first–century teachers across Canada. It was all a bit challenging without the Internet for most of the time, but by the end of that first summer we sent three chapters and the introduction to our editor in October as promised.

What we did not anticipate was that our initial face-to-face writing would become outdated so rapidly. Technology was shifting what was happening in the field. We felt like we were at a turning point and racing against the clock. The first three chapters had to be rewritten to reflect those changes.

In retrospect, that summer was a luxury. The three of us never met together again, although Susan and Joanne met on occasion as geography was not as great an obstacle. Nevertheless, our threesome became a dynamic writing partnership over the next two years.

To collaborate and to write about curriculum and assessment in the twenty-first century, we found we needed to become twenty-first–century learners ourselves. We wrote much of the book on Google Docs. We would meet on Skype to discuss and revise the text. Of course this wasn't a perfect method; for example, we ran into frustrations with formatting the many figures and tables when we uploaded them in Microsoft Word to send to Oxford.

We learned so much from the teachers in this book, and the many more who do not appear in the text yet were so generous with their time and thoughts. We knew few of these teachers before we started; we still have never met them in person. In fact, we found many of them through Twitter. We would come across an interesting tweet and send the person a direct message. Once we had made contact, we would Skype or Google chat with the person. Often the teachers we contacted had blogs that we would follow or had websites to explore. Sometimes someone would recommend someone else that we should talk to. And so we each developed a personal learning network.

As we wrote this book, we became excited by what we were hearing and seeing. We believe it is time for a new story in education. What we didn't know was that a new story was already unfolding in many places across Canada. We liked what we saw. These teachers were amazing, innovative, thoughtful professionals. They took risks and tried interesting things—but at the same time they were grounded in sound principles of teaching and learning.

Where do we go from here? Will things continue to change so rapidly that we can't keep up? Rapid change seems inevitable indeed. We believe that this book offers the basic tools for curriculum/assessment design that can act as the bedrock for the uncertainties of the future. We offer you a vision, however temporary, of twenty-first–century education and invite you to be a part of it.

Acknowledgements

Writing this book has been a fascinating and challenging experience. We are so grateful to the educators who shared their stories and insights with us—their experiences made this book possible. We thank them for their expertise and their willingness to show how the new story of education is happening across Canada today.

We thank the reviewers who all had a strong vision of curriculum/assessment in the twenty-first century; their visions enriched ours. Their thoughtful comments made a significant difference in our revisions and made for a lively dialogue among us. Michael Savage has had extensive experience with these ideas and was very helpful both during the writing and review process. We also thank our editors from Oxford University Press.

Finally, we thank our partners and family members. Without the support and patience of Michael Manley-Casimir, Stephen Sprague, and Mark Kolohon we could not have sustained the focus and energy this project required. Thank you.

Introduction: The Twenty-First–Century Learning Experience

This book is for twenty-first–century educators who need to be accountable but also want to offer students rich, rigorous, and relevant educational experiences. The educators from across Canada whom you will meet in this book are doing exactly this—balancing accountability and relevance. They work toward student improvement at the same time as they innovate within their classrooms to help students reach their full potential. They are teachers with a passion for teaching and with a moral purpose—they care deeply about their students and their growth. Many are exploring the potential of technology to enhance the learning in their classrooms and in their professional lives. And they are striving, as learners themselves, to improve their own practice.

Our goal is to help educators understand the relationships among *curriculum, instruction,* and *assessment* and how to interweave the three to foster a twenty-first–century learning culture. Curriculum, instruction, and assessment are often discussed in separate conversations. A curriculum book might mention assessment, but it is not a central focus. Similarly, an assessment book may offer information on psychometric principles, how to create a variety of assessment tasks, and how to create effective assessment tools such as rubrics and checklists, but rarely are these tasks and tools connected to curriculum design. Yet a third book might focus on instructional strategies without considering curriculum or assessment. We think our book is different because we look at curriculum, instruction, and assessment as an interdependent system.

We chose the title *Interweaving Curriculum and Classroom Assessment: Engaging the Twenty-First–Century Learner* because we wanted an image or metaphor that would convey concisely how curriculum, instruction, and assessment are interdependent and dynamic parts of a system. Our metaphor is of a tapestry—hence "weaving." Curriculum, instruction, and assessment are threads that are seamlessly interwoven to create a rich learning experience.

In Canada, education is a provincial responsibility and there have been few pan-Canadian conversations. Each province has different policies and favoured practices. Yet across the country there are many similarities—similarities that can also be found in international education systems. This book presents a perspective on education that is relevant to the current trends and policies found across Canada and beyond.

A Framework for a New Story for Education

We live in a world that is changing in fundamental ways given globalization and rapid technological advancement. We know what educators from across the globe are doing and we can learn from each other. Every day new technology applications provide teachers and students with ways of learning that were not imaginable in the near past. These conditions call upon educators to create a new story for the twenty-first century.

And students themselves want change. Most telling is student engagement in schools. Levels of student social, academic, and intellectual engagement are generally low. The "What Did You Do in School Today?" survey of 32,000 students from across Canada found that intellectual engagement dropped from 60% in Grade 6 to 30% by Grade 10. Attendance declined steadily from 90% in Grade 6 to below 50% by Grade 12 (Willms, Friesen, & Milton, 2009).

To participate in the creation of this new story, it is helpful to understand the change process (Fullan, 2013). The Story Model framework (Drake, 2010) is one way to understand this process (see Figure I.1).

The Story Model describes a change process in expanding contexts from the personal to the social, cultural, global, and universal. The frames of the Story Model represent ways of knowing. Our knowing is filtered first through a frame informed by our personal experiences. The students in your class will all learn a bit differently because they will connect new knowledge with their unique past experiences. Your personal frame will also affect your own learning. The second frame is a cultural frame; culture is defined as the set of values and beliefs that drive group life in the particular culture we live in. The cultural assumptions we make and act upon are often taken for granted. In this book we explore learning through the frame of Canadian cultural diversity. You

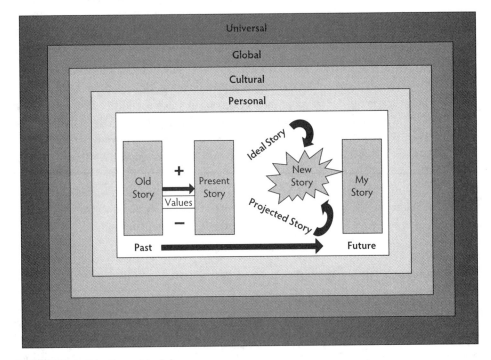

FIGURE I.1 The Story Model

and your students may have many more specific cultural frames, such as nationality, community, geographic region, language, race, ethnicity, or religion. The third frame is the global frame. In the twenty-first century, we are all connected to and affected by global conditions, and the global frame is evident in education. Students in classrooms around the world collaboratively engage in tasks ranging from peer editing to sharing ideas about solutions to global problems. The outer frame is the universal frame. This frame reminds us that, regardless of our differences, we are all human beings with similar needs, drives, and emotions. In education, for example, the focus on bullying derives its impetus from a fundamental human need to belong and to be accepted. The first three frames suggest our knowing is informed by individual or social differences; the universal frame also informs our ways of knowing and speaks to the aspects that connect us to others.

There are four assumptions to the Story Model:

1) All humans make meaning through story. When we talk about a "story" we are describing a general story that captures the essence of most people's experiences (although the actual individual story will be different for each of us, given the frames of knowing described above). As well, there is always an emerging new story as the world continues to unfold in amazing and unpredictable ways.

2) The present story, or "now," is in a state of change or transformation. Some parts of the old story remain relevant while others have become dysfunctional. A catalytic question is "What parts of the old story no longer work and why?"

3) The process of creating the new story is a dialectical one. We shift back and forth between two opposites or polarities until the two polarities are reconciled or synthesized and a new story becomes the taken-for-granted way. For example, whole language and phonics have often been seen as two polarities. In the new story, phonics is taught in the context of whole language. Rather than either/or, it is both/and.

4) Humans can create a new story based on a new set of values and beliefs that are consciously chosen collectively. Each of us can choose to participate in the creation of the new story. Wearing seatbelts is a good example. Initially, as a "new story," people had to train themselves to wear seatbelts. Now, wearing seatbelts is so embedded in our culture that it has become an expected behaviour rather than an emerging new story. The change in behaviour came about through the combined forces of research on safety, public education, and legislation and enforcement. Given these forces, people's perceptions shifted back and forth between initial doubt and resistance (old story) to acceptance (new story). There are many new stories in the making that are currently changing our personal and public lives. They include the sexual orientation story, the smoking cessation story, women's increased equality (which is not true for all countries), and recently the story related to bullying.

What Is the Old Story?

In the past century, two seemingly opposite approaches or polarities dominated education. This resulted in a dialectical process between the two polarities that represented two different, sometimes conflicting or competing, beliefs and resulting behaviours. One of these approaches we shall call the **traditional approach**, although it is also called the transmission or **factory model** approach. The alternative approach is called the **constructivist approach**. Sewell (2005) differentiated between the two as *outcome-based* and *experience-based* approaches, respectively.

Albertan educators Sharon Friesen and David Jardine (2009) elaborate on the traditional and constructivist models of education in an interesting paper for the Western and Northern Canadian Protocol. For them (and us) it is important to understand the assumptions that underlie the traditional and constructivist models of education to move forward into the twenty-first century.

The traditional model of schooling is grounded in the principles outlined by American mechanical engineer Frederick Taylor (1911) who sought to make factory work more efficient. Taylor's principles included standardization; small, highly specific tasks; hierarchical roles; and compliance from the workers. Philosophically, the traditional orientation is grounded in **analytic philosophy**, propounded by John Locke (1693) and Francis Bacon (see a collection of Bacon's major work, edited by Vickers, 2002). Analytic philosophy focuses on logically precise language to describe phenomena. Mandated content-based curriculum outcomes reflect this idea. Such curriculum assumes that knowledge is derived from **empirical research** and the application of the **scientific method**. The mind is viewed as a blank slate (*tabula rasa*)—the teacher transmits established knowledge to an empty vessel. From a psychological perspective, the learning process is considered a physiological mechanism of stimulus response. This paradigm reflects the views of behavioural psychologists who saw human learners as passive beings who respond to positive and negative reinforcements (Thorndike, 1911; Skinner, 1954, 1968). Thus, the teacher was seen as an expert who transmitted knowledge, and the students were passive learners working in isolation in individual seats. All students received the same curriculum delivered at the same time in the same way (usually by lecture); knowledge was organized into disciplines; the three Rs (reading, writing, and arithmetic) represented the fundamental learning blocks that students must attain first; knowledge acquisition was evaluated based on paper-and-pencil measures (tests); standardized tests allowed for rank-ordering of students in a class, region, province, or country; and competition and power were underlying values.

In contrast is the constructivist approach. In the 1930s, **progressive education** was a popular constructivist approach grounded in the work of John Dewey (1938, 1966). Through a pragmatist lens, Dewey emphasized democracy, problem solving (with the scientific method), and student growth. Psychologist Jean Piaget's work (1963) recognized that stages of cognitive development influenced learning. Later, Lawrence Kohlberg (1981) introduced stages of moral and personal development. Lev Vygotsky's (1978) concept of social constructivism broadened the theory of constructivism—we make meaning by interacting with others; learners construct their own knowledge through interactions with their teachers and peers.

From this perspective, students connect their learning to past experiences; knowledge is indeterminate and there is not one right answer; and the teacher is a facilitator who interacts with students. Since learning is a social endeavour, students may work in groups, and large projects are favoured as a way of learning; integrating the curriculum helps students learn the knowledge and skills necessary to complete the project. Students learn at different paces and at different times, which is addressed through differentiation. Assessment revolves around performance demonstrations, and teachers give ongoing feedback to students. Collaboration and equity are underlying values.

Education policy and practice during the twentieth century shifted between the traditional approach and the constructivist approach, much like the swinging of a pendulum. A look at how policy and practice changed in Ontario is typical of most jurisdictions in North America (see Figure I.2). Across North America, neither the traditional nor constructivist orientation endured completely; elements of each remained as policy and practice shifted.

In general, this is how the pendulum swung throughout North America. A period that focused on academic content and accountability ignited concerns that the students were unmotivated to learn, which prompted a shift in policy toward a more student-centred model of curriculum (i.e., a more constructivist model). Then, a period of implementation of the constructivist model stirred public questions about academic rigor and assessment standards. This lack of confidence shifted attention back to a more standardized,

Year	Approach	Policy/Practice Change
1840–1936	Traditional	Drive for standardization and segregated disciplines
1937–1950	Constructivist Progressive	Progressive elementary curriculum and the enterprise method (project based)
1951–1966	Traditional	Back to scientific segregated curriculum
1967–1974	Constructivist Progressive	Hall-Dennis Report influences humanized decentralized curriculum
1975–1993	Traditional	Back to traditional approach to increase accountability
1994–1997	Constructivist Progressive	*The Common Curriculum* approach organizes learning into four broad subject areas
1998–2003	Traditional	*The Ontario Curriculum* emphasizes rigorous segregation and standards
2004–present	Both	Synthesis of traditional and constructivist progressive

FIGURE I.2 Shifting between Traditional and Constructivist Approaches
Source: Adapted from Clausen & Drake (2010).

content-based curriculum and testing for accountability purposes. In the mid-1990s, for example, there was a profound shift toward accountability across North America and internationally. Large-scale testing became the trusted measure of academic achievement and top-down, mandated, standards-based curriculum became the norm. Yet the public was still uncertain and dissatisfied. Had the accountability agenda narrowed the curriculum? Were students engaged in their learning? Were students prepared to succeed in a global economy?

Toward the New Story

For many educators, twenty-first–century education demands a new story (Friesen & Jardine, 2009; Barbar, Donnelly, & Rizvi, 2012). The new story does not seek to dismiss the old—it would be unwise to throw the baby out with the bathwater! We need to identify and build into the emerging new story the positive aspects from the traditional and constructivist paradigms that are still very much with us. But the new story must also consider the power of technology to accelerate learning and be open to new and perhaps unimaginable innovations that promote learning. It will be a dialectical process, and one that is disrupted from the margins (Horn, 2013).

We have the power to create this new story. Indeed, Canadian media and technology guru Donald Tapscott (2012) urges Canadians to see this time in history as an exciting opportunity to do just that. Creating the new story does not happen overnight—there will be resistance, as is inevitable in any change process. Indeed, to make it happen educators who believe in this vision need to make it "My Story" through our practices as educators. The teachers you will meet in this book offer wonderful examples of how each of us can be a part of creating the new story within the confines of our provincial cultural story.

Our Stories

Susan Drake is a full professor at Brock University in the Faculty of Education. She holds a Master of Education (M.Ed.) in foundations of teaching and learning from Brock University and a Ph.D. in curriculum from the University of Toronto. She has been in education for over 40 years and has taught at all levels. She spent half of her career as a teacher, primarily teaching physical education and health and English in secondary school. In the second half of Susan's career at Brock's Faculty of Education she researched innovative curriculum and assessment practices in the context of educational reform. She is particularly interested in technology as a powerful influence on pedagogy.

Joanne Reid also worked as a secondary school educator, teaching English, history, and social science for many years. She took on many different roles, including literacy resource/student success teacher and school improvement coordinator. Currently, Joanne is working in the area of literacy and large-scale assessment. She is also a doctoral student who is interested in assessment and integrated curriculum. She is particularly focused on the collaborative writing process.

Wendy Kolohon taught elementary school for 15 years, during which she taught all subjects and grades, including a self-contained classroom for students with special needs. Wendy has two specialist qualifications in reading and special education. She was a system lead teacher at the board level for six years, where she facilitated K–12 teachers and administrators working with new curriculum and assessment models such as those represented in this book. Her Master's research focused on interdisciplinary planning, teaching, and learning. Currently she is an administrator at a K–12 school.

The Chapters Ahead

In Chapter 1 we discuss the relationship among curriculum, instruction, and assessment in the traditional and constructivist approaches to education. We look specifically at models of curriculum, instruction, and assessment through a traditional and constructivist lens. We also offer guiding principles for sound assessment practices regardless of paradigm. To finish, we offer a view of the new story that is emerging across Canada given the dramatic changes in technology. We take a **both/and approach**; that is, we believe that synthesizing the best of both the traditional and constructivist approaches provides a strong foundation for accountable and relevant curriculum in the twenty-first century.

In Chapter 2 we explore two topics: knowing your students and knowing your curriculum. With respect to curriculum, we define the concepts of "Know, Do, and Be" (KDB) and look at how to identify them in curriculum documents. The "Know" is Big Ideas and Enduring Understandings, the "Do" is twenty-first–century skills, and the "Be" is how we want students to be in the world, for example, living as ethical citizens. We develop the concept of the KDB umbrella as a way to synthesize what is most important to know, do, and be according to policy and curriculum outcomes. We explore how the architecture of a unifying framework for K–12 curriculum influences and aligns the KDB. Chapter 2 also considers why it is important to really know your students and offers ways to do so.

Chapter 3 discusses the three steps of the backward design process: (a) determine the learning goals using provincial curriculum documents; (b) design a rich performance assessment task and create appropriate assessment tools to assess the demonstration of student learning; and (c) create daily learning experiences that will prepare students to demonstrate the learning goals. We offer integrative thinking as a skill that is necessary in backward design. In this chapter we walk through the design of a sample disciplinary curriculum unit. Although we use Grade 10 history as an example, we intend the sample to be generic and applicable to all grades and subjects. Assessment is interwoven throughout the design. We finish with a discussion on assessment for learning (AfL).

Chapter 4 explores inquiry learning and integrated models. We use examples from the field to demonstrate the principles of inquiry learning from both a disciplinary lens followed by more interdisciplinary examples. We then explore interdisciplinary or integrated models of learning. We look at a rationale for this type of learning in the twenty-first century, including recent research to support such models. We present a continuum of integration as a way of distinguishing the many different ways that educators are designing and implementing curriculum. We offer many examples of teachers who are integrating the curriculum to motivate and engage students while also addressing curriculum mandates.

Chapter 5 further explores the concept of integrated curriculum. First we look at the five Ws: what, why, where, when, and who. Then we look at the how. Here we walk through the development of an integrated unit. We use Grade 4 as a target grade, but we hope that the reader sees that the skills can be applied to any grade and any level. AfL is interwoven throughout the unit. We follow the unit with a discussion of how assessment in an integrated context is different than in a disciplinary one.

We wondered if Chapter 6, the final chapter, should actually appear first in this book because this chapter is about you—the twenty-first–century educator. We look at personal stories and the living contradiction that teachers experience when they can't be the teacher they aspire to be. We explore Fullan's (2013) concept of twenty-first–century learning through the eyes of the educators we interviewed across Canada. Finally, we return to "Your Story." Who are you as a teacher? What are your values? In what ways are you willing to commit to creating a new story?

Professional Discussion Questions

1) How do the frames of learning around the Story Model (see Figure I.1) affect your understanding of education?

2) Read Friesen and Jardine's (2009) in-depth analysis of the old and new stories in education. Identify the values and beliefs behind the practices of the factory model of schooling and the constructivist approach. What has been your experience as a student? How do you think people learn best? The article is available at http://education.alberta.ca/media/1087278/wncp%2021st%20cent%20learning%20(2).pdf.

3) The "new story" also affects teacher education. Read Susan Drake's (2010) article "Enhancing Canadian Teacher Education Using a Story Framework." To what extent is your personal experience of teacher education reflective of the "new story"? The article is available at http://ir.lib.uwo.ca/cgi/viewcontent.cgi?article=1012&context=cjsotl_rcacea.

4) The future of education is a topic of lively conversation and creative exploration. There are many YouTube videos available on twenty-first–century education. How do these videos influence the way you think about your role in education? (See, for example, Sir Ken Robinson [www.ted.com/talks/lang/en/ken_robinson_changing_education_paradigms.html], the New Brunswick Department of Education [www.ourschool.ca/21st-century-education-in-new-brunswick-canada], and the Alberta Department of Education [http://education.alberta.ca/department/ipr/curriculum.aspx].)

1

Toward a New Story of Curriculum, Instruction, and Assessment

In this chapter, you will learn about:

- Descriptions of curriculum, instruction, and assessment
- Existing models of curriculum, instruction, and assessment
- A new story for education in the twenty-first century

In this chapter, we will explore approaches to curriculum, instruction, and assessment through the lens of the Story Model presented in the Introduction. This will help us understand where we have come from in order to see where we are going as we create a twenty-first–century story for education. Finally, we will explore what the new story looks like as it is emerging in practice.

What Is Curriculum?

Definitions of curriculum range from content, a set of subjects, or a program of studies to everything that is taught in school. Curriculum can be formal or informal. Formal curriculum is outlined in provincial Ministry of Education documents and course syllabuses. Informal curriculum includes the knowledge, skills, and attitudes gained in extracurricular activities and outside school activities. As well, there is the hidden or unintended curriculum—what students learn through what is said and not said by their teachers and peers, such as gender roles and how to play the "game of school" successfully.

Curriculum reformist and progressive educator Hilda Taba (1962) suggested that all curricula have certain elements such as a diagnosis of needs, objectives, selection and organization of content, and effective ways to teach that content, followed by a program of evaluation to see if objectives have been achieved. Instructional strategies are a part of the curriculum design process.

Other theorists focus on experiences—the experience itself enhances student growth (Tanner & Tanner, 1995). However, not all experiences are educative (Dewey, 1938). As explained by curriculum theorist Peter Hlebowitsh (2005), an educational experience must be "by design (and by operation, and ultimately, by effect) responsive to the nature of the learner, to the values of society, and to some framework of useful and empowering knowledge" (p. 8).

Joseph Schwab (1983), professor of education and the sciences at the University of Chicago, focused on curriculum development/revision as a deliberative endeavour. For

Snapshot of Informal Curriculum

When students conduct collaborative action research, education can shift from being student-centred to student driven. Such an example is that of four Aboriginal Grade 10 students from Timmins High and Vocational School who attended the 2012 provincial Student Research Symposium in Toronto.

At the symposium, these students learned the principles of action research and then designed an evocative research question based on their own experiences as Aboriginal youth who had relocated to further their education. Their research question was "What are the experiences that Aboriginal youth have as they transition to Timmins High and Vocational School?"

Following standard research procedure, the students administered a survey to 62 interested and self-identified Aboriginal students. Survey questions sought information on demographics, daily challenges, inclusion, the transition process, and related supports.

The researchers were surprised to discover that the surveyed students had similar experiences to their own. As members of the school's Aboriginal Youth Advisory Committee (AYAC), the researchers set up a series of activities to address the concerns of the students. They invited speakers to share their knowledge of cultural traditions and celebrations, and they also held an Anishinaabe Olympics. The researchers did not stop there. More Aboriginal students joined the AYAC, and non-Aboriginal students joined the Olympics. A student outreach team presented the research to Cochrane High School students and staff. One of the AYAC members travelled to her home community to share the research results with local education directors, who in turn offered practical suggestions for further implementation.

This example of collaborative action research shows the power of informal student-driven education and its positive effects on the school and community. This project was a part of the Ontario Ministry of Education's SpeakUp initiative to promote student voice.

him, curriculum designers need to consider four interconnected commonplaces: learners, teachers, the subject matter, and the milieu (educational environment). Schwab cautions curriculum designers that when one of these commonplaces changes, the other three also change. If, for example, the teacher changes, then there is a corresponding change in the learners, content, and environment. If curriculum designers concentrate on only one or two commonplaces, the result is an unbalanced curriculum. In other words, Schwab sees curriculum design as an interconnected and dynamic system.

Still other theorists move beyond the school building and what happens in schools. Canadians Jean Clandinin and Michael Connelly define curriculum as "life" (1992, p. 393). William Pinar and his colleagues stretch the definition of curriculum to include symbolic representations that refer to institutional and discursive practices, structures, images, and experiences. These representations can be explored in many ways, such as politically, racially, autobiographically, theologically, and through gender (Pinar, Reynolds, Slattery, & Taubman, 1995).

We agree with and use the definition of curriculum provided in the International Baccalaureate Learner Profile (International Baccalaureate Organization, 2009). Curriculum is

- what is to be learned (the written curriculum), which we consider curriculum content,
- how it is to be learned (the taught curriculum), which we consider instruction, and
- how it is to be assessed (the learned curriculum), which is assessment.

This definition recognizes the balanced triad of content, teaching methodologies, and assessment practices, which all work together in an interdependent and systematic way.

MODELS OF CURRICULUM

In the 20th century, curriculum policy shifted back and forth in various degrees between traditional and constructivist approaches. Here we explore four models: the traditional model and three that are associated with constructivism—project-based learning, holistic education, and social reconstruction.

The Traditional Model

The traditional approach to education was described in the Introduction. The teacher is usually the person at the front of the class lecturing, while students sit in separate seats in rows and listen. The teacher delivers the content to the students, so lessons are teacher-centred. Much of the work for students involves memorization. Students learn alone, with limited social interaction. Behaviour and learning are reinforced by rewards and restrictions. Learning is evaluated by pencil-and-paper measures and sometimes standardized tests. This method of direct instruction can be efficient for large groups and for a portion of the population, usually university-bound academics, and there remains a place for some of the practices from this model today.

Project-Based Learning

Although "doing a project" is often used as an instructional and assessment task, **project-based learning** is a more comprehensive approach that is grounded in constructivist learning, content mastery, and critical thinking. Students in project-based learning classrooms do not learn content in a traditional transmission method and then apply that knowledge to a project. Instead, they learn *while doing* the project, because the project is the vehicle for simultaneous instruction and application. Students apply an inquiry process to answer an open-ended "driving question" that arises out of their genuine interest and desire to know. The problem or question comes first. It determines what content knowledge and skills students need to solve/answer it. For example, a student built a wind turbine to see if it could provide sufficient power to run her iPod.

In addition to an in-depth exploration of content, project-based learning incorporates **twenty-first–century skills** such as inquiry and research, critical thinking and problem solving, organization, collaboration, and communication. Because student voice and decision making are valued components of project-based learning, engagement and relevancy are likely.

Project-based learning meets accountability requirements through the assessment of process *and* product. Students often work together to produce a publicly presented product, demonstration, or performance. Learning is assessed on an individual basis using criteria on a rubric that makes learning targets clear.

Many examples of projects as well as assessment tools and strategies are posted online. Rich sources of information and examples include the Buck Institute for Education (www.bie.org), the International Education and Resource Network (www.iearn-canada.org), and Edutopia (www.edutopia.org/project-based-learning). Alberta Learning offers background information on inquiry-based learning online (http://education.alberta.ca/media/313361/focusoninquiry.pdf). Canada's SchoolNet Project-Based Collaborative Learning Teachers' Guide (www.tact.fse.ulaval.ca/ang/html/projectg.html) offers historical and theoretical information as well as implementation strategies.

Snapshot of Classroom Project-Based Learning

David Wees from British Columbia described an example of project-based learning from his Grade 9 math class. He posed a driving question: "What would be the best cellphone plan for him to buy?" The question took students 10 weeks to answer and involved them in many different layers of mathematical inquiry and application. Students were required to research and problem solve.

First, they researched the multitude of choices and narrowed them down by developing criteria as the basis for evaluating a good cellphone plan. To establish criteria, they had to determine a number of factors, such as the typical usage for someone of David's age. They needed to graph the equation of intersecting lines (curricular outcome), which usually required several attempts. Students constantly came up against new considerations, such as adding texting or call display to the plan.

AfL (assessment for learning, which will be discussed later in this chapter) occurred throughout discussion and observation as students made their own comparisons and judgments. Students were making meaning (constructivist) when they judged whether their plans made sense. Each student presented answers based on his or her unique assumptions, and each student offered a choice that was plausible, well-reasoned, and backed by evidence. David was pleased with the level of student engagement in the task and with students' understanding of the processes they used. Students were guided by an assessment rubric based on the standard rubric for the International Baccalaureate Middle Years Programme for Mathematics. The rubric focused on problem solving, particularly related to graphing, and on communication.

A variation of David's rubric can be found at https://docs.google.com/document/d/1rHWkPaW4k_stmLLntMzOhJ8n6cROneGmqP3SEcOVLKc/edit?usp=sharing.

Holistic Curriculum

Holistic curriculum considers teaching the whole child—body, mind, and spirit. The basic philosophy is that everything—subjects, mind, body, spirit—is interconnected (Emerson, 1903; Huxley, 1970; Miller, 2007). Psychologists Abraham Maslow (1970) and Carl Rogers (1969) were influential in offering the concept of humanism as a fundamental aspect of education.

In practice, the holistic model enacts most of the qualities of a constructivist classroom within the context of the whole child. In Toronto, Equinox Holistic Alternative School is dedicated to the holistic teaching and learning philosophy, allowing for the child's mind, heart, body, and spirit to be engaged in his or her day-to-day learning. The Equinox School is based on the seven principles in John P. Miller's (2007) book *The Holistic Curriculum*; the principles are organized around connected learning: community, earth, inner, body–mind, subject, intuition, and inquiry. Storytelling is an important part of their teachings, as is outdoor education. Kindergarten children spend most of their day outside, while the students in Grades 1 to 6 take part in weekly afternoon outings to local parks, ravines, and woodland areas, observing and interacting with their environment (Toronto District School Board, n.d.).

Teachers in a subject area can also teach holistically. Spanish teacher Michelle Metcalfe from British Columbia trained as a primary teacher but ended up teaching high school Spanish. At first she taught in a traditional way that emphasized structure and grammar. Prompted by the realization that storytelling captured her students' attention, she discovered the **teaching precision through reading and storytelling** (TPRS) method (see http://en.wikipedia.org/wiki/TPR_Storytelling for more information). Thanks to Michelle's implementation of this program, Spanish classes at her school grew from two classes to a full program requiring two full-time teachers. TPRS is a holistic program in which students

Snapshot of Holistic Education

The Waldorf schools are a good example of what holistic education looks like (www.waldorfanswers. org). The first Waldorf school was founded by Austrian philosopher, scientist, and artist Rudolf Steiner in 1919. Today there about 900 Waldorf schools and kindergartens in 60 countries. The early years focus on active learning, Grades 1–8 focus on emotional involvement and imagination, and high school focuses on independent thinking. The same teacher stays with the student over several years. The whole child is considered to be a spiritual being (body, soul, spirit). There is a main lesson every day that integrates English, math, geography, history, science, and the arts. There is an emphasis on using the head, heart, and hands. Students paint, draw, sing, and play music, and storytelling is a key method for teaching. Writing is taught before reading as it evolves out of art. Reading is not taught until Grade 2, where it evolves naturally. Over 32 Waldorf schools are established across Canada, with schools in British Columbia, Alberta, Ontario, Quebec, and the Maritimes (www.maplesplendor.ca/waldorf_schools.htm).

learn a language through reading and storytelling, without a structured grammatical component. It is an acquisition/immersion-based model. Current brain research and kinesthetic movement influenced TPRS. The purpose is to "acquire" the language, not "learn" the language. Every word used in the classroom is one that students understand, or will eventually, in context; the language is introduced in holistic ways. It is a student-centred approach based on a complex questioning method taught in a personalized and compelling way. Students ask questions to create stories about themselves as central characters. Applying a mastery approach, the class does not move ahead until everyone has 80% proficiency.

Social Reconstruction

The purpose of **social reconstruction** is to change society by challenging barriers that limit access and success. "Critical theory aims to disclose all forms of injustice and inequity in schooling by revealing the interest served by the knowledge and the human action brought to bear in the school setting" (Hlebowitsh, 2005, p. 78). Some theorists, like Peter McLaren—studying life in schools in a rough area of Toronto—developed a theory of **critical pedagogy** as a way to teach. This theory explores how knowledge is constructed and who benefits from this knowledge (McLaren, 1989).

How do teachers approach teaching for social justice? Some begin with critical literacy as a twenty-first–century skill to be infused into different subject areas. There are classical questions that we need to ask of all texts to determine what version of culture, history, and everyday life will count as official knowledge: How is "truth" represented, and whose interests are served? Who is disadvantaged and who benefits? Who is excluded from this version? (Janks, Dixon, Ferreira, Granville, & Newfield, 2013).

Snapshot of Social Reconstruction in the Classroom

Manitoba teacher Cara Zurzolo applied for a grant from the Asper Foundation; her Grade 8 and 9 classes were selected to be one of 10 urban schools to participate in the Holocaust and Human Rights Education Program. This three-hour a week, 13-week program looked at the history of the Holocaust as well as human rights, leaders such as Mahatma Gandhi and Martin Luther King, Jr., and other upstanders—individuals who act to make a positive difference in the life of an individual or inspire change in the community (www.tvdsb.ca/programs.cfm?subpage=155749). The term *upstander* comes from the organization Facing History and Ourselves (www.facinghistory.org). Cara ensures critical literacy is taught and practised in other contexts, too. For example, she includes the stories and history of First Nations people in her curriculum, providing an opening for listening to Canada's founding people, whose voice is missing in the canon. She is teaching the "Big Idea" of human development and civilizations (Know) and critical literacy (a twenty-first–century skill). Cara is also very interested in the Be component of the Know, Do, Be (KDB). She hopes her students will become upstanders, too.

Snapshot of Social Justice in the Classroom

Teaching for social justice often goes beyond questioning assumptions to initiating social action. When Grade 12 student Mitch Redden in rural Nova Scotia realized that his social network friends were not real friends to whom he could turn for help with problems, his teacher Steven Van Zoost asked how he and his peers could change this (Van Zoost, 2012). Van Zoost's Grade 12 English students created a face-to-face social network called realfriends that helped change the school culture to a more open and social one. The social action project started as a series of socializing activities with 30 students and ended up with 240 students from one school plus other interested people. Then students got involved in common causes. Ultimately, 240 students performed a laughing flash mob to get the attention of the other students and educate them about the Children's Wish Foundation. Van Zoost challenged students to think about equity issues during the planning of realfriends; their reflections are expressed in a published book of essays about the experience. Mitch Redden won the Nova Scotia Premier's Power of Positive Change Award in June 2011 for his efforts. The story can be found in a two-part documentary at www.stevenvanzoost.com.

Brazilian educator, philosopher, and influential critical pedagogy theorist Paulo Freire outlined his philosophy in his famous book *Pedagogy of the Oppressed*, published in 1970. Literacy through education could change the lot of the oppressed, who were poor and illiterate, but education needed to change from a banking model (a transmission-based model, i.e., traditional) to a transformative model (new story) where people could connect their personal stories to the cultural story or social contexts in which they were embedded. The marginalized could rise above their oppressed state by recognizing the power differentials, and use their knowledge to level the playing field. Feminist, postcolonial, and queer theory all emerged from this worldview.

Critical theory has had a powerful impact on education. Today the Organisation for Economic Co-operation and Development (OECD) evaluates the success of international countries on two counts—school achievement and equity (Schleicher, 2010). The OECD came to an optimistic conclusion that education around the world is improving because most countries are putting their resources and energy into both aspects. Access to educational opportunities balances wealth in determining education achievement (OECD, 2011).

All Canadian provinces are concerned with equity and have policies such as differentiated instruction and assessment to this end. Aboriginal education or First Nations students and schools on reserves in Canada are an exception regarding equity. Aboriginal education is a federal responsibility rather than a provincial one. There are wide disparities in financial support, and the result is significantly inferior schooling compared to provincially funded schools (Assembly of First Nations, 2010; Auditor General of Canada, 2011).

Curriculum for social justice is not without caution or critique. Journalist Cynthia Reynolds (2012) wrote a devastating critique entitled "Why are schools brainwashing our children?" in *Maclean's* magazine. In it she offered examples of debatable teaching practices in the name of social justice, such as protesting oil pipelines and celebrating polygamy. According to her article, faculties of education have a strong commitment to curricula for social justice, but teachers—especially new teachers—need training to understand the care and sensitivity these topics demand. Teachers may avoid such pitfalls by looking at resource guides like the global human rights curriculum available through Amnesty International (Amnesty International, 2012).

What Is Instruction?

In this section, we will take a broad look at instruction to clarify traditional and constructivist views of curriculum delivery. These contrasting views of instructional design are found in Table 1.1.

An *instructional strategy* refers to a learning activity that the student experiences in the day-to-day life of the classroom. Across Canada, the written provincial curriculum documents may suggest possible instructional activities to meet outcomes. However, it is usually the local curriculum designer (the teacher) who makes curriculum come alive through the design of appropriate and meaningful instructional strategies and activities. In other words, teachers have the responsibility for and the opportunity to create a curriculum that it is relevant and effective for the particular students in their classrooms.

APPROACHES TO INSTRUCTION

Most effective teaching strategies are generic in nature and can be applied in various contexts. For some, classroom instructional strategies are techniques that a teacher selects according to a learning task. Examples of such strategies are metaphors, Venn diagrams, advance organizers, co-operative learning, explicit cues, inferential questions, physical models, manipulatives, and practice at summarizing and note taking (Dean, Hubbell, Pitler, & Stone, 2012).

For others, teaching strategies are much broader than specific techniques and are identified as models of instruction. Within the different models, teachers would choose specific strategies to teach the curriculum. Below we describe some "models" based on *Strategies and Models for Teachers: Teaching Content and Thinking Skills* (Eggen & Kauchak, 2012) and *Instruction: A Models Approach* (Estes, Mintz, & Gunter, 2011).

TABLE 1.1 A Comparison of the Traditional and Constructivist Instructional Design Perspectives

Traditional	Constructivist
• Teacher-centred delivery (e.g., transmission, lecture, demonstration)	• Student-centred discovery/inquiry (interactive process between student and teacher)
• Focused on student retention	• Focused on student thinking skills
• Whole-group focus	• Individual student/small group focus
• Teacher plans time, activities by asking "What are students doing today?"	• Students develop skills for autonomy and self-direction: teacher asks, "What will students take away in the long term?"

As with curriculum, models are rarely purely one or another in practice. Perhaps it is helpful to see them more as a continuum. Direct instruction, programmed learning, and mastery learning are based on the assumptions underlying traditional education; the other models are grounded in constructivist assumptions. In the twenty-first century, teachers use instructional strategies from any model according to whatever best fits the leaning goals, the students, the classroom environment, and so on. This is a both/and context rather than an either/or context. Let's briefly go over some of the various strategies:

- *Direct instruction* is appropriate for teaching procedural skills, such as math problem solving and map reading. The teacher demonstrates and explains, and the student moves from guided practice to independent practice.
- *Programmed learning* is individual, self-paced learning. Tasks are broken into a series of small, sequential segments; the learner receives immediate feedback at each step of the process. Technology can provide instant feedback.
- **Mastery learning** is founded on Benjamin Bloom's (1956) taxonomy of learning objectives. Clearly defined objectives are organized into small sequential units. Students perform the skills again and again until mastered. Mastery learning can be delivered by a variety of methods, including direct instruction, independent learning, or learning with others.
- *Lecture* is a way to transmit organized bodies of knowledge in a brief time period. Discussion can be a way to review previous knowledge, present new knowledge, monitor comprehension, integrate previous knowledge into new information, and summarize information for consolidation.
- *Group work* and co-operative learning encourage student-to-student interaction and promote social development and critical thinking. An example of a group-work strategy is think-pair-share. Students answer the teacher's question silently, then pair up to share ideas. In **co-operative learning**, students take on defined roles that encourage interdependence and accountability. One example is the jigsaw strategy. Students form expert groups to learn about one part of the topic, after which the expert groups dissolve. New groups form, containing an expert from each former group, so that students share their "expert" knowledge of the topic with each other.
- In the **guided discovery model**, students are guided to uncover concepts and enduring understandings. The teacher provides a conceptual framework and provides examples and nonexamples of the concept to be taught. The second stage is open ended, with students observing and making comparisons of the teacher examples. In the convergent stage, the teacher asks students more specific questions to guide them to the understanding of the concept. In the last stage, the teacher guides students to the definition, which students apply in a new context.
- The **concept attainment model** is focused on the development and elaboration of concepts through the development of critical thinking skills. The teacher selects examples and nonexamples, and students create a hypothesis for the concept. The teacher then provides more examples and nonexamples. Students analyze their existing hypotheses to see if they are valid; students may develop new hypotheses.

Students can now identify the essential characteristics of the concept. Models can be used for the scientific method to test hypotheses.

- In **inquiry learning**, the focus is on teaching problem-solving skills and self-regulation. Responsibility lies with the learner. The teacher reviews prior knowledge and presents a problem, then students devise a plan to solve the problem. Students implement their strategy (which may require some scaffolding from the teacher) and discuss and evaluate the results. In more student-centred inquiries, the students identify the problem themselves and work to solve it.

DIFFERENTIATION OF INSTRUCTIONAL STRATEGIES

A constructivist approach recognizes that students learn at different rates and in different ways. This basic belief opens the door to the differentiation of instruction and assessment—a process called **differentiated instruction (DI)**. The Ontario Ministry of Education defines differentiated instruction as a "method of teaching that attempts to adapt instruction to suit the differing interests, learning styles, and readiness to learn of individual students" (2011, p. 58). Respected DI researcher Carol Tomlinson (2001) offers four broad categories for teachers to consider for differentiation in a mixed-ability classroom (see Table 1.2). Note that teacher action includes both instruction and assessment.

TABLE 1.2 Differentiated Learning Strategies for Teaching and Assessing

Categories	Focus	The DI teacher . . .
Cognitive	How does the student think and learn?	• Uses research-based instructional strategies • Encourages demonstration of learning through a variety of challenging tasks (products) that have similar criteria for success • Allows for choice for completion of a task that will take a similar amount of time and is based on similar learning outcomes
Intellectual	What is the student's preferred learning style?	• Knows students' readiness, interests, and preferences • Differentiates instruction and assessment tasks to ensure students are challenged appropriately.
Group orientation	To what degree does the student prefer to work with others?	• Provides flexibility for learning: whole class, groups, alone, with the teacher, or a combination of these configurations • Groups and regroups • Develops a culture of shared responsibility for learning
Environmental	What does an invitational learning environment look like?	• Creates an inviting space with opportunities for students to work alone or in groups • Customizes space for specific learning, such as readiness, interest in a concept, or learning preferences • Uses technology effectively • Provides a variety of useful resources • Creates a code of conduct collaboratively with students

Source: Based on Tomlinson and Imbeau (2010) and Ontario Ministry of Education (2010a).

Snapshot of DI in the Classroom

Heather Best teaches Grade 4 in Ontario. In her class, six students are English language learners, three others arrived with no record of prior schooling, and four different students are identified with special learning needs. "As a demonstration of the diversity in my class, I have seven guided reading groups. Within each group, there can be a range of two to three benchmarks."

Heather describes how she differentiates her math lessons:

I start with differentiated diagnostic activities. For example, with the English language learners, I wanted to see if they have the necessary vocabulary, such as denominator. With the newcomers I can't start where curriculum expectations would suggest is appropriate for the grade. I have to figure out what is appropriate for these kids' experience. I use manipulatives often for this. The diagnostic assessment tells me how to group students.

I do a lot of preparation beforehand, setting up centres and preparing materials for the groups. I invite someone from each group to be the "helper/go-to person" for another group. If someone in Group A needs help and I'm not there, the students know who to go to in Group B. If Group B runs into problems, there is someone in Group C to help. These leadership roles change often. Students feel empowered in the role, and teaching someone else reinforces their own learning. Besides, I just can't be everywhere at once. I introduce the concepts with a mini-lesson, usually using modelling with the whole class, and I explain what groups will do at their centres. Then I move from group to group; I'm constantly moving. It's a juggling act. I probably move every seven to ten minutes.

I always have my clipboard with me. I'm writing down anecdotal observations constantly. Our reporting requires specific examples that I gather from work samples. My notes inform both my assessment and instruction because they tell me where a student is now and where we need to go next.

PERSONALIZATION

In the emerging new story, differentiation has been extended to personalization. Barbara Bray and Kathleen McClaskey, co-founders of Personalize Learning (www.personalizelearning.com), have explained the differences among differentiation, individualization, and personalization:

- In *differentiation*, students are all striving toward the same learning goal, but possibly in different ways. The teacher targets instruction and adapts assessment based on different groups of learners.
- In *individualization*, the teacher is responsible for modifying instruction to meet the needs of the individual learner. Both differentiation and individualization start with the teacher making the modifications for the student.
- By contrast, *personalization* starts with the learner. Personalization means that individual learners own and drive their learning based on their goals, passions, interests, and how they learn best. Their passions take them on different paths, even though they share the common "big picture" learning goals of the curriculum. The teacher is a facilitator or guide.

Personalization can be confused with individualization because both consider the learner as a separate being rather than a member of a group. However, the philosophical underpinnings of each are distinct regarding the locus of motivation and control. Table 1.3 makes clear the differences among differentiation, individualization, and personalization.

TABLE 1.3 Personalization versus Differentiation versus Individualization

Personalization	Differentiation	Individualization
The Learner ...	**The Teacher ...**	**The Teacher ...**
drives his or her own learning.	provides instruction to groups of learners.	provides instruction to an individual learner.
connects learning with interests, talents, passions, and aspirations.	adjusts learning needs for groups of learners.	accommodates learning needs for the individual learner.
actively participates in the design of his or her learning.	designs instruction based on the learning needs of different groups of learners.	customizes instruction based on the individual learner.
owns and is responsible for his or her own learning, which includes his or her voice and choice on how and what to learn.	is responsible for a variety of instruction for different groups of learners.	is responsible for modifying instruction based on the needs of the individual learner.
identifies learning goals for the learning plan with guidance from the teacher.	identifies the same objectives for different groups of learners.	identifies the same objectives for all learners with specific objectives for individuals who receive one-on-one support.
develops the skills to select and use the appropriate technology and resources to support learning.	selects technology and resources to support the learning needs of different groups of learners.	selects technology and resources to support the learning needs of the individual learner.
builds a network of peers, experts, and teachers to guide and support learning.	supports groups of learners who are reliant on the teacher to support learning.	understands the individual learner is dependent on the teacher to support learning.
demonstrates mastery of content in a competency-based model.	monitors learning based on Carnegie unit (seat time) and grade level.	monitors learning based on Carnegie unit (seat time) and grade level.
assessment *as* learning	assessment *for* learning	assessment *of* learning
becomes a self-directed learner who monitors progress and reflects on learning based on mastery of content and skills.	uses data and assessments to provide ongoing feedback for groups and individual learners to advance learning.	uses data and assessments to confirm progress and report what the individual learner learned.

Snapshot from Outside the Classroom: Personalization in Action

Nine-year-old Sam is an example of personalized learning—not in a classroom, but in a collective (Thomas & Brown, 2011). Sam likes to play with software called Scratch that helps young people understand programming. He quickly learned how to create an avatar and play a game. He took a summer class to learn the Scratch program better. Then he joined a collective by posting his game online where it was accessible to thousands of other players who could play and modify it. He could remix other people's programs—but noted that he had to make major changes to improve them. Sam, according to Thomas and Brown, learned a lot about programming. In addition, he learned the twenty-first–century skills of collaboration, communication, and citizenship through giving and receiving constructive feedback on programs—other people's and his own.

What Is Assessment?

During the 20th century, assessment was often defined as evaluation and assessment. **Evaluation** is summative assessment conducted at the end of an instructional period to measure achieved learning. It is also the term used for standardized measures such as large-scale provincial assessments. In comparison, **assessment** is now considered classroom-based and includes diagnostic and formative feedback during the instructional period to improve learning.

Since knowledge is objective in the traditional model, it can be quantified; achievement can be measured through tests and pencil-and-paper tasks. Evaluation is normative; students are ranked against each other on a **bell curve** in norm-referenced grading. The proportion of students who achieve at various levels is predetermined by the curve's distribution (see Figure 1.1a). The majority of students' grades fall in the middle range of the bell curve as average, while only a small percentage of students' grades fall at either end of the curve. Thus, students are sorted; the model assumes that only a few will be drastically unsuccessful, but also that only a small proportion of students succeed in ways that allow them access to scholarships and higher education and the higher-paying, higher-status jobs.

A constructivist approach requires a different assessment philosophy and practice. Over the course of the 20th century, research about brain functionality and cognitive development and learning, along with an interest in equity and inclusion, challenged the assumptions of the traditional model. A different assumption emerged: If learners are active, self-motivated builders of their own understandings, all students can learn and succeed in different ways and in different areas. As part of this shift toward a more constructivist approach, curriculum was revised and teachers employed a broader range of instructional strategies. In contrast to norm-referenced grading, criterion-referenced grading presumes that all students are eligible to achieve at a high level. Distribution of grades looks like the **J curve** (see Figure 1.1b). However, there grew increasing tension in some teachers' minds around the misalignment between their constructivist daily classroom instructional practices

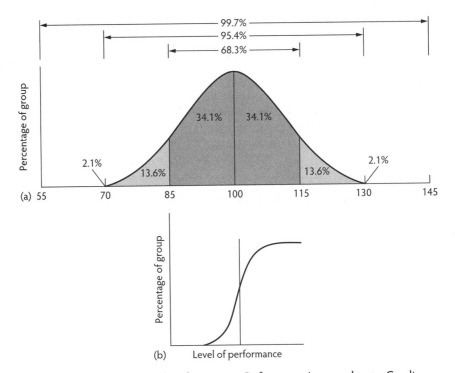

FIGURE 1.1 Norm-Referenced and Criterion-References Approaches to Grading
Source: http://www.doctorramey.com/musings-by-dr-ramey/horse-psychics-chic-horses-spy/attachment/iq-bell-curve-03/

and the more traditional systemic assessment practices of unit tests, exams, and large-scale testing (Harris & Brown, 2009; Leighton, Gokiert, Cor, & Heffernan, 2010).

Then, in 1998, Black and Wiliam published a seminal work entitled "Inside the Black Box: Raising Standards through Classroom Assessment." This article was a meta-analysis of studies about formative assessment. **Formative assessment** refers to strategies that make student learning visible so that the teacher as well as the student can take steps to improve performance. Black and Wiliam concluded that formative feedback provided during the learning phase was a powerful influence on academic achievement. This was followed by the Assessment Reform Group (2002) from the UK, who developed principles for formative assessment. While this conclusion about the power of feedback may seem obvious today, the Black and Wiliam study and the Assessment Reform Group rocked the education world at a time when large-scale testing for accountability purposes was popular. The study became the catalyst for the new story in assessment.

The Black and Wiliam study proposed that assessment could be used to enhance student learning, not just evaluate it. The emphasis was on individual improvement, not on sorting and grading. The assumption underlying assessment changed to "All learners can succeed" in an appropriate context if given appropriate and effective tools. The assumptions of the role of the teacher also changed. It was not enough for the teacher to create an assessment task. Rather, the teacher needed to gather, dialogue, and act on ongoing information to help all students meet the success criteria. Just as instruction required differentiation, so too did assessment (Reeves, 2011).

In short, the main difference between the old story and the new story is the purpose of assessment. In the old story, evaluation is a final judgment. Quebec's *Policy on the Evaluation of Learning* (Quebec Ministry of Education, 2003) captures how assessment is an integral part of an ongoing learning process when it states that "students do not learn in order to be evaluated: they are evaluated so that they can learn more effectively.... Thus, evaluation of learning has an essential pedagogical function.... Evaluation is considered a component of the learning process rather than a distinct concept" (p. 12). Statistically, it meant that educators could evaluate using a J curve, where most of their students were in the high success range.

In a powerful article, assessment expert Lorrie Shepard (2000) explained how curriculum, instruction, and assessment were brought together under constructivist learning theory to promote what she called "a learning culture." Figure 1.2 is an adaptation of her work.

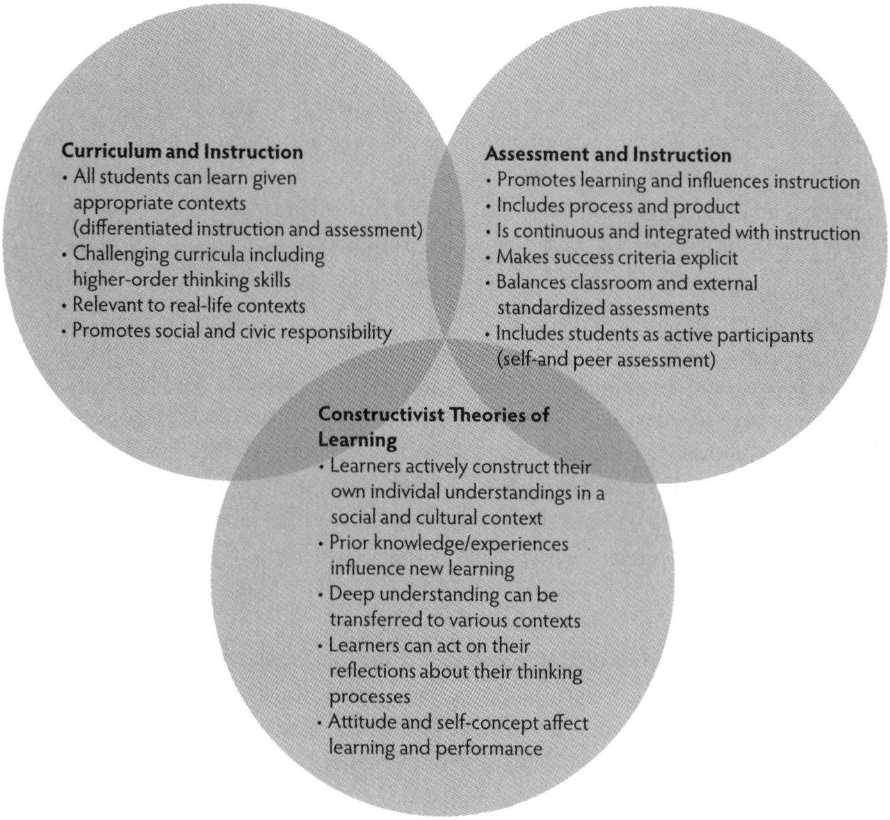

Curriculum and Instruction
• All students can learn given appropriate contexts (differentiated instruction and assessment)
• Challenging curricula including higher-order thinking skills
• Relevant to real-life contexts
• Promotes social and civic responsibility

Assessment and Instruction
• Promotes learning and influences instruction
• Includes process and product
• Is continuous and integrated with instruction
• Makes success criteria explicit
• Balances classroom and external standardized assessments
• Includes students as active participants (self-and peer assessment)

Constructivist Theories of Learning
• Learners actively construct their own individal understandings in a social and cultural context
• Prior knowledge/experiences influence new learning
• Deep understanding can be transferred to various contexts
• Learners can act on their reflections about their thinking processes
• Attitude and self-concept affect learning and performance

FIGURE 1.2 Assessment as a Component of the New Story of Learning Theory and Curriculum Change

Source: Adapted from Shepard, L. (2000), p. 8

Note how the figure shows instruction as a part of both curriculum and assessment. We agree with this view. For an accountable curriculum, instructional strategies need to be connected both to critical learning as described by curriculum documents as well as to valid and reliable assessment that determines if the students have acquired that critical learning. In this book, you will see instructional strategies as they are connected to official curriculum documents and also as they serve as assessment tasks and tools.

ASSESSMENT WITH A TARGETED PURPOSE

Canadian assessment researcher/author Lorna Earl writes that "purpose is everything" (2003, p. 12) when it comes to assessment. Across Canada, assessment definitions and practices have shifted to reflect the idea that different purposes require different practices. Earl describes three approaches to assessment: assessment of learning, assessment for learning, and assessment as learning.

Assessment of Learning (AoL)

Evaluation in a classroom context is called **assessment of learning (AoL)**. This type of summative assessment may be tests or may take another form such as portfolios or rich performance assessment tasks where students demonstrate their learning. The purpose of AoL is to report on *achieved* learning. Usually results are communicated with numeric or letter grades, with limited if any descriptive commentary. Often summative assessment indicates how one student ranks in relation to others. Results are often used to determine promotion and access to scholarships and programs. When AoL is standardized, such as in large-scale testing, results are used to make judgments about system accountability and student performance in relation to set standards (e.g., provincial expectations/outcomes/competencies).

AoL has been the predominant form of assessment and continues to be an important way to compare students across larger groups and systems. However, as curriculum shifts to a more constructivist approach that accommodates diverse learning needs, the purpose of assessment is also shifting from measuring achievement to promoting learning. Today, there is growing interest in using summative evaluation for formative purposes, such as diagnosing learning gaps for future remediation. For example, some school boards administer standardized reading assessments and use them to prepare students for provincial assessments.

Assessment for Learning (AfL)

In **assessment for learning (AfL)**, assessment information is used to enhance learning (Black & Wiliam, 1998; Brookhart, Moss, & Long, 2008; MacPhail & Halbert, 2010; Shepard, 2000). Formative in nature, assessment for learning occurs continuously throughout a learning period as descriptive feedback about performance in relation to clearly understood criteria. Assessment tasks are designed to make both the process and attainment of learning visible to the teacher and, importantly, to the student him or herself (Hattie, 2009). Feedback (assessment without grades) focuses on strengths, areas of confusion, and next steps for growth. Comparisons with other students are irrelevant; what matters is the individual's progress toward the learning goal.

The theme of this book is the connection among curriculum, instruction, and assessment. A twenty-first–century view of assessment, especially AfL, includes what traditionally might be identified as the territory of instruction. For example, Black and Wiliam (2004) suggest these low-tech methods to assess learning as part of instruction:

- Questioning for higher-order thinking
- A no-hands policy (the teacher asks whomever, whenever, rather than calling on volunteers who have raised their hands)
- Traffic lights (students hold up red, yellow, or green cards to indicate level of understanding)
- Exit cards or one-minute essays (students submit short reflective pieces at the end of class to summarize what they have learned or to identify areas of confusion).

AfL goes beyond implementation of such strategies, however—it reflects a commitment to a moral purpose. The spirit of AfL really is a philosophy based on the belief that everyone can learn and that the teacher's responsibility is to actively support learning, not just report it (Earl, Volante, & Katz, 2011). AfL redefines the roles of teacher and student by emphasizing their mutual commitment as collaborative learning partners (Black, Harrison, Lee, Marshall, & Wiliam, 2003; Gipps, 1999; Popham, 2008). Teachers see where, when, and how to target instructional strategies to meet differentiated student needs, and students understand where and why learning gaps exist and how to remedy them.

Assessment as Learning (AaL)

Assessment as learning (AaL) is focused on developing self-assessment and metacognition. In AaL, the goal is for students to monitor their own learning. Through frequent self-assessment, students develop the metacognitive skills (thinking about one's thinking) to reflect on their successful achievements, identify what they have not yet learned, and devise and implement learning strategies that are effective for them. Eminent New Zealand researcher John Hattie (2009) finds the strongest influences on learning are metacognitive and self-directed strategies. For Lorna Earl (2003), AaL is the ultimate goal of assessment and should be taught and practised often to develop metacognitive skills and student autonomy.

In much of this book we will use AfL as a shorthand term that includes both assessment for learning (diagnostic and formative) and assessment as learning (self-assessment and metacognition). We do this because AfL is the umbrella term most commonly used in much of the literature to include both types of assessment, and AaL is subsumed under AfL. We do differentiate between AfL and AaL as defined in this chapter when we are describing specific instructional/assessment strategies in the Canadian context since all provinces use an AfL, AaL, and AoL framework.

Table 1.4 shows how purpose—why you are assessing—has implications for *what* is assessed, *when* assessment is done, *how* assessment is carried out, and *for whom* assessment is conducted (Earl, 2003).

TABLE 1.4 How Purpose Affects Assessment Practice

	Assessment for Learning (AfL)	Assessment as Learning (AaL)	Assessment of Learning (AoL)
If your purpose is . . .	. . . to identify learners' current level of performance, to set future learning goals, and to identify the next steps to get there, then do formative monitoring.	. . . to build reflection and self-assessment skills, then build students' self-assessment capacity.	. . . to make summative judgments about performance in relation to provincial standards, then conduct a final evaluation.
What is assessed?	Content knowledge, disciplinary skills, learning strategies, and attitudes Criterion-referenced	Content knowledge, disciplinary skills, learning strategies, and attitudes Criterion-referenced	Content knowledge, disciplinary skills Can be both criterion-referenced and norm-referenced
When does it occur?	Frequently; before (diagnostic) and during instruction (ongoing)	Frequently; before (diagnostic) and during instruction (ongoing)	After instruction at key stages (e.g., end of unit or year)
Who does the assessing?	Teacher, peers, self	Peers, self	Teacher
How is learning communicated?	Temporary grades, anecdotal descriptions/rubrics, checklists	Journals, exit cards, anecdotal descriptions/rubrics, checklists	Grades, anecdotal description on report card
How is assessment information used?	By the student and teacher to determine current achievement and set future learning goals in relation to outcomes identified in provincial curriculum guidelines By the teacher to target and differentiate instruction	By students to provide feedback to peers, to monitor their own progress, to reflect on strategies (metacognition), and to set learning goals Can be motivating	To make judgments about students' performance in relation to provincial standards for grade promotion, program placement, or scholarships Information can be shared with parents/guardians, school and district staff, and other educational professionals (e.g., for the report card or purposes of curriculum development)
Teacher and student roles	Teacher and student are collaborative, interactive partners; process of continual reflection and review about progress Teachers adjust their plans and engage in corrective teaching in response to formative assessment of and from students Students respond to feedback to improve learning	Teacher scaffolds experiences to allow for gradual release of responsibility Students develop increasing independence as they develop skills to determine their own level of achievement Students use assessment information to improve learning	Teacher is judge

PUTTING IT ALL TOGETHER

Above, we have described the three approaches to assessment as if each were neatly distinct and separate. Such categorization would not be accurate; all three types of assessment are interactive. For example, Socratic questioning is a well-established traditional method of instruction, but student answers provide rich information about their current understandings; thus, questioning is also a way to informally assess (AfL). Assessment can offer instructional opportunities. When students participate in the design of their assessment tool, like a rubric, and apply it to samples of work including their own, their understanding deepens. These activities clarify the characteristics of exemplary performance, helping students understand **assessment criteria** and how performance moves from one level to the next. Students become more effective self-assessors as a result. Thus, effective assessment comprises all three interconnecting approaches operating as dynamic components of a system.

Guiding Principles of Assessment

KEY ELEMENTS OF FAIR ASSESSMENT PRACTICES

Principles for Fair Student Assessment Practices for Education in Canada (Joint Advisory Committee, 1993) is a foundational document that outlines essential standards for fair assessment. Other excellent resources offer more complete coverage of the technical aspects of assessment than you will find here (see, for example, Airasian, Engemann, & Gallagher, 2012; McMillan, Hellsten, & Klinger, 2010; and Popham, 2008). We briefly discuss three key elements of effective assessment practices below: validity, reliability, and fairness.

Validity

Validity refers to the trustworthiness of the judgments that can be made based on the assessment data. Has the assessment provided sufficient information and the right kind of information to support the conclusion? In other words, to what degree does the assessment method measure what it is supposed to measure? For classroom teachers, the best insurance of validity is to plan assessment tasks simultaneously with the curriculum objectives, then plan instruction that will support students in the development and, ultimately, in the demonstration of these outcomes. This method of curriculum planning is called "backward design" and is described in depth in Chapters 3 and 5. Backward design ensures that (a) assessment tasks are consistent with the learning goals, and (b) that students will have had the opportunity to learn whatever knowledge and skills are needed to be successful on an assessment task (Black et al., 2003; Cooper, 2006, 2011).

Reliability

Reliability is the degree of consistency of the assessment results. Any assessment will have some degree of error because many noninstructional factors influence a student's performance—health, mood, setting, confusing instructions, luck. But if a student's performance results are consistent across multiple assessments in the same domain when

Snapshot from the Classroom: Improving Reliability

Teachers can improve the reliability of their assessments through **moderated marking**, an activity this Grade 6 teacher described as "professionally exciting":

First, my division partners collaborated on the development of a writing task and its assessment rubric. We chose to focus on a writing task. Once we had student work, we selected samples as reference points for levels of performance. Then we began marking, first in pairs, then individually, stopping often to compare our scores. This was supposed to reinforce a common understanding of the criteria. We were dismayed to discover how variable our scores were at first. Instead of looking only at the work itself, we were considering effort or letting background knowledge of the students influence our marking. Also, we had to overcome initial defensiveness. Even though we had worked together for years, sometimes one of us felt offended when her judgment was challenged. We became more consistent and less biased when we focused on actual student performance in light of criteria and exemplars rather than comparing student to student, or taking student work personally.

The complexity of moderated marking among teachers, particularly the tension between the *tacit* knowledge of personal and professional experience and the *explicit* knowledge provided by external artifacts such as rubrics and exemplars, is explored by Wyatt-Smith, Klenowski, and Gunn (2010). The researchers analyzed the recorded conversations among groups of primary and secondary school teachers as they compared their scoring decisions with state standards. The researchers concluded that "much more is in play than a set of stated expectations" (p. 72) in the search for consistency in teacher judgment. Social interaction, respect for and understanding of assessment artifacts, and the teachers' unspoken experiential knowledge all influence assessment decisions.

it is assessed in different ways (e.g., projects, tests, oral presentations) and by different assessors then a fairly reliable judgment about proficiency can be made. These results are a fairly reliable, although never an exact indicator of a student's proficiency.

Fairness

Fairness means that all students have an equal opportunity to succeed regardless of gender, prior knowledge, teacher bias, or any other factor unrelated to what was taught and is being assessed. Teachers stress the importance of being fair, but "fairness" is a slippery concept in practice. When researchers investigated the practices of 77 Ontario and Saskatchewan teachers, they found that the teachers agreed with statements about criterion referencing but did not necessarily follow these principles in their grading practices (Tierney, Simon, & Charland, 2011). In granting a grade, teachers also considered such things as the type of course, individual improvement during the course, and ranking students for postsecondary selection (norm-referenced). In addition, opinion and practices varied widely around the inclusion of non-achievement factors (e.g., attendance, effort) in grading. The researchers concluded that "It seemed that teachers were driven in their practices by a sense of what was fair for students, which may have included a host of unexamined assumptions, rather than a sound understanding of grading principles" (p. 224).

Teachers can ensure fairness when they are guided by sound assessment principles and by being transparent about the assessment criteria from the outset. Fairness is more likely when all students have had sufficient and appropriate opportunity both to learn and to demonstrate their learning. Fairness does not always mean standardization—the same assessment task or the same assessment criteria for everyone. Indeed, one of the criticisms of standardized testing is that such tests are unfair because they do not take student individuality into account. By knowing your students, you can differentiate for students with exceptionalities.

ASSESSMENT, MOTIVATION, AND LEARNER IDENTITY

The data from the *What Did You Do in School Today?* study confirms that students are generally bored in their classrooms (Willms & Friesen, 2012). How can we engage and motivate students? Designing rich tasks and providing appropriate instructional scaffolding are two parts of the answer. Tapping into learner **motivation** also increases engagement and the way we deliver assessment information. Assessment is an emotional business that affects motivation and learner identity and effort (Brown, 2011; Kearns, 2011; Marsh & Martin, 2011; Pulfrey, Buchs, & Butera, 2011; Stephan, Caudroit, Boiché, & Sarrazin, 2011).

Psychologist Carol Dweck (2006) uses the ideas of "fixed" and "growth" mindsets to explain the links among motivation, effort, and identity. Students with a fixed mindset believe their success is the result of innate intelligence and talent, qualities that are genetic or "fixed." When such students encounter difficulty, they are baffled, discouraged, and feel powerless. Thinking like this—"I'm just like my dad. I'm just no good at math"—discounts the value of practice and effort. By contrast, students with a growth mindset view failure as a temporary condition because they believe that their abilities can improve with persistent effort; they welcome tackling challenges and overcoming difficulties as an opportunity for learning, and they see practice as an effective strategy to achieve eventual success. Assessment feedback that focuses on the student's visible actions and actual work rather than on assumed actions and personal attributes fosters a growth mindset.

Assessment can feed a success orientation when it acknowledges competencies as much as pointing out areas for improvement. Indeed, the idea of "appreciative assessment" advocates accentuating the positive by "catching students doing something right" rather than using assessment as a "gotcha" moment. Neal (2012) writes, "Appreciative assessment, then, is all about helping students find and build on their unique abilities and

Snapshot from the Classroom: Building a Growth Mindset

Ontario math educators Laura Inglis and Nicole Miller (2011) helped their students develop a growth mindset by using problem-based instruction. Their students deconstructed work samples from the provincial standardized test. "Students enjoyed using exemplars.... They were able to identify the levels scored for each piece of work and were able to cite specific examples on how to improve each answer.... The added advantage was that students were evaluating work based solely on the work, as opposed to being asked to evaluate their friend's work which, in Grade 6 particularly, can become quite political!" (p. 9). Subsequent scores on the provincial tests increased 12% (Grade 3) and 4% (Grade 6). According to Inglis and Miller, students attributed their success to improved problem-solving strategies rather than innate talent; they developed confidence and expanded their explanations. In short, as they became effective assessors, they also became better mathematicians and vice versa.

aptitudes by providing positive, supportive feedback with a focus on capabilities and possibilities . . . students feel good about their accomplishments and are motivated to work on their challenges" (p. 7)

Table 1.5 shows what teachers can do and how they can communicate assessment information so that students develop a stronger sense of self-efficacy (i.e., develop a growth mindset).

REPORTING AND GRADING

The dialectic shifting between two different perspectives as discussed in the Story Model is highly visible in the area of grading and reporting. At the moment, North American education retains much of the traditional competitive mark culture. But in the twenty-first century, a new story focused on nurturing a learning culture is challenging this paradigm. The highly charged debate about large-scale testing is symbolic of the divergent stories related to assessment.

Grading can provoke tension when teachers and students feel caught between these seemingly contradictory cultures that operate simultaneously in schools today. Teachers must meet accountability demands and provide quantified measures of achievement at prescribed intervals. Grades are important to students, too. They can be an external affirmation of accomplishment. As well, students compete for grades that determine access to scholarships and programs. This is the traditional assessment culture, which continues to exert much influence (Earl, Volante, & Katz, 2011).

At the same time, teachers are encouraged to apply more constructivist, interactive teaching practices and to devote the majority of their time and energy to descriptive, formative assessment focused on growth. Some teachers are turning to class web pages,

TABLE 1.5 Productive Teacher Feedback

Teacher Action	Productive Teacher Feedback
Help students to see when they have succeeded through their own efforts rather then through talent, luck, or teacher help.	"You spent a lot of time going to different sources, and that is why you got such rich results." "You put a lot of effort into making your presentation board attractive and informative."
Focus on the observable, not assumed effort.	"I noticed that you wrote two drafts of this report. That's why your ideas are so clear." "I see you in the gym practising at lunchtime. No wonder your layup is improving."
Give specific and descriptive feedback. Identify specific strategies for improvement. Link successful outcomes to the use of specific strategies.	"You have structured your paragraph well around a clear main idea. Your next step is to add description by using adjectives and adverbs." "You used a thesaurus efficiently to add nuance and variety to your word choices."
Give (and get) frequent feedback as soon as possible. Circulate among students, observing, listening, and probing.	"I know you're just starting, but how's the research going so far?" "What should I be looking for in your work?"
Make the goal clear. Post outcomes in class. Provide exemplars so that students can self-assess.	"When you compare your essay to this sample, how are they similar? What is missing in yours?" "Our learning goal today was making accurate observations. How do your notes about this experiment demonstrate this goal?"
Let the students know how their work has improved by connecting to their previous work. Show them how their future work can improve.	"Your graphing has improved. This time you remembered to label the axes. Next time, focus on plotting data points more precisely."
Include students in deciding what their next steps should be.	"Your lap time was four minutes. Your goal is two minutes. What steps could you take to close this gap?"
Balance positives and negatives.	"Your oral presentation was well done. You really knew your topic and your voice was very strong. Next time, look at the audience when you speak."
As a teacher, model a growth mindset.	"I'm having trouble with this camera. Perhaps you can show me how. I'd like to learn."

Source: Adapted from McMillan, Hellston, & Klinger (2010), pp. 134–137.

electronic student portfolios, and student-led conferences to communicate with parents beyond the report card and the hasty conversations at parent–teacher night. They feel a stressful disconnect when their abundant assessment information is reduced to a single number or letter. Reconciling assessment policies, traditional and newer constructivist practices, and teacher values can be challenging (Crossman, 2007; Harlen, 2005; Nolen, 2011; Pope, Green, Johnson, & Mitchell, 2009; Steinberg, 2008).

We can offer no pat solutions to this struggle. However, we believe that strong, clear alignment among the three components—curriculum outcomes, assessment tasks, and instruction—can help ensure that however reductive, grading provides valid evaluation information. Ideally, a grade should be an affirmation of information that has been accumulated and communicated through ongoing formative assessment. Whether levels, letters, or percentages, grades should communicate effectively and accurately the degree of competency demonstrated in the student's most recent work (Winger, 2009; Guskey, 2003; Marzano & Heflebower, 2011; O'Connor, 2011; Erikson, 2011). As Brookhart writes, "The main issue is not what scale to use, how often to report, how many grades to combine, or how to combine them. These secondary issues can be decided only after you answer the main questions: What meaning do we want our grades to convey? and Who is (are) the primary intended audience(s) for this message? . . . grades are not about what students earn; they are about what students learn." (2011, p. 12).

The Emerging New Story

As you read in the Introduction, there is a call for a new story in education—one that is emerging now. A story is never static; it always has one foot in the past and another in anticipation of the future. What does this new story look like? According to Canadian change theorist Michael Fullan (2013), there are three interconnected Big Ideas in the new story: technology, the new pedagogy, and the teacher as change agent.

In this book, we explore the emerging new story based on Fullan's framework, as well as the literature, policy documents, and Internet resources such as blogs, YouTube videos, webinars, and podcasts. Most importantly, we include interviews conducted with twenty-first–century teachers across Canada. In upcoming chapters, you will hear more about these teachers and the educational landscape they inhabit. Indeed, some of the impetus for change will come from the disruption of the system by educators at the margins who are implementing effective innovations (Horn, 2013). Get a glimpse of this landscape by looking at Chapter 6 before going on to Chapter 2.

TECHNOLOGY

Technology is creating new professions and transforming others, including education. Some boards of education have been enthusiastic adopters; others are cautious, often because students know more than their teachers about technology, reversing roles in sometimes uncomfortable ways (Mishra & Koeler, 2006). But according to Fullan (2013), resistance is not only detrimental, it is futile.

The twenty-first–century classroom is a connected networked classroom. Technology is ever-present, not as bells and whistles but as tools to engage students and enhance learning. Students bring their own personal devices (BYOD) such as laptops, tablets, e-readers, iPods, or mobile phones along with pens and paper. Thousands of educational apps offer interactive ways to learn through gaming and social networking. As an example, google (note the verb) "Bloom's digital taxonomy" and see the myriad applications that teachers and students can use at each level of the taxonomy. Digital video exercises that are found in online textbooks make instruction and assessment seamless.

Classrooms are also global in nature. Students collaborate with students from around the world on things ranging from editing each other's work to problem solving. Access to learning is achieved anywhere, anytime through virtual schools, online lessons (e.g., the Khan Academy), and even university courses via a MOOC (massive open online concept) from a highly reputable university like Stanford or the University of Toronto. Students are not restricted to course offerings in their local schools.

Given this potential for a personalized approach to education, the role of teacher and student is shifting. The teacher is no longer the expert or even the facilitator of learning. They are unnecessary to transmit information. Students can connect to experts in their areas of personal interest, such as learning to play an instrument by watching an expert on YouTube. However, students *do* need teachers to help them learn ethical and responsible use of technology.

NEW PEDAGOGY

For us, the new pedagogy is about deep learning. The new pedagogy is constructivist in nature and often is project-based. It keeps the best of what we have learned about education but is also transformed by technology. The emerging new story follows the path of the Story Model. Rather than two either/or choices grounded in two different ideologies (traditional and constructivist), there will be a synthesis or reconciliation of seemingly opposite approaches, resulting in a both/and approach. False dichotomies will be recognized as possible in a both/and world (Barbar, Donnelly, & Rizvi, 2012). Teachers will then be able to choose instructional and assessment strategies that best fit the needs of the students in front of them.

John Hattie's (2009, 2012) work on visible learning is based on a synthesis of over 800 meta-analyses related to student achievement. He measured the influence of 138 educational factors on student achievement. The results confirm that there are best practices in both the traditional and constructivist approaches. For example, phonics, direct instruction, and mastery learning were highly effective practices alongside creativity programs, co-operative learning, and reciprocal teaching. High on Hattie's list was AfL: self-report grades, formative evaluation, and feedback and metacognitive strategies. Examples of the both/and approach are in Table 1.6

TABLE 1.6 Education as a Both/And Enterprise

Both	And
Three Rs	New literacies
Phonics	Whole language
Quantitative reporting	Qualitative reporting
Disciplinary	Interdisciplinary
Lecture/direct instruction	Inquiry/project-based learning
Evidence based	Intuitive innovation

Teachers will need to integrate twenty-first–century skills such as collaboration, communication, critical thinking, problem solving, and creativity to activate deep learning. As well, "The integration of technology and pedagogy to maximize learning must meet four criteria. It must be irresistibly engaging; elegantly efficient (challenging, but easy to use); technologically ubiquitous; and steeped in real-life problem solving" (Fullan, 2013, p. 33). That is, learning tasks must engage students, be simple and also challenging, be accessible through technology 24/7, and require real-life problem solving. In this book we offer examples of teachers who are using a new pedagogy.

TEACHER AS CHANGE AGENT

The third Big Idea is the teacher as a change agent. Hattie (2012) describes this teacher as a person with agency who, acting much like a chemical catalyst, increases the learning of both students and him or herself. The central feature of agency is evaluation. The teacher needs to be able to assess his or her impact on student learning. Hattie calls this "know thy impact." Rather than learning about a number of different strategies, Hattie claims that teacher education students should learn "how to evaluate the impact of their learning on students," then how to apply different and multiple strategies for the students in front of them. Teacher professionalism is crucial to student learning (Hargreaves & Fullan, 2012).

INTEGRATIVE THINKING

We add one more Big Idea: **integrative thinking**. How can we best connect all the parts that are necessary for the new story? Former dean of the University of Toronto's Rotman School of Management Roger Martin (2007) defines integrative thinking as a way to bring together the either/or dichotomy by synthesizing the best of the two seeming opposites. For Martin, it is a key skill for the twenty-first century. For us, integrative thinking is crucial to being able to build a new story—to bring both the old and new together in ways that make education better than other models alone.

Conclusion

In this chapter we explored different models of curriculum, instruction, and assessment. The models are built on different sets of beliefs and assumptions that are grounded in constructivist or traditional educational practices. These beliefs and assumptions have usually been considered to be either/or approaches. We ended the chapter by exploring a new story of education in the twenty-first century. In this new story, the seeming contrasting views of the two different paradigms are seen as false dichotomies leading to a both/and approach. We take the best from both stories to create a new story that is enhanced by technology. The ultimate goal of education is student learning.

Professional Discussion Questions

1) Consider the examples of traditional and constructivist teaching presented in this chapter. What has been your experience as a student? How do you think that people learn best?

2) What does curriculum mean to you? Instruction? Assessment?

3) Describe your best assessment story. Which elements of assessment described in this chapter are present/missing in your story?

4) Does the new story as described in this chapter have any meaning for you? Do you agree a new story is needed? Do you see it differently from the description in this chapter?

2

Know Your Curriculum Documents and Know Your Students

In this chapter, you will learn about:

- A process to acquire an in-depth understanding of curriculum documents
- What is most important for students to Know, Do, and Be
- Essential questions
- A unifying framework
- The KDB umbrella
- The role of outcomes in curriculum documents
- Unpacking curriculum outcomes
- How to know your students

In this chapter, we explain two preliminary steps for designing curriculum. The first step is to explore relevant curriculum documents in depth to get an overview of the broad curriculum, then focus in on a specific grade level. It is easier to design an aligned curriculum for a grade when you see the big picture. But the curriculum documents only tell half the story. The second preliminary step involves knowing your students. Then, you will be ready to explore how to design a relevant and engaging curriculum unit in the next chapter.

To write this chapter, we studied curriculum documents from different provinces and subject areas. Although such documents are frequently revised, we looked for patterns based on historical and current trends across Canada and internationally. While we found many commonalities in philosophy and approach across documents, we also saw differences in terminology and the way mandates were presented. Even across subject area documents within one province there is sometimes a difference in terminology.

To have a shared understanding and a common language in which to discuss Canadian curriculum and assessment, we adopted the term **outcomes** to describe what students are expected to learn; the term includes the different provincial terminologies such as **prescribed learning outcomes**, **expectations**, **standards**, and **competencies**. We use the concepts of Know (K = knowledge), Do (D = skill) and Be (B = trait)—the KDB—to make meaning of the outcomes. Finally, we use the AfL, AaL, and AoL terms that we introduced in Chapter 1 to discuss curriculum design.

Know Your Curriculum

EXPLORING THE KNOW, DO, AND BE FRAMEWORK

The **KDB framework** is a simple but useful way to talk about curriculum documents. In this section, we expand on the terms Know, Do, and Be to provide a common vocabulary. We offer many different examples of KDB and follow this discussion with another section on how to identify the KDB in your curriculum documents.

The Know

As a most basic definition, the Know comprises the content that is mandated in curriculum documents by subject and grade level. Knowledge is sometimes classified as subject area knowledge.

Another way to look at knowledge is to look at the four categories of knowledge as defined by Lorin Anderson and colleagues (2001):

- *Factual* knowledge is essential facts or elements.
- *Conceptual* knowledge goes beyond facts and involves Enduring Understandings and Big Ideas. Conceptual knowledge is the underlying idea behind something.
- *Procedural* knowledge is how to do something: methods of inquiry, skills, techniques, or strategies. Students need to know how to do complex skills (and it is crucial that teachers teach all the subsets of these skills).
- *Metacognitive* knowledge is awareness of one's own thinking process—how one learns best. It represents the core of assessment as learning.

Deep learning is the goal of the new pedagogy. Hattie (2012) proposes a framework for deep learning and compares it to the four categories above:

> There are three major levels of achievement outcome that teachers need to consider when they prepare, teach, and evaluate their lessons: the surface knowledge needed to understand the concepts, the deeper understandings of how ideas relate to each other and extend to other understandings; and the conceptual thinking that allows surface and deep knowledge to turn into conjectures and concepts upon which to build new surface and deep understandings (p. 77).

Hattie sees single ideas and several ideas as surface knowledge, and relating ideas and elaborating ideas as deep knowledge. Students must have a certain amount of surface knowledge before they can move to the more challenging tasks of deep learning. At this point, students can understand taught concepts in a more integrated and coherent way. Finally, students can activate metacognition to understand and monitor their own cognitive processes. The differences between categories are not clear-cut and not necessarily sequential. Deeper learning involves thinking of criticisms or alternatives, proposing experimental tests, and proposing a problem and solution with a critique of the solution (Bereiter, 2002).

Hattie's (2012) research shows that the expert teacher can determine which subject matter is surface knowledge or deep knowledge, and that the number of years of experience is not predictive of this ability.

THE STRUCTURE OF KNOWLEDGE

With its emphasis on concepts, the new story in education sees knowledge differently from the factual subject-based curriculum of the traditional story. Figure 2.1 presents the structure of knowledge as interpreted by concept-based curriculum researcher Lynn Erickson (1995). Erickson herself was influenced by the seminal work of curriculum theorist Hilda Taba. In this graphic representation, facts are at the bottom of the hierarchy. Many provincial outcomes are stated at the factual level, where a topic consists of related facts. Traditionally, a topic is often the focus of a curriculum unit. In Erickson's structure of knowledge, above a topic is a concept that is made up of a number of topics; we call a concept a Big Idea. Above a Big Idea is an Enduring Understanding, sometimes called a generalization, principle, or essential learning; we would like to see units planned around Big Ideas and Enduring Understandings rather than topics. At the highest level is theory.

The Know and the Do are connected. Erickson's structure of knowledge coincides with a revised version of Bloom's taxonomy, another hierarchical way to organize knowledge. Students apply lower-level thinking skills when they remember facts. Students use higher-order thinking skills such as analysis and judgment at the higher levels of knowledge. This is one of the strongest arguments for concept-based teaching.

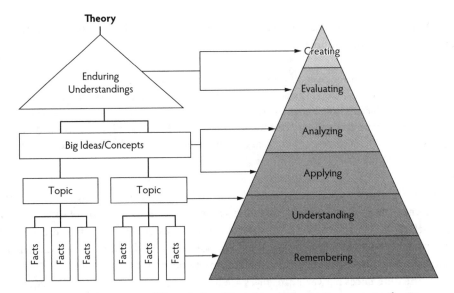

FIGURE 2.1 The Structure of Knowledge (Know) and How It Connects to the Do

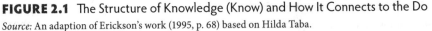

Source: An adaption of Erickson's work (1995, p. 68) based on Hilda Taba.

BIG IDEAS

For the purpose of this book we define a **Big Idea** as a concept made up of one or two words. (We recognize that some documents identify Big Ideas as statements that connect concepts, but we use the term Enduring Understanding for these statements.) Big Ideas are broad, abstract, and do not change over time (Erickson, 2005). A Big Idea is represented by many different examples. "Systems" is an example of a Big Idea. It may be a human system or a natural system, an ecosystem, a body system or systems in the body, a governmental system, a family system, a technological system, or a school system. Each system shares several characteristics: They are composed of interrelated parts that make up a whole and that may be connected to other systems. A system such as a government system may change, but the general characteristics of the concept of "system" are enduring.

As an example, consider the six fundamental Big Ideas underlying the social sciences content for K–12 in *The Ontario Curriculum* (Ontario Ministry of Education, 2000, 2004, 2005a, 2005b):

- Systems and structures
- Interaction and interdependence
- Environment
- Change and continuity
- Culture
- Power and governance

Within these Big Ideas are interrelated concepts such as patterns, environment, co-operation, change and continuity, globalization, cause and effect, urbanization, diversity, and conflict.

By 2013, the revised social sciences document for Grades 1 to 8 was designed with the twenty-first century in mind (Ontario Ministry of Education, 2013). Six fundamental Big Ideas were identified as foundational to the development of historical thinking and geographic thinking:

- Significance
- Cause and consequence
- Continuity and change
- Patterns and trends
- Interrelationships
- Perspectives

These Big Ideas are further focused in the subdisciplines of the social sciences. Significance or importance in social studies, for example, is identified as historical significance, spatial significance (geography), political significance, economic significance, and legal significance.

What is the difference between a Big Idea and a topic? A topic is usually a specific example that can fit under a larger, more abstract interdisciplinary concept. Table 2.1 shows the difference between a topic and a Big Idea. Table 2.2 offers some examples of Big Ideas

TABLE 2.1 The Difference between Topics and Big Ideas

Examples of a Topic		Big Idea
Women's movement	→	Citizenship and structure
Butterflies	→	Life cycles
Electricity	→	Energy
Canada's trade connections	→	Structures
Medieval times	→	Heritage and citizenship

TABLE 2.2 Examples of Big Ideas in Subject Areas

Science	Math	Social Sciences	Art
Matter	Patterns	Patterns	Line
Energy	Interactions	Community	Colour
Systems and interactions	Order	Co-operation	Texture
Interdependence	Cause and effect	Globalization	Form
Sustainability and stewardship	Probability	Ecosystems	Space
	Ratio	Ecology	Balance
Change and continuity	Proportion	Urbanization	Perception
Model	Model	Sustainability	Repetition
Cycle	Quantification	Conflict	Angle
Organism	Theory	Ideology	Motion
Replication	Scale	Economic/political/legal systems	Light
Order	Symmetry	Diversity	Rhythm
Population	Change	Democracy	
Cause and effect	Constancy	Justice	
	Spatial sense	Rights/responsibilities	
	Uncertainty		

English (Literature)	Technology	Music	Physical Education
Power	Aesthetics	Harmony	Stability
Conflict	Control	Rhythm	Locomotion
Passion	Environmental sustainability	Melody	Manipulation
Perception		Perception	Body awareness
Cause and effect	Ergonomics	Form	Spatial awareness
Patterns	Function	Tempo	Effort awareness
Character	Innovation	Timbre	Relationship
Order	Mechanics	Tone	Gravity
Emotion	Power and energy	Pattern repetition	Motion
Change	Safety	Form	Force
	Structure		Healthy living
	Systems		Safety

in different subject areas. It is informative to see that many are cross-disciplinary and aren't actually discipline bound.

The role of Big Ideas in language arts and math can be confusing, since these subjects can be the processing vehicles for other content areas such as science and social studies. For example, students may be learning the Big Idea of interdependence in science but use communication skills to write up a report on an experiment. Students learn content from social science about immigration and use math to calculate population change. However, language arts and math have their own conceptual Big Ideas. The Big Ideas of identity or conflict between good and evil are common themes in literature. Many mathematicians see distinctive disciplinary Big Ideas in their subject. Manitoba's curriculum differentiates between Big Ideas and topics. Topics include algebra, financial mathematics, geometry, logical reasoning, measurement, number, probability, relations and functions statistics, and trigonometry. Big Ideas are change, constancy, number sense, relationships, spatial sense, and uncertainty (Manitoba Ministry of Education, 2009, p. 7). Identified processes are skills that include communications, connections, mental mathematics and estimation, problem solving and reasoning, technology, and visualization.

Schwartz (2007) claims that students have shown a steady increase in mathematical performance since the 1990s, a period when teachers began to focus on conceptual understandings. The biggest challenge now in shifting from teaching the procedure (algorithm) to the concept (Big Idea) has been getting teachers themselves to develop a conceptual understanding of mathematics.

ENDURING UNDERSTANDINGS

In a hierarchy of the structure of knowledge, **Enduring Understandings** are above Big Ideas. Enduring Understandings may be called generalizations, principles, or essential learnings. An Enduring Understanding connects Big Ideas and shows relationships. It reflects a conceptual understanding, and it is what lasts—what a student remembers long after the lessons and facts are forgotten. Like a Big Idea, Enduring Understandings are abstract, timeless, and represent the essence of teaching and learning. Enduring Understandings are found in curriculum documents as overall or broad-based outcomes and are the most important things for students to learn. They often sound very simple, but are quite profound. Here are some examples:

- The arts are set within a social, cultural, and historical context.
- Humans have an impact on ecosystems.
- Global issues require global actions.
- Citizenship comes with rights and responsibilities.
- Earth's surface changes over time.
- Ancient societies influence present-day cultures.
- There is a relationship between nutritional choices and physical activity.
- There are widespread effects of technology on society.
- Physical activity contributes to healthy living.

Enduring Understandings hold truth when they are supported by examples, but they are not absolutely true. University lecturer Andrea Milligan and doctoral student Bronwyn Wood (2010) work in the social sciences in New Zealand. From their observations, students can only work at the level of conceptual understanding when they are engaging in higher-order thinking. They offer five important observations about Big Ideas and Enduring Understandings:

- Concepts are contestable.
- The selection of conceptual understanding makes some aspects of the social world more important at the same time as it makes other aspects less important.
- Concepts are value-laden.
- Concepts are contextual and mean different things in different contexts.
- Conceptual understandings are theoretical frameworks (people analyze and synthesize at this level).

Determining Big Ideas and Enduring Understandings is interpretive work (if they are not identified in the documents for you). From Milligan and Wood's perspective, concepts are not destination points—there is never final and complete understanding of a Big Idea or Enduring Understanding. As a final destination, the Big Idea would be reduced to a fixed and static endpoint (a collection of facts) that does not require higher-order thinking. Rather, Milligan and Wood urge us to think of conceptual understandings as transition points. A Big Idea doesn't just act as an anchor for a unit of study; it is the beginning of an ongoing, in-depth inquiry and critique of the concept expressed more fully as an Enduring Understanding. Enduring Understandings make current learning relevant to the learner's future.

ESSENTIAL QUESTIONS

Enduring Understandings should lead to rich questions. In backward design, these questions are called **Essential Questions** (Wiggins & McTighe, 2005). It is the students' task to explore the questions that emerge from the Enduring Understandings (based on provincial outcomes). The Essential Question needs to be a rich, complex question with no single right answer. Thus, students will be challenged to use higher-order thinking to address it. The question can be the beginning of, and can provide the underlying structure for, inquiry-based, problem-based, and project-based curriculum. Essential questions cut to the core and touch the heart (McKenzie, 2005). Examples of effective Essential Questions include the following:

- What is love?
- What does it mean to be a citizen?
- How do cause-and-effect patterns manifest themselves over history?
- What is the difference between wants and needs?
- How can fractions be used in real life?
- What does it mean to explore?

- When should society control individuals?
- What causes change?

Developing a unit from a central driving question rather than outcomes is another approach associated with project-based learning. The question emerges from the problem at hand. Some good driving questions suggested by The Driving Question website (http://pbl-online.org/driving_question/dqexplore/dqexplore1.html) include the following:

- Do we have too much freedom?
- How does the place we live in affect how we live?
- What is good writing?
- How can we stop the spread of infectious disease?
- Why do things cost so much?

The Do

Some skills are subject specific (e.g., adjusting a microscope lens, serving a volleyball, attaching a clarinet reed) and need to be acquired to apply other learning. However, there is increasing consensus that students also need to perform complex cross-curricular skills to live successfully in a contemporary world. These skills are often called the "twenty-first–century skills" and that is how we will refer to the Do concept in this book.

WHAT ARE THE TWENTY-FIRST–CENTURY SKILLS?

Twenty-first century skills are loosely defined but have the same goal: to prepare a student to be a productive and participatory citizen of the twenty-first century. Many governments from countries as seemingly diverse as the United States, Hong Kong, South Korea, Singapore, and Finland have adopted the twenty-first–century skills framework.

In May of 2012, C21 Canada published *Shifting Minds* (www.c21canada.org), its vision for public education for the twenty-first century. Members of the board are from both the private and public sectors. The Canadian School Boards Association has approved this document (Martellacci, 2012) and it has become quite influential. Based on solid research, *Shifting Minds* provides a comparison of twenty-first–century education frameworks from the OECD (Organisation for Economic Co-operation and Development), British Columbia, PEI, Alberta, and the Partnership for 21st Century Skills out of the United States. Building from this research, C21 identified twenty-first–century competencies with targeted outcomes and a rationale for the necessity of these competencies:

- Creativity, innovation, and entrepreneurship
- Critical thinking
- Collaboration
- Communication
- Character
- Culture and ethical citizenship
- Computer and digital technologies

Despite the almost universal acceptance of twenty-first–century skills as crucial for students of the twenty-first century, the skills have not yet been defined very well (Fullan, 2013). And a skill like "design thinking" as a component of problem solving has a new significance in the educational landscape. In the twenty-first century everyone can access information, so the difference in determining success is going to be who can create the best design—be it a business plan, a chair, or a pair of shoes (Boss, 2013; Pink, 2005). This lack of precision makes the skills difficult to teach and to assess. Educators around the world are working toward common definitions and assessments.

The goal of an international research project called Assessment and Teaching of 21st Century Skills (http://atc21s.org) is to create valid and reliable assessments for the twenty-first–century skills. Led by researcher Dr. Patrick Grifford from the University of Melbourne, this project is sponsored by Cisco, Intel, and Microsoft, companies that are interested in building a skilled workforce. Four founder countries are also involved: Australia, Finland, Singapore, and the United States. More recently Costa Rica and the Netherlands have joined.

Although some educators might believe that the corporate sponsorship of this consortium biases its results, we think this project is of key importance. First, there is a common definition of the twenty-first–century skills across many countries. Second, the project has moved from the conceptual to the practical by developing assessments for collaborative problem solving and ICT literacy (i.e., learning in digital networks). For example, PISA (the Programme for International Student Assessment) measured digital reading in 2009 and 2011. As well, PISA measured problem solving (paper based) in 2003, dynamic problem solving in 2012 (computer based), and will measure collaborative problem solving (computer based) in 2015.

PISA testing is highly influential in the world of educational reform because it tests 15-year-old students from as many as 70 countries and allows for comparisons of educational systems. When PISA assesses digital literacy and collaborative problem solving, it means that these twenty-first–century skills are becoming less abstract and more well defined; they are becoming established and will be targeted for direct instruction in classrooms around the world.

Still, we are left with the question of what does a twenty-first–century skill look like? Definitions are often in flux as we develop further understanding. You can see in the definitions of problem solving as presented in 2012 by Michael Davidson, OECD Directorate for Education and Skills, how understanding and precision are emerging. In 2003, the OECD defined problem solving like this:

> An individual's ability to use cognitive processes to confront and resolve real, cross-disciplinary situations where the solution path is not immediately obvious and where the literacy domains or curricular areas that might be applicable are not within a single domain of mathematics, science or reading (Davidson, 2012).

In 2012, problem-solving competency was expected to be computer based and was defined like this:

> An individual's competency to engage in cognitive processing to understand and resolve problem situations where a method or solution is not immediately obvious. It includes the

willingness to engage with such situations in order to achieve one's potential as a constructive and reflective citizen (Davidson, 2012).

A typical problem was to organize the seating at a dinner party that fulfilled a number of complicated conditions of who was to sit beside whom. The task was done on the computer by dragging different "people" around the table until they sat in the right places.

By 2015, PISA will look at a collaborative problem-solving competency, which will measure how well an individual works with two or more others to solve a problem. Draft categories of the problem-solving process for this task are exploring and understanding, representing and formulating, planning and executing, and monitoring and reflecting. Students will be measured on their collaborative competency in establishing understanding, taking action, and establishing organization during the process.

Teachers will be more familiar with the **higher-order thinking skills (HOTS)** that are end goals in most twenty-first–century curriculum. But what do HOTS look like? How do you assess them? Renowned curriculum and assessment theorist Susan Brookhart (2004) includes the following in her definition of HOTS:

- Analysis, evaluation, and creation
- Logical reasoning
- Judgment and critical thinking
- Problem solving, creativity, and creative thinking

We agree with Brookhart, and we use the term HOTS to refer to the higher levels in **Bloom's revised taxonomy** (see Table 2.3). In the traditional model, **Bloom's taxonomy** (1956) was a useful tool that helped teachers create learning objectives and connect them to rich performance assessment tasks. Although not originally intended as a hierarchy, educators interpreted it this way. More recently, educators recognized that Bloom's taxonomy did not go far enough to incorporate the necessary twenty-first–century skills. Revised by a number of academics, the modified version of the original taxonomy is widely used (Krathwohl, 2002). In Bloom's original, synthesis was the highest level; the highest level of thinking is now creating—the generation of new knowledge.

Table 2.3 shows developmental patterns and also gives a starting point for designing tasks that demand a certain level of thinking. It is this developmental pattern that we see matched up with the structure of knowledge in Figure 2.1. However, we must take care to avoid oversimplification. Summarizing, for example, is usually associated with lower-level understanding, but summarizing can be a HOTS if the task requires analysis and evaluation to organize ideas and to distinguish main ideas from supporting details.

Finally, to assess a HOTS we need to deconstruct the selected skill to determine the criteria for success. Once we know these criteria, we are better able to devise teaching activities and rich performance assessment tasks and tools to address the criteria.

TABLE 2.3 Bloom's Revised Taxonomy of Thinking Skills

Remembering	Understanding	Applying	Analyzing	Evaluating	Creating
Lower-level thinking →		→	→	**Higher-level thinking**	
Retrieving, recognizing, recalling relevant knowledge from long-term memory	Constructing meaning from oral, written, and graphic messages through interpreting, exemplifying, classifying, summarizing, inferring, comparing, and explaining	Carrying out or using a procedure through executing or implementing	Breaking material into constituent parts, determining how the parts relate to one another and to an overall structure or purpose through differentiating, organizing, and attributing	Making judgments based on criteria and standards through checking and critiquing	Putting elements together to form a coherent or functional whole; reorganizing elements into a new pattern or structure through generating, planning, or producing
		Associated Task Action Verbs			
Recall	Discuss	Apply	Analyze	Check	Construct
List	Classify	Execute	Organize	Assess	Design
Name	Summarize	Implement	Attribute	Estimate	Create
Identify	Compare	Use	Categorize	Rank	Improvise
Repeat	Explain	Perform	Investigate	Justify	Invent
Quote	Infer	Practise	Experiment	Argue	Compose
Label	Interpret	Demonstrate	Distinguish	Evaluate	Generate
Recognize			Examine	Critique	Plan
					Produce

Source: Adapted from Saskatchewan Ministry of Education (2010), p. 14. Retrieved from https://www.edonline.sk.ca/bbcswebdav/library/curricula/English/Renewed_Curricula.pdf. Used with permission of Saskatchewan Ministry of Education.

The Be

When the pendulum swung from a more holistic, integrated approach to a standards-based approach in the mid-1990s the Be component disappeared from curriculum outcomes—at least explicitly. A circulating myth told of the end of the careers of the unfortunate outcome-based gurus of the day when a school was sued by a boy's parents. The boy had done well academically, but he had failed to be a nice person and thus did not graduate. Whether there is any truth to this story we do not know, but it sums up the climate of the times. Education in the mid-1990s was to be objective and value free. All standards were to be measurable and observable. Success was measured through standardization.

But not everyone endorsed this vision. In 1999, UNESCO published a report of the International Commission on Education for the 21st century called *Learning: The Treasure Within.* Author Jacques Delors (1999) presented a powerful plea to view education in a broader context than measurable objective outcomes and standardization. He offered four pillars of education for the twenty-first century: learning to know, learning to do, learning to be, and learning to live together.

Fortunately, more and more evidence is accumulating to connect enhanced academic performance with the Be (Adams, 2013). If students come to school feeling safe, for example, they are more likely to learn. Scientific evidence from 69 studies has supported the effectiveness of 33 different character education programs to enhance the academic goals of schools (Berkowitz & Bier, 2011). A meta-analysis of socio-emotional learning (SEL) in 213 school-based programs from K–12 showed significant improvement in academic performance, social and emotional skills, attitudes, and behaviour when these techniques were used (Durlak, Weissberg, Dymnicki, Taylor, & Schellinger, 2011).

Most educators today recognize that the Be is important. Indeed, Fullan (2013) is calling for character education and citizenship as key twenty-first–century platforms. According to the Action Canada report *Future Tense* (2013), Quebec and Alberta teachers perceived the most character development in their curriculum, but generally Canadian teachers say they personally put more emphasis on the importance of character development than they felt their curricula did. Teachers also felt the curriculum put more onus on them than on parents for character development.

Character education has become an integral part of Ontario's K–12 program, and in some jurisdictions it is infused into various subject areas. The York Region District School Board in Ontario, for example, describes character education as interwoven through every aspect of school life, from how students and staff members greet one another to how discussions evolve in all subject areas at all levels to expectations of conduct during sports activities. The focus is on safe schools, anti-bullying, and ethical conduct (York Region District School Board, n.d.). A teaching resource on literacy for adolescents addresses self-regulation, a facet of the Be, through both AaL and giving student voice in the classroom (EduGAINS, 2012).

In Quebec, the Be is addressed through cross-curricular personal and social competencies. Quebec lists intellectual and behavioural attitudes for students to acquire and cultivate as they carry out their tasks (see Table 2.4). The student achieves his or her potential and co-operates with others.

In the Manitoba Social Studies documents, outcomes are labelled as knowledge, skills, and values. For example, in the Grade 7 Social Studies course "People and Places in the World" (Manitoba Ministry of Education, 2006), the following value-based outcomes are identified in the citizenship strand:

- Respect the inherent dignity of all people.
- Acknowledge that the rights of citizenship involve limitations on personal freedom for the sake of the collective quality of life.
- Be willing to contribute to their groups and their communities.
- Be willing to take action to support quality of life for all people around the world.

TABLE 2.4 Attitudes that Promote the Development of Twenty-First–Century Competencies

Intellectual Attitudes	Behavioural Attitudes
Curious	Autonomous
Open-minded	Self-disciplined
Creative	Committed
Ingenious	Shows initiative
Takes intellectual risks	Sense of organization
Tolerant of ambiguity	Perseverance
Interest in comparing ideas	Makes an effort
Critical thinking	Concern for a job well done
Realistic	Listens to others
Intellectually rigorous	Respect for self and others
Objective	Respect for intellectual property
Methodical approach to work	Co-operative
Concern for accurate, precise language	Concern for major contemporary issues

Source: Adapted from Quebec Ministry of Education (2007), p. 20.

Since the Be is value-laden, a potential problem is determining whose values are considered the "right" values or which values are worthy of cultivating. This question is particularly true in a multicultural country like Canada.

THE RELATIONSHIP AMONG THE KNOW, DO, AND BE

When we view education as a system, we see connections among the many different elements that are treated as separate entities in the traditional model. We propose that education is three interconnected, dynamic, simultaneous systems:

- Curriculum, instruction, and assessment
- The Know, Do, and Be
- Assessment of, for, and as learning

These three systems interact with each other like woven threads of a tapestry. To make the mix more complex, the boundaries of subject areas are also blurring in an age when interdisciplinary Big Ideas, and twenty-first–century skills are most important to learn.

When we look across curriculum documents, we see how the Know, Do, and Be are interdependent. Take, for example, the revised Ontario social studies curriculum document for Grades 1 to 8 (Ontario Ministry of Education, 2013). The introductory material describes a twenty-first–century context where the educator creates a classroom environment considering the Self/Spirit of the student and the development of cognitive, emotional, social, and physical domains. Threaded throughout the curriculum, the Know is represented by Big Ideas found in the content knowledge. The Do is disciplinary thinking (historical and geographical) and inquiry thinking. The central goal of the curriculum speaks to the Be: The student is to be an "informed, productive, responsible and active citizen in their own communities and in the world" (p. 3).

Understanding Curriculum Documents

Now that you understand the concepts of the KDB it's time to apply them to an understanding of your curriculum documents. When you are planning your unit, you will need to analyze curriculum documents to determine the KDB components.

UNIFYING FRAMEWORK

In Canada, curriculum documents are designed at the provincial level and include both the introductory material (front matter) and desired outcomes for appropriate grade levels. The introduction may provide a **unifying framework** that encompasses common goals for K–12. (In Quebec, the final year is called CEGEP. We use the term K–12 to include CEGEP unless we are talking specifically about Quebec.) Also included in curriculum documents is a stance on classroom assessment.

Together, the introductory material and the learning outcomes form the curriculum that educators are responsible for teaching. These documents are not a "living" curriculum. Curriculum comes alive only when it is implemented with real students in real classrooms.

A unifying framework is valuable because it acts like an umbrella over the entire K–12 curricula. This umbrella tells us what is most important for students to know, do, and be by the end of their school experience. A unifying framework offers a big picture of the goals of education for that province. We interpreted the introductory material of curriculum documents from across the country to identify a unifying framework that focuses on twenty-first–century skills that cut across the K–12 curriculum. While the twenty-first–century skills are defined slightly differently among provinces (Action Canada, 2013), we focus on the similarities among them.

The Atlantic provinces use a graphic representation of a cube that acts as a unifying framework to show the Essential Graduation Learnings. All teachers in all subject areas from K–12 are to incorporate these Essential Graduation Learnings in their teaching. The Essential Graduation Learnings are listed below with our interpretation of this particular learning as a Do or a Be; some of these can be categorized as both Do and Be. The Know comes from the content in different subject areas.

- Aesthetic expression (Do)
- Citizenship (Be)
- Communication (Do)
- Personal development (Be)
- Problem solving (Do)
- Technological competence (Do)

Alberta, Saskatchewan, and Quebec use concentric circles to represent similar ideas of what is most important to Know, Do, and Be. C21 Canada uses a similar graphic to describe their vision for the 21st Century learner. Based on these frameworks, we offer a picture of the 21st Century learner in Figure 2.2

In Ontario, the strategic direction announced in January 2013 by Michael Fullan at the annual Ontario Education Research Symposium offered a unifying framework that included six Cs: character education, citizenship, communication, collaboration, critical thinking, and problem solving and creativity. As in the other provinces, the six Cs transcend the disciplines. Ontario also threads an assessment philosophy through each subject area document from K–12. In the introductory material of each Ontario curriculum guideline there is an achievement chart that is to be used for grading and reporting. *Growing Success* (Ontario Ministry of Education, 2010b) is a policy document that mandates AfL, AaL, and AoL for all grades at all levels. Quebec has taken a similar approach in using assessment to unify curriculum (see Quebec Ministry of Education, 2003).

THE KDB UMBRELLA

We use the image of an umbrella as an overarching organizer for the curriculum. The umbrella identifies what is most important to Know, Do, and Be in a particular context

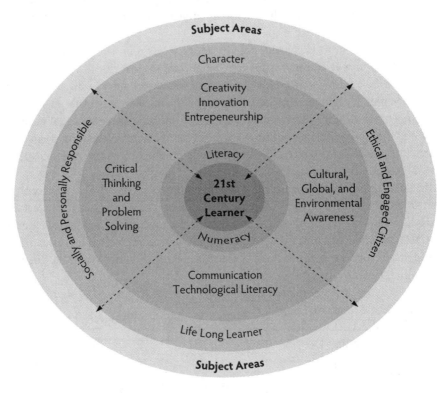

FIGURE 2.2 The 21st Century Learner

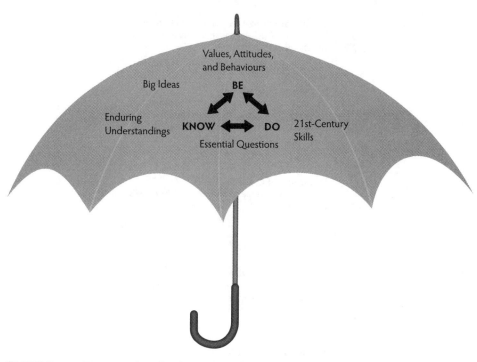

FIGURE 2.3 The Template for the KDB Umbrella

(see Figure 2.3). The KDB umbrella can be created at many different levels—from a unifying framework for all subjects, to a specific subject area from K–12, to the unit you are planning to teach.

Your umbrella will include the Know (Big Ideas, Enduring Understandings) and the Do (twenty-first–century skills) as well as the Be (the most important values, attitudes, or behaviours you would like students to demonstrate). When you are planning a specific unit you will also include the Essential Question(s) to guide the unit planning. Regardless of whether your umbrella is created for the entire K–12 curricula or for a specific unit, *less is more*. If the umbrella is cluttered with details, it will not be as useful in your planning.

SPIRALLING CURRICULUM OUTCOMES WITHIN A SUBJECT AREA

Not all outcomes are created equal. The most important things to Know, Do, and Be spiral throughout the curriculum. They are usually identified as overall outcomes. Outcomes are repeated because they represent what is most important for a student to learn during his or her time in school. Inquiry and research skills run through all grades of science and social science at increasingly complex levels. Figure 2.4 shows how one outcome in English spirals from K–12 to more sophisticated levels as students move through the school years.

English Language Arts Curriculum Outcome
Students will use language to enhance the precision
and clarity of their own and others' writing.

by the end of Grade 12:
Students will, independently and collaboratively,
revise selected texts of their own and others
for cohesion and clarity, demonstrating control
of a range of appropriate stylistic features.

by the end of Grade 9:
Students will, independently and collaboratively,
use a range of strategies and techniques
to revise selected drafts for cohesion, clarity
and impact.

by the end of Grade 6:
Students will, independently and collaboratively,
use a range of strategies and techniques
to extend and clarify selected drafts.

by the end of Grade 3:
Students will, independently and collaboratively,
make revisions to selected drafts for meaning
and clarity of expression.

FIGURE 2.4 The Atlantic Canada Framework for Essential Graduation
Source: Atlantic Provinces Education Foundation (2001), p. 17.

Similarly a Big Idea may reappear over the years to be taught with different content. For example, the Big Idea of "systems and interactions" spirals through life sciences in characteristics of how living things grow (Grade 1), growth and change in plants (Grade 2), growth and change in animals (Grade 3), habitats (Grade 4), human organ systems (Grade 5), biodiversity (Grade 6), interactions in the environment (Grade 7), sustainable ecosystems (Grade 9), to diversity of living things (Grade 11) (Ontario Ministry of Education, 2007, 2008a, 2008b).

Since the twenty-first–century skills are interdisciplinary, you will find them in more than one subject area. Similarly the twenty-first–century skills spiral across the curriculum and throughout grades. Communication appears in all curriculum documents. As evidenced in Table 2.5, English teachers are no longer the only ones responsible for teaching communication skills.

UNPACKING THE INDIVIDUAL OUTCOMES

A general rule is that the nouns in the stated outcomes represent the Know, and the verbs represent the Do. Most curriculum outcomes are complex when they are deconstructed. The more complex the outcome, the more you need to go beyond the noun and verb analysis.

TABLE 2.5 How a Twenty-First–Century Skill Connects across Subject Areas in Atlantic Canada

Subject Area Outcomes for Communication	Essential Graduation Outcome for Communication
Science Students will communicate an understanding of the major concepts and principles of science and technology.	
Mathematics Students will demonstrate an understanding that graphs are one method of representing a quantitative relationship and realize that a relationship may also be shown with a verbal description, a formula, a table of values, and/or a set of ordered pairs.	Graduates will be able to use the listening, viewing, speaking, reading, and writing modes of language(s), and mathematical and scientific concepts and symbols to think, learn, and communicate effectively.
English Language Arts Students will speak and listen to explore, extend, clarify, and reflect on their thoughts.	
Music Students will demonstrate understanding of the use of language as lyrics for songwriting.	
Social Studies Students will be able to organize information garnered from various sources, including maps, charts, graphs, globes, print and media texts, and the arts.	

Source: Adapted from Atlantic Provinces Education Foundation (2001), p. 14. http://www.ednet.ns.ca/files/reports/essential_grad_learnings.pdf

There may not be an explicit Be evident in an outcome because outcomes are written to be observable and measurable, but often there is an implicit Be. Consider the unpacking of the outcomes presented in Table 2.6. The verb is in bold and represents a Do. The nouns are italicized and are part of the Know.

FINDING THE KDB IN CURRICULUM DOCUMENTS

Identifying the KDB is interpretive work and a good collaborative exercise. Discussions around the meaning of each outcome using a KDB lens are usually rich and illuminating. Deep understanding of outcomes ensures that you are teaching what you are committed to teaching and not just checking off an outcome as covered in a peripheral and superficial way (which is a common practice).

Finding the Know

If your curriculum document has named the Big Ideas and Enduring Understandings in specific areas, you need to identify outcomes that are connected to these concepts. Otherwise, you will need to interpret the outcomes yourself to find a conceptual focus for your upcoming

TABLE 2.6 Unpacking Learning Outcomes

Outcome	Know	Do	Be
Describe how *studies of the depletion of the ozone layer* and the *increase in acid rain* have led to *innovations and stricter regulations* on *emissions from cars, factories, and other polluting technologies* Nova Scotia, Grade 5, Science	Studies of depletion of the ozone layer, increase in acid rain Innovations and regulations Emissions (cars, factories, other polluting technologies) **Possible Big Idea:** Cause and effect	Describe the relationship between the two	Environmental stewards (implicit)
Analyze the impact of *knowledge acquired from historical events on the future of contemporary societies* Saskatchewan, Grade 9, Social Studies	Knowledge of historical events Impact of knowledge acquired from historical events on future and contemporary societies **Possible Big Idea:** Cause and effect	Analyze Predict	Critical thinker Value historical events
To **understand** *life situations* with a view to **constructing** a *moral frame of reference* Quebec, Level 1 to 6, Moral Education and Personal Development	Life situations Moral frame of reference **Possible Big Idea:** Moral frame of reference **Enduring Understanding:** Successful humans act in ways that are consistent with a personal moral framework	Understand Construct	Act in ways that are consistent with a personal moral framework
Compare and **contrast** how *social values* are **communicated** in *several drama forms* and/or *styles of live theatre from different times and places* Ontario, Grade 7, The Arts	Social values Different types of drama forms Styles of live theatre from different times and places **Possible Big Ideas:** Social values Culture Social Values **Enduring Understanding:** Societies past and present use or have used drama to communicate social values	Compare and contrast	Historically literate Geographic

unit. Looking at the introductory material of your document and at the Big Ideas chart in Table 2.2 should be helpful. Enduring Understandings are often (but not always) found in the overall outcomes.

Once you have identified one or two concepts—Big Ideas and Enduring Understandings—you will need to think about how a student will demonstrate his or her understanding and how various levels of understanding could be made visible. What do you, the teacher, need to know about concept development to assess a student's progress? What types of instructional activities could students do to build knowledge and deepen understanding? What kinds of formative assessment can you give to encourage greater sophistication of knowledge and skills? The paradox is that in order to identify a Big Idea and think about teaching it, you need to know what it looks like from an assessment perspective—what are the criteria that demonstrate understanding? Clearly, instruction and assessment are interwoven here.

An emerging twenty-first–century issue is the assessment of concept development—which represents a departure, since the old story has been concerned largely with the accumulation of facts. Table 2.7 shows a rubric for conceptual development of a Big Idea and Enduring Understanding. In this combined rubric, development moves from the concrete to the abstract level. At ascending levels, the student makes more connections, reflecting more interdisciplinary conceptualization. Note that the creators of this rubric used five levels to describe concept development rather than the more typical four levels. There are many different ways to create rubrics, as discussed in Chapter 3.

Finding the Do

Finding the twenty-first–century skills in curriculum documents requires a different process than finding the Know. There are a number of twenty-first–century skills, and there will always be at least one such skill present in every document. Since these skills are interdisciplinary, you will find the same ones, such as communication, in more than one subject area. The knowledge in a subject area can be specialized, but disseminating that knowledge requires communication, whether it is a written essay, an oral presentation, a piece of art, or a graph.

These twenty-first–century skills occur across curriculum documents. Some of them will be easy to recognize and others less so.

- Communication: reading, writing, speaking, listening (with a variety of "texts")
- Higher-order thinking skills: problem solving, reasoning, critical thinking, research, inquiry skills, integrative thinking, creative thinking
- Design and construction: creative thinking, combining information in innovative ways, application of imaginative planning
- Disciplinary literacies: numeracy, scientific, historical, geographical, arts, movement, health, financial
- New literacies: technological, media, critical, environmental, financial, visual, movement

We see certain complex skills repeated over and over again in curriculum documents, whether in a disciplinary guideline or an overview of the policy for K–12. These skills are not necessarily labelled and described—this is where the curriculum designer comes in.

A twenty-first–century skill is a complex interdisciplinary skill with many parts. Sometimes the parts of a complex skill can be found as outcomes clustered together in

TABLE 2.7 Rubric for Concept Development and Enduring Understandings

Level of Understanding	Beginning	Developing	Competent	Proficient	Expert
Big Ideas	Can state the Big Idea in communication.	Can restate the definition of the Big Idea in her or his own language.	Can give examples and nonexamples of the Big Idea	Can provide key attributes of the Big Idea.	Can link the Big Idea with other related concepts.
Example	Migration	"Migration is movement of living things for a real purpose."	Examples: Butterflies Whales Salmon Nonexamples: When a subdivision is built Fires Accidents	Beneficial Change Large groups Movement Purposeful Causes Effects Universal	"People and animals migrate to improve their chances to meet their needs."
Enduring Understandings	Defines and provides examples of the Big Idea.	Identifies a relationship between two or more Big Ideas.	Explains the relationship as conditional (e.g., if/then, cause/effect, part/whole)	Provides novel examples of Enduring Understandings within a discipline.	Provides novel examples across disciplines.
Example	Butterflies Whales Salmon	"Animals move around to get what they need."	"Animal migration is about reasons and results."	"We studied whale migration in class but migration happens a lot in biology, for example, with butterflies and even people."	"Migration in animals is like the Westward movement in history."

Source: Based on the work of Tomlinson et al. (2009), p. 88.

the documents. Alternatively, the parts of the skill may be scattered throughout, in which case the curriculum designer must cluster the outcomes together. Each part of the skill or individual outcome can be taught separately, but it is good to understand the outcomes as parts of a whole.

Research is a good example of a complex cross-disciplinary skill. Each discipline takes a slightly different perspective and puts its own stamp on research procedures. Stripped down, however, the procedural steps of research are similar. Table 2.8 compares the most basic steps in the scientific method and research in the social sciences.

You can see in Table 2.9 that the basic steps of the creative process are similar to those of the research process in science and the social sciences. Each subset of skills is described, allowing the teacher to imagine possibilities for scaffolding instructional and assessment activities to develop them.

Although some argue that creativity cannot be taught, and think that describing a creative process in lockstep detail defies the very nature of creativity, we like the direction that the newer curricula are going. Indeed, creativity is on every nation's list of twenty-first–century skills that we have seen.

Finding the Be

The Be is not necessarily explicit in the outcomes, but is usually implicit. A problem with assessing the Be is that it is not clear how to measure it in an objective way. Ontario has dealt with this dilemma by identifying the Be as learning skills and work habits. To signal the importance of the learning skills, they appear at the front of a student's report card.

Snapshot from the Classroom: Teaching and Assessing Creativity

Creativity is a key twenty-first–century skill. In Ontario high school teacher Steve Fralick's class, creativity is seamlessly interwoven throughout his curriculum, instruction, and assessment. Curriculum documents for the Arts stress critical analysis and the creative process—skills that Fralick recognizes all students can demonstrate regardless of their level of performance. He uses the steps of the creative process to plan curriculum and assess student achievement. In his Grade 10 guitar class, students write and perform a song as a performance assessment task that is rich in instructional possibilities. The project has many steps reflecting the process shown in Table 2.9 from inspiration and planning to deciding on tools and technology to modify the song based on feedback. There is plenty of formative assessment feedback along the way, including peer and self-assessment. Fralick continually asks students where they are currently in the creative process and what he should be looking for in their work at that stage. Because students have co-constructed the assessment rubric with him at the outset, they know how to apply assessment criteria to answer his questions.

TABLE 2.8   Subset of Skills in Research for Science and Social Sciences

Science	Social Sciences
Identify a worthwhile problem	Identify a worthwhile problem
Ask a good question	Ask a good question
Research the problem	Gather data to answer the question
Construct a hypothesis	Organize and analyze data
Conduct an experiment	Make conclusions
Analyze results	Communicate results
Make conclusions	Use correct terminology and the guidelines provided in recognized style manuals in producing written reports and/or audiovisual presentations and in citing sources
Accept or reject the hypothesis	
Communicate results	
Use correct terminology	

TABLE 2.9   The Creative Process

Stage of Process	Possible Activities for the Student
Challenge and inspire	Generate creative ideas as a response to the teacher, other students, or any stimulus as a creative challenge.
Imagine and generate	Generate possible solutions to the creative challenge. Some possible strategies are brainstorming, thumbnail sketches, choreographic sketches, musical sketches, and mind mapping.
Plan and focus	Create a plan for a work of art. Determine and articulate a focus and choose an appropriate art form.
Explore and experiment	Explore a range of elements and techniques. Make an artistic choice for a work.
Produce preliminary work	Produce a preliminary version. Share the preliminary work with peers and teacher and seek their opinions and responses.
Revise and refine	Refine the initial work on the basis of students' own reflection and others' feedback.
Present and perform	Complete the art work and present/perform it for an audience (e.g. their peers, a teacher, the public).
Reflect and evaluate	Reflect on the degree of success of the work with reference to specific aspects that went well or that could be improved. Use the results of this reflection as a basis for starting another arts project.

Source: Adapted from "The Creative Process" in Ontario Ministry of Education (2010c), p. 16.

TABLE 2.10 Learning Skills Observation Checklist

Category	Observed Behaviours	Date of Activity Comments			
		Amir	Ben	Cathy	Dan
Responsibility	Completes assignment on time				
	Completes homework				
	Demonstrates appropriate behaviour in class				
Organization	Established monthly learning goal in journal				
	Manages time effectively to complete tasks				
	Maintains an orderly workspace and notebooks				
Independent work	Uses class time to focus on tasks				
	Follows instructions				
Collaboration	Takes on appropriate and fair amount of work in group tasks				
	Plays various roles (leader, recorder, organizer, etc.)				
	Shares ideas, information, expertise, and resources				
	Shows respect for others				
	Shows willingness to help others				
Initiative	Shows a positive attitude to new tasks				
	Generates and acts on ideas				
	Shows willingness to take risks, try new things				
Self-regulation	Sets goals and checks own progress in learning log				
	Asks for help when needed				
	Completes self-assessment portion of assignments				
	Perseveres when facing difficult work				

Source: Based on Ontario Ministry of Education (2010b), p. 11.

The observation checklist based on Ontario learning skills seen in Table 2.10 offers concrete, observable criteria that describe what a teacher could be watching for, and helps students understand what learning skills and work habits look like.

Defining the Be is the first step. What does it look like in practice? What constitutes as evidence for such a quality as *initiative,* for example? In London, Ontario, the Managing Information for Student Achievement (MISA) group developed a number of videos showing examples of what each learning skill looks like. The evidence is found in specific student behaviours. Table 2.11 offers the criteria for "initiative" and some suggested evidence. Evidence then can be used to "measure" initiative as an aspect of the Be, and this can be used to report qualitatively.

TABLE 2.11 Student Evidence to Show Initiative

Criteria for Initiative	Suggested Evidence
Looks for and acts on new ideas and opportunities for learning	Student signs up for a student conference to discuss next steps Follows through with plan
Demonstrates the capacity for innovation and a willingness to take risks	Student uses math manipulatives Student makes choice for culminating activity
Demonstrates curiosity and interest in learning	Student looks at an anchor chart posted in the room and uses it as a guide for problem solving
Approaches new tasks with a positive attitude	Student begins the culminating project promptly and meets checkpoint deadlines; student shows his or her thinking in front of peers
Recognizes and advocates appropriately for the rights of self and others	Student works collaboratively in a reading buddy activity; older students advocate for the needs of younger students

Source: Adapted from MISA (2012).

Know Your Students

Although an educator may use the same curriculum document multiple times, a unit of study changes each year because of the uniqueness of the students and the dynamic global issues impacting their world. The curriculum can be relevant only when it connects to students' interests and experiences. To create a relevant curriculum, it is important to know your students.

Teachers can collect various pieces of information to illuminate the strengths and needs of an individual learner to inform the planning process. They can learn a lot from official student records before meeting the students. These records include provincial test scores, standardized or aptitude test results, previous report cards, and classroom assessments. Individual education plans that outline specific physical or learning accommodations and modifications that need to be addressed are also included. Portfolios from previous years can provide a rich picture of a student's proficiency and interests.

POSSIBLE SOURCES OF STUDENT BACKGROUND INFORMATION

Possible sources of information that can be compiled on a student profile include the following:

- Review of OSR (official school record), including current and previous report cards
- Consultation with parents
- Consultation with previous teacher(s)

- Consultation with support team
- Classroom observation checklist
- Educational assessments (e.g., pretests related to curriculum)
- Multiple Intelligences Survey or Learning Style Inventory
- Work samples, assignments, and projects
- Portfolios
- Teacher–student conference
- Peer and self-assessments
- Interest survey

Once the students are in the class, the teacher can learn from the students themselves. What are they interested in? What matters to them? An informal conversation—perhaps about extracurricular activities—is a good starting point. Questions, interviews, and self-descriptions are also helpful. A more formal method of collecting this information is using student interest surveys, either commercial online versions or teacher-designed electronic documents created through a web-based application like SurveyMonkey.

It is good to know about the students' social, cultural, and socioeconomic backgrounds. This is particularly true if you notice unusual behaviour. Does a student get a good breakfast each morning? Is something happening outside of school that is affecting behaviour? How might the home situation affect the student's classroom experience? Does the curriculum acknowledge the background of the student? For example, if you teach Aboriginal students, do you acknowledge their unique culture and include representations of the diversity of Aboriginal peoples? In today's multicultural classrooms, it is challenging but crucial to be aware of the socioeconomic and cultural characteristics of your students. Home visits and integrating the expertise of family members can be ways to value students' personal and cultural knowledge.

STUDENTS' PRE-KNOWLEDGE AND SKILLS

Getting to know your students also involves **diagnostic assessment**. Diagnostic assessment provides information about what students already know and can do, their preferred learning styles and multiple intelligences, and their general interests. The assessment happens before instruction and is considered to be one of the two planks of assessment for learning, the other being formative assessment. It is important to do a wide range of diagnostic assessments and keep an open mind. Diagnostic information can come from various sources.

Determining Current Content Knowledge and Skill Level

What do the students already know and what can they already do with regard to the targeted outcomes? To ascertain this information, a teacher designs and administers diagnostic or pre-instructional assessments (AfL) as part of the unit of study, perhaps using a KWL strategy (students brainstorm what they already *know*, what they *want* to know, and how will they know when they have *learned* it).

Getting to Know your Students Using Student Profiles

An idea that is taking off in the UK is the one-page profile (Smith, 2012). This profile is a living document that travels with a student through his or her school career and is updated frequently. There are three questions. The first question is "What do other people appreciate about me (character, gifts, talents)?" Friends, families, and teachers answer this question. The student, with a parent, answers the second and third questions: "What is important to me (interests, activities, people, classroom activities)?" and "How can someone support me?" Teachers who use this profile say it is not just another piece of paper; it helps them personalize the curriculum and build relationships with students because they can talk to students about their goals and interests.

Another important consideration is to determine the level of technological literacy of students in the classroom. Educators can use the technological tools familiar to students to teach them how to manage information and apply twenty-first–century skills to new and unpredictable situations. Students may also teach peers (and their teacher) the skills they have acquired, resulting in a collaborative and reciprocal learning community. Still, technology itself is not useful unless it is used as part of an instructional strategy to meet clear curricular goals.

Learning Preferences

There are a variety of ways that both the teacher and student can explore learning preferences. The Ministry of Education in Ontario recommends that teachers consider the following areas.

LEARNING STYLES

There are many different theories on **learning styles**. One popular approach used by educators, called VARK, suggests that there are three kinds of learning styles or modalities: auditory learners, visual learners, and kinesthetic/tactile learners (Fleming & Mills, 1992). There are free online learning styles inventories that teachers can administer to their students (e.g., http://learning-styles-online.com/inventory/#online). Older students could take the VARK questionnaire, which can be found at www.vark-learn.com/english/page .asp?p=questionnaire.

MULTIPLE INTELLIGENCES

Another way to get to know your students is through Howard Gardner's (1983) **multiple intelligences**. Gardner challenged the traditional understanding that intelligence is fixed and can only be measured through the student's logical and linguistic abilities. Multiple intelligences support the idea that individuals can demonstrate their intellectual abilities in eight different ways (verbal/linguistic, visual/spatial, musical/rhythmic, intrapersonal, interpersonal, logical/mathematical, bodily/kinesthetic, and naturalist). Multiple intelligence surveys can be found online.

TRIARCHIC INTELLIGENCES

The theory of **triarchic intelligences** is based on the work of Robert Sternberg (1988, 1997). Students all have three intelligences and use them to different degrees:

- Analytical: logical
- Practical: applied in a real-world context
- Creative: innovative

The goal is to balance the three as well as strengthen them. An inventory of these intelligences can be found at www.schultzcenter.org/pdf/sternberg_inventory.pdf.

ENVIRONMENTAL PREFERENCES

How do students work best? Alone or with others? In a structured or flexible work setting? With bright or dimmed lights? With ear buds for music or white noise? Some researchers question the idea that students have fixed learning styles, but many agree that providing multiple ways to learn does improve student learning (Hattie, 2012; Willingham, 2004). Teachers find thinking about learning preferences, however, enables them to design creative instructional strategies and assessments.

Teachers can record the information they learn about their students on a student profile. Student profiles allow for the consolidation and analysis of the various pieces of information to illuminate the strengths and needs of an individual learner, and can inform the planning process to support all learners. Table 2.12 is an example of a teacher's class profile.

Teachers can use data to create a responsive and student-centred learning environment. They can accommodate the learning needs of the students in their class by planning various activities to capitalize on student strengths. As well, teachers can provide opportunities for students to work outside their comfort zones. Students also benefit from knowing themselves as learners; knowing their preferred ways of learning is a form of assessment as learning.

Cooper (2011) offers one caution about accumulating information about students. He points out that teachers need to gather diagnostic data with a purpose. It is easy, for example, to administer a multiple intelligences survey and apply it superficially rather than giving it deep thought about how to use it effectively to actually support learning. Another caution is raised in the stories of teachers Helen Pereira-Raso and Mary (see Snapshot box).

Conclusion

In this chapter, you have learned two important preliminary steps for designing a curriculum: knowing your curriculum, knowing your students. In each step there is a lot to consider. The next chapter will describe the three steps of backward design.

TABLE 2.12 A Sample Class Profile

Student	Learning Style/ Preference	Strengths	Needs	Instructional Strategies	Assessment Strategies
Abdul	Bodily/ Kinesthetic Logical/ Mathematical Intrapersonal	• inquiry • problem solver • reflective • technological skills • independent thinker	• support with communication • literacy skills	• hands on • small groups • inquiry based • interactive white board	• use of technology • project based
Aleisha	Auditory Interpersonal	• explaining ideas • class discussions • working in groups • collaborating	• problem solving • analyzing • communicating in writing	• technology (iPod with headphones) • response journal • literature circles • co-operative learning	• oral responses • video project (e.g., podcast) • debate • project presentation
Josh	Visual/ Spatial	• artistic creations • graphic representations	• inquiry • problem solving • analyzing	• anchor chart creation • graphic organizers • individual technological device	• portfolio • game creation • aesthetic products
Zoe	Tactile Logical/ Mathematical Interpersonal	• creating models • reflective • problem solving • analyzer	• communicating in writing • public speaking	• co-operative learning • open-ended problems • goal setting	• aesthetic products • portfolio • virtual models

Source: Adapted Ontario Ministry of Education (2011), p. 39.

Snapshots of Knowing Your Students

Helen Pereira-Raso teaches in an Ontario high school. During conversations with her colleagues, she realized she had judged her students before she even met them. She had been influenced by Ontario school record data or by other teachers. She decided she needed to hear from the students themselves. Although she had always felt that she had listened carefully and created spaces for students to share in her classroom, now listening took a new form. Today, Helen listens with a purpose, and she is fully present and engaged. She listens to how and what students are thinking and why they are thinking it. She listens for evidence as to how they are engaging with the material they are exploring in class. She listens to understand and take cues of where to go next in the learning process, knowing that at times this means that different students require different things. She engages in respectful conversations with her students, acknowledging the knowledge they bring to each class. Her listening reflects the deeper, more holistic way she sees her students.

Wendy, one of the authors of this text, worked with an intermediate teacher named Mary who was known to be thoughtful, inclusive, student centred, and reflective about her practice. At one time, Mary did not look at the official student records because she wanted each student to start with a clean slate. She didn't want to cloud her first impressions of them. However, during the latter part of a school year, as she was putting a document into a student's file, she noticed that the student had severe hearing loss. Mary was devastated that she had not accommodated this student's special learning need throughout the year. The student was shy and had kept quiet to avoid being singled out. Mary apologized to the student and made adjustments for the short time left in the term, and from that day forward she always read official records carefully beforehand to help her plan an inclusive learning environment.

Professional Discussion Questions

1) Big Ideas are different in different contexts or subjects. Explore how the Big Idea of rights and responsibilities could vary according to the context in which it is interpreted.
2) Looking at the chart for Big Ideas in different subject areas (Table 2.2), devise a chart of Big Ideas that are cross-disciplinary.
3) Creativity is a key twenty-first–century skill. Given a future where everyone has ready access to vast amounts of information, brainstorm how the creative process can be applied to disciplines other than the arts.
4) What should the role of schools be in cultivating the Be? What should the role of the teacher be?
5) Most curriculum outcomes are surprisingly complex when they are unpacked. Look at the outcomes in Table 2.6. Do you agree with our interpretation? Choose some in your provincial context to deconstruct.
6) Consider Helen and Mary's experiences described in the Snapshot box "Knowing Students in Different Ways." When can prior knowledge of students be beneficial, and when can it be detrimental? What ways of getting to know your students do you consider most useful?

3

Backward Design with Assessment in Mind

In this chapter, you will learn about:

- Identifying what are the most important things for students to Know, Do, and Be
- Creating a rich performance assessment task
- Creating daily activities/assessments to prepare students to demonstrate the KDB
- Creating assessment tasks and tools
- Aligning the three steps of backward design
- Infusing the spirit of AfL into your teaching
- Thinking like an assessor

Backward Design with Assessment in Mind

This chapter focuses on the **backward design process**, the stages of which are illustrated in Figure 3.1. Within each stage there are steps to negotiate—these steps are rarely linear but are presented as such in this chapter. We use a Grade 10 history unit to show how each stage is connected to ensure alignment. We follow this with a detailed exploration of the

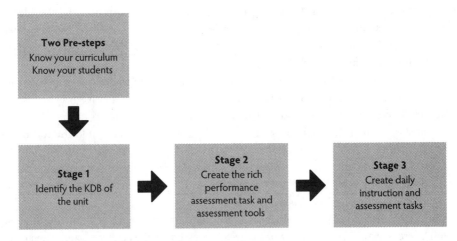

FIGURE 3.1 Stages of Backward Design

interwoven assessment. *The history example is an example only; the process can be applied to any subject area at any level using appropriate curriculum documents.*

There are two preliminary steps followed by three stages in the backward design process. (In Chapter 5 there will be three pre-steps when we do interdisciplinary planning.) What differentiates backward design from other methods of curriculum design is the emphasis on assessment as part of the early planning.

Applying Integrative Thinking

Integrative thinking (Martin, 2007) is a skill that curriculum designers bring to the backward design process. It is the ability to see in two dimensions simultaneously and to bring the best of both dimensions together. To create a rich and accountable curriculum we need to be able to see both

- with a wide angle lens and a zoom lens,
- the big picture and the more narrowly focused picture, and
- the broad introductory material and the specific grade-level outcomes for one unit

The **Hoberman sphere** is a good metaphor for integrative thinking. The sphere can be expanded or compressed. You can see the ball expanded as a big picture or compressed as a focused one—it depends on your perspective.

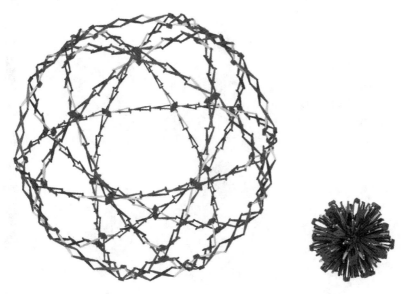

FIGURE 3.2 Hoberman Sphere
Source: Copyright 1993 Charles Hoberman.

Designing the Curriculum

Each stage of backward design has several steps within it, which are identified in Figure 3.3. Although we present the three stages in a linear manner, there are interconnected steps within the stages. You will need to go back and forth continuously between steps and even stages. For example, you may have decided on a topic and Essential Question before you begin the planning, but either or both of these may change when you choose your outcomes or as you proceed further with the planning. The goal is to align your curriculum at every stage, from the initial selection of the KDB to ensuring the culminating

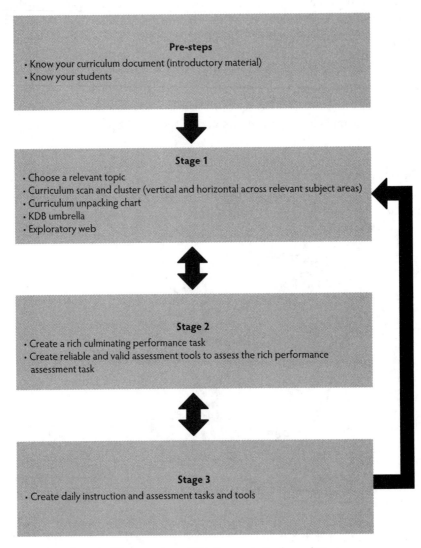

FIGURE 3.3 A Detailed Description of the Stages in Backward Design

rich performance assessment task (RPAT) provides evidence of the KDB. Finally, the daily activities and assessments need to enable the student to demonstrate the KDB.

Let's walk through the steps as if we were planning a unit, keeping the assessment basics—validity, reliability, and fairness—in mind. Here we walk through a sample unit called "The Canadian Person of Influence Video Library" (based on the Ontario curriculum for Grades 9 and 10, "Canadian and World Studies"; Ontario Ministry of Education, 2005a). Although we apply the process to Grade 10 history, the intention is to show a generic process that is suitable for any subject and any grade. We begin with the pre-steps and then walk through the three stages of backward design (Figure 3.3).

THE PRE-STEPS

The pre-steps involve knowing your curriculum and knowing your students.

Know Your Curriculum

The first step in knowing your curriculum is to explore the introductory material or front matter of relevant documents to discover the KDB for all courses under that umbrella.

Scan the pages in the introductory section of a document with a wide-angle lens. *Scan* means "scanning," not doing an in-depth read. Educators often highlight key words, phrases, or sentences on the hard copy pages or online. If there is a K–12 unifying framework for all subjects, it will usually be included in the introductory material, yet the introductory material is also specific to the subject area.

What you learned about the KDB in Chapter 2 guides this scanning process. What stance does the document take on twenty-first–century skills in its unifying framework? What KDB can we expect to find spiralling through the curriculum? What is the philosophy for the subject? Does it align with a unifying provincial framework? What is emphasized—Constructivist teaching? Democracy? Social justice? Critical literacy? You can note what you have found about the KDB in a chart such as Table 3.1, which gives a brief overview of the introductory material from K–12 for history.

Know Your Students

You are designing this unit for your Grade 10 history class. The course is compulsory, and student motivation and academic proficiency in this class vary. The cultural composition of your school is diverse; 42% of students have arrived in Canada within the last five years. You cannot assume that students have much prior knowledge about Canadian history. Thus, diagnostic assessment of knowledge and of attitudes toward Canadian practices will be important. Because six of the 24 students use translation software regularly on their own devices, oral communication, especially as "rehearsal" for written work, is part of daily practice. For this unit, you hope hands-on application of research skills, particularly using computers, will make the class more student centred and increase engagement. While a common textbook provides a foundational reference, differentiation of resource materials to meet various levels of literacy skills and learning preferences is necessary. You anticipate that the Internet, particularly online collections of primary source materials, will prove invaluable.

TABLE 3.1 Looking for the KDB in the Introductory Material (History)

Social sciences in Ontario are integrated from Grades 1 to 6. There is no Grade 9 history.

Grade 7—New France, British North America, Conflict and Change

Grade 8—Confederation, Development of Western Canada, Canada: A Changing Society

Grades 10 and 11—Communities: Local, National, and Global; Change and Continuity; Citizenship and Heritage; Social, Economic, and Political Structures; Methods of Historical Inquiry and Communication

Know—Big Ideas

- Systems and structures
- Interactions and interdependence
- Environment
- Change and continuity
- Culture
- Power and governance

Do—Historical inquiry

- Ask appropriate questions
- Plan investigations to answer those questions
- Use appropriate research methods selected from a variety of methods
- Locate relevant information from a variety of sources (distinguishing between primary and secondary sources to determine their validity and relevance, and to use them in appropriate ways)
- Organize, analyze, interpret, and apply findings (consider chronology and cause-and-effect relationships)
- Communicate findings in a variety of written, oral, and visual forms

Be—Informed, responsible, and active Canadian citizens in the twenty-first century

BACKWARD DESIGN: STAGE 1

Identify what are the most important things for students to Know, Do, and Be at the end of the learning period.

Choose a Relevant Topic

This may be done now or after the scan and cluster. If you know the curriculum well, you will have good ideas. But be prepared for some surprises as you explore the outcomes in depth. You may find that you want or need to revise your topic to fit the outcomes.

Curriculum Scan and Cluster

The purpose of a scan and cluster is to determine the critical learning or KDB in the mandated outcomes. The clustering is the process of chunking together outcomes into meaningful bundles. Natural groupings of outcomes will emerge as you scan and then cluster. These bundles will align with the work you have done with the introductory material.

The first step is a *vertical scan and cluster*. This step usually involves scanning a disciplinary document two grades below and one grade above the target grade. You are looking for patterns of what has been expected of the student and what will be expected the following year. Using the wide-angle lens, what is critical for students to learn? Again, a highlighter is useful to identify key words, phrases, or outcomes. Are there outcomes that connect to the KDB in the introductory material? For example, are communication outcomes evident in each grade level? Inquiry outcomes? Research outcomes? What are the Big Ideas? Enduring Understandings?

Table 3.2 shows the cluster of outcomes selected after a vertical scan from two grades below and one grade above Grade 10 history (there is no Grade 9 history in Ontario). The scan revealed that the topic of influential Canadian people was a consistent focus.

A *horizontal scan and cluster* involves scanning across a grade level. In some disciplinary work, it is helpful to integrate across the strands. In language arts, for example, you will want to scan reading, writing, speaking, and media literacy for similar goals across the discipline. In the history example here, we found that exploring the influence of individuals, usually Canadians is important across all strands in history and is also in the introductory material of the curriculum documents. In every subject, you will find that communication will span across strands. The clustering involves recording the outcomes you are choosing to bundle together. Generally, the horizontal scan and cluster is done for interdisciplinary work; you will see this process in Chapter 5.

The clustering or bundling of outcomes can be interpretive work, depending on how your province has already organized outcomes in the curriculum documents. In some provinces you will need to cluster together many outcomes and identify the bundle in some meaningful way, as you can see in Table 3.2. In other provinces, much of this work has already been done; you only need to choose among a few overall outcomes. In any event, it is important that you record your outcome choices for planning the unit so that they are upfront and clear as you proceed with curriculum planning.

This scan and cluster process may seem tedious and frustrating on the first attempt. However, we think it is the most important part of creating a curriculum that is outcome based and accountable; once you are grounded in the outcomes, it is easier to let the creative juices flow to design a curriculum relevant for students. The scan and cluster gets easier to do each time, and there is a rewarding sense of satisfaction in fitting all the pieces together into a coherent plan.

Curriculum Unpacking Chart

Now that you have organized outcomes into bundles that loosely represent the KDB and are aligned with the introductory material, select a few broad-based outcomes that best represent your organizing process. It is time to use the zoom lens to identify exactly what you need to teach for students to meet the outcomes. Deconstruct the outcomes for the Know, Do, and Be. Remember that the nouns will tell you about the Know, the verbs about the Do, and the Be may be implicit in the outcomes (but usually explicit in the introductory material)—and there might not be a Be at all. Table 3.3 shows how this was done for our Grade 10 history example.

Table 3.2 Vertical Scan and Cluster for History, Grades 7 to 11

	Grade 7	Grade 8	Grade 10	Grade 11
Strand	British North America	Canada: A Changing Society	Heritage and Citizenship	Heritage and Citizenship
		Know		
Identity	Identify some of the themes and **personalities** from the period and explain their relevance to contemporary Canada (e.g., Graves, Simcoe, Brant/Thayendanegea)	Describe the key characteristics of Canada between 1885 and 1914, including social and economic conditions, **the roles and contributions of various people** and groups (e.g., Black Marconi, Beck, McClung, Carr, Johnson)	Assess how individual Canadians have contributed to the development of Canada and the country's **emerging sense of identity.** Assess contributions of **individuals** (e.g., Arthur Currie, etc.)	Explain how American **political and social identity** changed over time.
Cause and effect	Explain the historical impact of key events on the settlement of British North America. Outline the causes, events, and results of the War of 1812	Describe factors contributing to change.	Analyze the impact of the women's movement in Canada since 1914.	Analyze the ways in which American culture has been spread around the world.
Systems and Structures	Explain key characteristics in English life (e.g., family life, economic, social, institutions, First Nations, French settlers)	Describe key characteristics of Canada before 1885 and 1914, including social and economic conditions, the roles and contributions of various people and groups	Explain how the labour movement has affected social, economic, and political life in Canada.	Explain how American **political and social identity** changed over time

Do

	Grades 7 and 8	Grades 10 and 11
Historical Inquiry	Formulate questions Use primary and secondary sources Analyze, synthesize, and evaluate data Describe and analyze conflicting points of view Construct and use a wide variety of graphs, models, etc.	Formulate questions Gather information from a variety of sources (primary and secondary) Evaluate sources Organize information Formulate and use a thesis statement Interpret data (fact and opinion) Draw conclusions based on evidence—predict or generalize
Communication	Communicate the results of inquiries for specific purposes and audiences, using media works, oral presentation skills, etc. Use appropriate vocabulary	Communicate results of historical inquiries using appropriate terms and concepts and a variety of forms

K to 12

Be

	Grades 7 and 8	Grades 10 and 11
	Be contributing and responsible citizens in a complex society characterized by rapid technological, economic, political, and social change (curriculum document introduction)	Be responsible, active, informed citizens in the 21st century (curriculum document introduction)

Snapshot of Collaborative Curriculum Planning

Susan (one of the authors of this book) was involved in a collaborative project, designing a Grade 4 unit on medieval times. The clustering had gone really well, and the three teachers were amazed at how many outcomes fell into the Know, Do, and Be categories. There was just one outcome on pollution in medieval times that they could not squeeze in anywhere, so they left it out. The teachers felt a bit guilty about this, especially since a teacher's responsibility in this school was to check off the outcomes covered each day. The check-off chart was publicly displayed on the staff room wall. The principal was very proud of this "innovation," so it was hard to subvert it. To their surprise, the outlier outcome about pollution was actually covered by the students, who researched and reported on different roles and responsibilities in society, including waste removal.

Deconstructing the selected outcomes from the scan and cluster in the curriculum unpacking chart (Table 3.3) helped to make the KDB precise. It is very easy to gloss over the precise language in the outcomes and create assessments that do not effectively target the learning goal. "Oh, I did that" does not mean that you actually did what the outcome specified.

Let's take "Assess how individual Canadians have contributed to the development of Canada and the country's emerging sense of identity" as our selected outcome. This deconstruction will make explicit what you need to teach and still allow you to be creative in designing a meaningful curriculum. The concept of "evolving national identity" is a rich Big Idea that deserves a thorough unpacking for deep understanding. Once the concept is unpacked, students will be able to formulate questions for research (historical thinking) and to judge/assess whether or not a person has had influence on Canada's evolving national identity. In what spheres did this person have influence? Is/was the influence truly enduring? Does the influence need to be positive? How has national identity evolved? How does this individual's influence connect with the concept of an evolving national identity?

Students are required to demonstrate the skill of assessment (making a judgement), so this skill should be targeted for evaluation and reporting. Assessment is a higher-order thinking skill (HOTS) that needs to be taught to students (or reviewed) to establish validity. Similarly, historical thinking and communication skills will need to be taught or reviewed.

KDB Umbrella

Now that you have a good idea of what you are required to teach, you are ready to construct your KDB umbrella (see Figure 3.4). On your umbrella you will record the Big Ideas, Enduring Understandings, twenty-first–century skills and the Be that you plan to address in your curriculum design. It is important to remember that you don't have to include everything that you discovered in your Scan and Cluster and that what you do include you will need to teach and assess. Remember that this is an iterative process and that you can edit your umbrella if it is necessary for alignment.

A crucial question is what Essential Questions should focus or drive the unit planning? This question should emerge from the outcomes. In creating the curriculum, you

TABLE 3.3 Curriculum Unpacking Chart			
Unpacking Selected Broad-Based Outcomes for Grade 10 History			
Broad-Based Outcomes	**Know**	**Do**	**Be**
Assess how *individual Canadians have contributed to the development of Canada* and the *country's emerging sense of identity*.	Contributions of Canadians to the development of Canada and an emerging sense of identity **Possible Big Idea:** Emerging national identity **Possible Enduring Understanding:** National identity is a fluid concept that is influenced by people.	Assess	Informed Canadian citizen (implicit)
Formulate *questions* **Gather** *information* from a *variety of sources (primary and secondary)* **Evaluate** *sources* **Organize** *information* **Formulate** and **use** a *thesis statement* **Interpret** *data (fact and opinion)* **Draw** *conclusions* based on evidence—**predict** or **generalize**	Good question Primary source Secondary source Opinion/fact Thesis statement	Gather information from a variety of sources (primary and secondary) Evaluate sources Organize information Formulate and use a thesis statement Interpret data (fact and opinion) Draw conclusions based on evidence—predict or generalize	Historical inquirer
Communicate the *results of historical inquiries* using *appropriate terms and concepts* and a *variety of forms of communication*	Results of historical inquiries Variety of forms of communication Appropriate terms and concepts	Communicate	Informed citizen

may wish to include things that are not explicitly in the grade-level outcomes, but which are aligned with the introductory material/unified framework. Generally, this will involve twenty-first–century skills such as technological literacy, collaboration, creativity, and critical thinking. This method of backward design encourages you to include these broader interdisciplinary skills if they are appropriate for the unit.

The Essential Questions are clearly aligned with the KDB and emerge from the Know. Many teachers post the questions in a prominent place in the classroom and refer to them throughout the unit. Often teachers involve students in creating these questions and/or co-creating the assessment criteria. This ensures that students know what the unit is going to be about and often increases their sense of ownership.

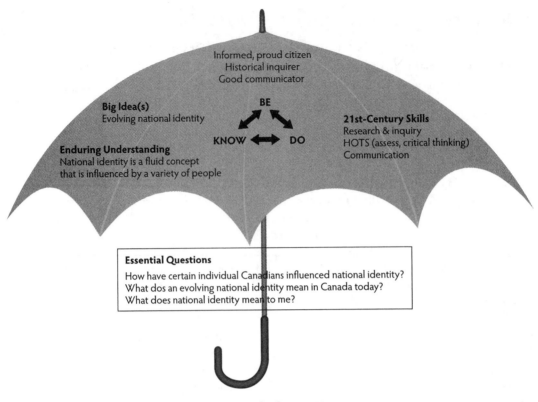

Informed, proud citizen
Historical inquirer
Good communicator

Big Idea(s)
Evolving national identity

BE

21st-Century Skills
Research & inquiry
HOTS (assess, critical thinking)
Communication

KNOW ⟷ DO

Enduring Understanding
National identity is a fluid concept
that is influenced by a variety of people

Essential Questions

How have certain individual Canadians influenced national identity?
What dos an evolving national identity mean in Canada today?
What does national identity mean to me?

FIGURE 3.4 The KDB Umbrella for the Person of Influence Unit

Exploratory Web

The scan and cluster work ensures that the curriculum will be aligned, coherent, and relevant to students. The KDB umbrella identifies the critical learning for the unit. It is this KDB that needs to be demonstrated in the RPAT that will act as a culmination of the unit and assessment of learning. We suggest creating an exploratory web (Figure 3.5) at this point to brainstorm for possible instructional activities, even if you think you know what your unit will include. The exploratory web is exploratory only—you are not tied to the ideas you come up with—but the web moves you from the abstractness of working with the outcomes without specific content to seeing the possibilities for the curriculum. As you move through curriculum design, you may find that the activities/assessments that you have brainstormed need to change to ensure alignment.

BACKWARD DESIGN: STAGE 2

In the next stage of backward design, your job is to create an RPAT as a culminating activity that allows students to demonstrate that they have learned the intended Know, Do, and Be. We will also create reliable and valid assessment tools to assess the RPAT.

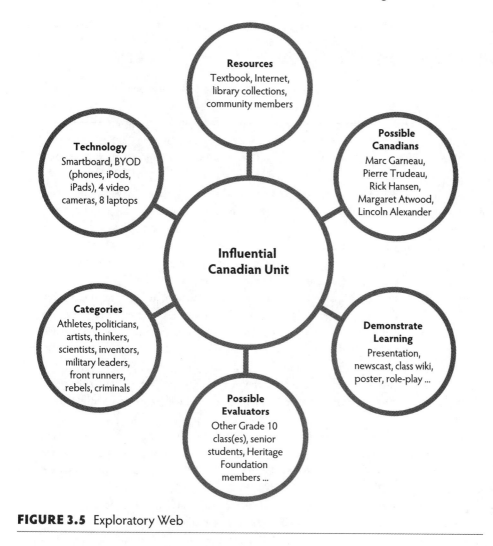

FIGURE 3.5 Exploratory Web

Create a Rich Performance Assessment Task

Sometimes a quiz or test is the most appropriate way to assess knowledge acquisition, but not all learning can be assessed "quantitatively." Some learning is skills based, complex, and integrated and is therefore better demonstrated by a performance and better assessed through qualitative description.

In an RPAT, students do something significant to show that they have learned the KDB (see the "Canada's Person of Influence Video Library" box for an example of an RPAT to go with our Grade 10 history example). A long unit may include several RPATs, but a culminating RPAT occurs at the end of the learning period and acts as a summative assessment. When someone is learning to drive, the culminating task is a performance; the learner is

Canada's Person of Influence Video Library

You have been invited to be on Canada's Person of Influence Committee to update the video library. Canada's Person of Influence Gallery focuses on individuals in the last century who have influenced what it means to be Canadian today. Not just anyone can make the list—remember, fame and influence are not the same thing. A famous person in the past may no longer have an impact on Canada's emerging identity today. Each potential nominee needs to be vetted by others on the committee. This project has three phases.

Phase 1: As a committee member, you will select one Canadian from the last 100 years who seems to have influenced the character of Canada regardless of any measure of fame. Develop questions and conduct research on that person. Then communicate that information; apply what you learned in the last unit about making a video by creating a 2–4 minute video for the other committee members to watch. Your video may take many forms: an interview with the person or with people who knew him or her, a monologue of the person in role, a video documentary, a eulogy—the choice is yours.

Your purpose is to communicate accurate factual information about your selected individual. Look for both primary and secondary sources. Through social media, see if you can actually connect to your person or someone who has been influenced by him or her. You are not trying to convince others that your person belongs in the video library. Indeed, your research might convince you that his or her contribution is not worthy of inclusion. Your purpose is to give viewers of your video enough "objective" information to allow them to make their own judgments as to whether the nominee deserves to belong in the Person of Influence Gallery. Your video will be posted on the Person of Influence wiki.

All members of the committee will view your video and will assess the contribution of your person according the criteria for determining influence created in class. Encourage others, such as parents, senior students, local historians, and community leaders, to visit the wiki. Seek their opinions as to who should be included or not.

Phase 2: After viewing all the videos, there will be a committee meeting to discuss each nomination. At that meeting, you will state and support your decision about including your person in the Gallery. Everyone should be prepared to offer their supported opinions and to reflect on the Big Idea of an evolving national identity. Each discussion will be followed by a vote on whether to include that nominee in the Gallery.

Phase 3: Finally, after viewing the videos and the culminating committee meeting, each committee member will post a blog that describes his or her understanding of *evolving Canadian identity*, using at least three influential Canadians as illustrative examples.

required to drive to demonstrate knowledge of the rules of the road and also the ability to apply that knowledge in an authentic setting. The driving test is an RPAT.

How do you know if the RPAT you have designed is "rich"? The checklist in Table 3.4 can help you assess the richness of your task design.

TABLE 3.4 Checklist for Creating a Rich Performance Assessment Task

- Is the task worth doing? Does it teach the KDB?
- Is it doable?
- Is the task engaging and fun?
- Is inquiry embedded in the task?
- Does it require the application of higher-order thinking skills (HOTS)?
- Does the task provide authentic opportunities for students to explore, enact, and reflect on the values and behaviours of a learner and a responsible citizen? (the Be)
- Is the task grounded in a real-world scenario/problem? Is it presented in an authentic way, even if it is a simulation?
- Are success criteria made explicit and clear to students, perhaps through co-construction of the assessment rubric with the students?
- Does the task allow for diverse approaches (e.g., individual or group settings, various presentation styles) that meet the diverse needs of your students and foster creativity?
- Does the task invite student voice and allow for student choice?
- Does the task encourage accountability and increase motivation by requiring students to demonstrate their learning to a public audience other than their teacher (or even their classmates)?
- Does the task value process along with product, particularly a process that leaves frequent opportunities for formative assessment, student revision, and reflection?

The first day that a unit is introduced, students should know what their final assessment task will be—whether it is a test, a traditional essay, or a performance demonstration. Students should also be introduced to the assessment tools. For example, they should be given any rubric that accompanies the rich performance assessment task or help to co-create one. The rubric should provide descriptors of what is expected. In the history unit, students would have a written description of the culminating task along with the checklist and rubrics.

If something is in the task that has not been taught, the task needs to be modified or the KDB needs to be rethought. For example, in the culminating task for the history unit students are asked to create a video. How to create a video needs to be addressed in class time since this is the assessment task. In the case of this unit, students had learned this skill in a recent class, so only a review was needed.

Create Reliable and Valid Assessment Tools to Assess the Rich Performance Assessment Task

There are several components to this project. We have included samples for the assessment of some of them.

An RPAT is "rich" because it is often complex. While exciting, it can seem overwhelming to some students. They will appreciate a summary checklist of the components to help track their progress, like the one presented in Table 3.5.

TABLE 3.5 Student Checklist for Person of Influence Project

Student Checklist for Person of Influence Project	Check-in dates
Choose one potential nominee—an important, influential Canadian of the last 100 years (no duplicates).	
Develop questions of various types to ask about or to your "influential" person.	
Conduct research to find answers to your questions. Include digital research. Can you connect with your nominee or with someone who knew or was influenced by him or her?	
Post your research findings and ideas in a 2–4 minute video on the wiki.	
Form a judgment about the extent and the nature of your nominee's influence on Canadian identity.	
Review all videos posted on the wiki and assess whether each featured person should be admitted to the gallery.	
Participate in the vetting committee meeting by stating and supporting your assessment of each nominee.	
Post on the blog a personal essay on your perceptions of the "evolving nature of Canadian identity" in the past 100 years (since 1914), supported by examples from the videos and committee meeting discussion.	

Rubrics can be used for instructional purposes and to provide targeted feedback (AfL) during the developmental phases. Table 3.6 offers a sample rubric for the video (the students have learned video skills in a previous class), and Table 3.7 shows a rubric for the committee meeting discussion.

TABLE 3.6 Sample Rubric to Assess Video

	Emerging	Developing	Proficient	Exemplary
Content (Knowledge) Does your presentation include relevant, sufficient, and accurate information?	Limited and overly general information is provided. Many facts are inaccurate or irrelevant.	Basic but vague information is provided. Some facts may be inaccurate or irrelevant.	Sufficient and usually specific information is provided. Facts are accurate and relevant.	Extensive specific information is provided. Facts are accurate, relevant, and thoughtfully chosen.
Inquiry & Planning Did you locate, select, and analyze information effectively?	Presentation shows evidence of limited research.	Presentation shows evidence of some research.	Presentation shows evidence of adequate research.	Presentation shows evidence of thorough research.
Did you plan your research, your questions, and the organization of the presentation effectively?	Ideas and information are presented with frequent and/or significant lapses in organization.	Ideas and information are presented with some lapses in organization.	Ideas and information are presented logically, perhaps mechanically.	Ideas and information are presented logically, coherently, and effectively.

Application Did your video make effective use of technology (camera angles, focus, transitions, sound, etc.)?	A limited variety of video techniques are used.	Some video techniques are used.	Some video techniques are used effectively.	A wide variety of video techniques are used purposefully and effectively.
Is your video creative? Did you use props, costumes, settings, and situations to engage your viewer?	Presentation makes no attempts to be creative, using no added features to generate interest.	Presentation attempts to be creative, using an added feature to generate interest.	Presentation is creative using some added features to generate interest.	Presentation is highly creative, using several added features to generate interest.
Communication Oral Skills Did you express your ideas clearly and effectively to achieve your purpose and engage your audience?	Language use indicates a limited awareness of purpose and audience.	Language use is variable, occasionally inappropriate for purpose and audience.	Language use is consistently appropriate for purpose and audience.	Language use is skillfully suited to purpose and audience.
	Delivery is interrupted by stumbles and pauses and is often inaudible.	Delivery is sometimes halting and inaudible.	Delivery is fluent and audible.	Delivery is fluent, expressive, and clearly audible.
	Eye contact, gestures, and facial expressions are rarely, if ever, used.	Eye contact, gestures, and facial expressions are sometimes used.	Eye contact, gestures, and facial expressions are used frequently.	Eye contact, gestures, and facial expressions are used purposely to achieve an effect.

Comments: (Self-evaluation/Peer evaluation/Teacher evaluation)

TABLE 3.7 Sample Committee Meeting Discussion/Concept Development Rubric

	Emerging	**Developing**	**Proficient**	**Exemplary**
Supported opinion— assessing the influence of a person on national identity	A thesis (opinion) is unclear. Some facts are presented, but they are not used to support an assessment of influence. There is minimal evidence of understanding of national identity.	A thesis (opinion) may be unclear. Assessment may be supported by many facts but little interpretation of those facts in relation to influence on national identity.	A clear thesis (opinion) is supported by different facets of influence. Commentary demonstrates a developing understanding of the complexity of emerging national identity.	A clear thesis (opinion) is supported by consideration of a wide variety of facets of influence. Commentary demonstrates a deep understanding of the complexity of emerging national identity.

Comments:

BACKWARD DESIGN: STAGE 3

Once the "big picture" task and assessment are determined, the instructional tasks follow. Table 3.8 shows daily activities that lead to the rich performance assessment task.

TABLE 3.8 Daily Instructional Activity/Assessment Chart

Learning Goals

Know

I can explain the Big Idea of evolving national identity.

Know and Do

I can assess how individual Canadians have contributed to the development of Canada and the country's emerging sense of identity.

Do

I can think like a historian (I can use appropriate methods of historical research to locate, gather, evaluate, and organize relevant information from a variety of sources. I can use various question types to construct my research plan. I can apply analytical thinking to literary representations of history).

I can communicate the results of my research through a video presentation.

Be

I can make judgments as an informed citizen.

Daily instruction/assessments Differentiation (DI)/Personalization	Outcomes	Connection to KDB and RPAT
Canadian Icon Quiz from Dominion Institute. **(AfL) Tool:** quiz scores	Gather information from a variety of sources.	Background information for culminating task
Snapshot biography. Gather names/icons from Dominion Institute Survey. **(AfL) Tool:** observation	Evaluate credibility of sources.	Think like a historian
Share effective strategy/research tool/resource (e.g., textbook index, Internet key word search, encyclopedia such as Wikipedia, obituary collections). **(AfL) Tool:** observation	Distinguish between primary and secondary sources.	Be an informed Canadian.
Exit card **(AaL)**		
Research bingo **(AfL)**	Gather information from a variety of sources.	Background information for culminating task
Create class master web. Analyze web. Who is missing? Is it skewed? Ethnicity? Geography? Gender? Who should be included? **(AfL)**	Identify explicit biases.	Think like a historian
Quads create game shows/quiz shows based on biographies **(AfL)**	Interpret and analyze information.	Be an informed Canadian
KWL chart **(AfL/AaL)**		
Tools for above: Observation and questioning		
DI/Personalization:		
Multimodal resources		
Mixed groupings		

Direct instruction on different types of questions	Formulate questions on topics and issues in history.	Historical inquiry
Review example interviews (e.g., talk show), noting questions. Categorize questions into organizer. Discussion. **(AfL) Tool:** Graphic organizer.		Begins process of assessing the influence people have on evolving national identity
Construct questions in pairs for possible use in their videos. **(AfL) Tool:** Peer and teacher feedback on possible questions		
DI/Personalization: additional time and more examples for question formation		
Class review of research rubric for historical inquiry.		
Poems: Small groups analyze "poems" for concept development of national identity. **(AfL) Tool:** peer assessment	Interpret and analyze information.	Know: Builds on concept of evolving national unity.
AaL: Exit card; what would you emphasize in a poem on national identity?	Identify different points of view and explicit biases	Do: Analysis
Symbols: Discussion: How are symbols used to express national identity (e.g., Olympic Games)? **(AfL) Tool:** questioning and observation		Be: Informed citizen
Student poll within class/community		
(AfL) Tool: interpretation of answers to the poll		
Learning stations with representations of Canada (e.g., songs/lyrics, fictional characters, travel brochures, artifacts). **Tool:** observation		
Differentiation/Personalization:		
Flexible grouping		
Team quiet students with more outgoing ones		
Review of video construction skills	Express ideas, arguments, and conclusions as appropriate for audience and purpose.	Technological literacy (front matter)
Co-construction of presentation rubric based on analysis of exemplars **(AfL/AaL)**		Prepares for video
Students		
• Plan the video presentation		
• Gather props/costumes if needed		
• Rehearse off camera		
• Make videotape		
• Revise based on self-assessment and peer feedback **(AfL)**		
Students upload final videos.		
• **(AoL)** Self, peer, external evaluators, teacher evaluation using rubric		

If you are creating a very long unit that will be divided into mini-units, you might consider creating another web now with the Essential Questions as organizers. You can plan the daily activities around the Essential Questions (see Figure 5.5 on page 139). Here we do not add this step because this history unit can address the Essential Questions in one unit rather than having several mini-units.

In this stage of designing daily activities, alignment is crucial. Do your activities align with the rich performance assessment task, and do they address the KDB? If the culminating task requires students to support an opinion, for example, does the instructional plan provide opportunities for students to learn, practise, and get feedback on their performance of the skill? If not, then you need to modify or omit the activity or go back to the drawing board and change your KDB to allow for the activity. Although this seems very prescriptive, it is amazing how tightly the curriculum can be aligned as a whole and be made relevant to students at the same time.

We continue with the sample history unit with the instructional plan that shows how assessment and instruction work together. AfL, AaL and AoL are added to the template to identify the type of assessment. DI stands for differentiated instruction/assessment. Often an effective assessment task has differentiation or personalization built into it by offering student voice and choice in process and product.

Learning Goals and Success Criteria

With learning goals and success criteria, both students and the teacher have a clear and shared understanding of what is expected in a demonstration of the learning. The learning goals/success criteria should address the question, Why are we learning this? The learning goals/success criteria for our Grade 10 history unit are identified at the top of Table 3.8, and for an interdisciplinary curriculum they are shown in Tables 5.6 and 5.7.

The Ontario Ministry of Education has defined and described the expected use of learning goals and success criteria in Ontario schools (2010d). **Learning goals** are short statements that encapsulate the KDB of a lesson, learning cycle, or unit of study. They answer the question, What are we learning? The learning goals are developed based on the curriculum outcomes (expectations), although the outcomes are not simply rewritten. Instead, teachers unpack the curriculum into manageable chunks so students can move forward (the scan and cluster process should be helpful here). The learning goals are phrased in student-friendly language from the learner's perspective. For example, "We are learning to write an opinion piece," or "I can use the inquiry process to conduct an investigation."

Success criteria explicitly outline the "look fors" to achieve the learning goal. The criteria are written in student-friendly language and make learning and successful achievement transparent and attainable. Teachers co-construct success criteria with students to promote student ownership of the learning. If students have some prior knowledge and skills, the teacher can have the students brainstorm success criteria in groups. The class consolidates their thinking in an organized anchor chart that can be posted in the classroom. At the beginning of a new learning cycle, anonymous work samples can be used to promote a discussion about quality work. The success criteria are drawn out of the class discussion. Success criteria are reviewed and revised throughout the unit of study based on new learning and further developed understanding.

The Ontario Ministry of Education sees a continuum leading from learning goals, to success criteria that are co-constructed by students and teacher, to descriptive feedback based on the success criteria, to self- and peer assessment, to individual goal setting. This continuum intentionally connects the learning goals to metacognition and goal setting (AaL). Hattie and Timperley (2007) support the purposeful connection between meaningful feedback and specific learning goals and success criteria. They caution that the use of peer, self-, and teacher assessment should be based on learning goals and success criteria rather than on the student attributes.

Rubrics and Success Criteria

Rubrics are used as an assessment tool to share the broad criteria required for the achievement of a given task. Table 3.9 demonstrates how the assessment requirement on a rubric is expanded into success criteria to provide a clear path toward achievement.

TABLE 3.9 Rubric Criteria and Success Criteria

Rubric criterion: Students use problem-solving skills with a high degree of effectiveness.

Learning goal: I can use a variety of skills proficiently to solve a problem effectively.

Success Criteria (the "look fors" and the necessary steps to achieve the learning goal)

- Deconstruct the problem to understand what it is asking and the important information I will need
- Make a connection to a similar problem
- Make a plan to solve the problem
- Select an appropriate problem-solving strategy (e.g., make a model, guess and check, create a table or chart)
- Select and gather appropriate tools
- Carry out my plan
- Monitor my success and make revisions as I go
- Communicate my learning in an appropriate way (writing, pictures, technology)
- Reflect and see if my solution is reasonable and made sense
- Reflect and see if my method was effective to solve the problem or if there was a better choice

Create Assessment Tools for Daily Instructional Activities/Assessments

There are many times that assessment will be informal. The teacher watches and listens. Observations can be recorded more formally on an observation sheet—perhaps observing a few students a day. Observations for each student will be completed over time.

At other times, assessment and instruction converge when tools are used as both as instructional activities and as formative assessment. Here are three examples:

- A bingo card can be used in a variety of ways. Once categories are established, students gather information to fill in the cells. The challenge level can be adjusted by including "free" spots. The bingo card allows instruction on categorization, research strategies (gather, select, organize, summarize information, and cite sources), and resources (see Table 3.10). Differentiation results when students choose their own categories or individuals, or even the number and placement of the "free" spaces. As students compare and amalgamate bingo cards, they begin acquiring content knowledge. Simultaneously, the bingo cards can be useful for formative assessment of research skills and content knowledge. As well, the teacher can observe how students work alone and with others.
- The class brainstorm web in Figure 3.6 is an instructional activity that reinforces and organizes the content knowledge that surfaced with the bingo cards. It becomes an assessment tool when the teacher or students use it to gauge their own learning gaps.
- Forming questions is a challenging skill, one that is at the heart of historical inquiry. Initially, Table 3.11 could be used to support the teaching of the taxonomy

TABLE 3.10 Sample Influential Canadians Research Bingo Card

	Political/ Military Leaders	Entertainment, Culture, Sports	Science/ Inventors	Activists/ Reformers	First person to . . .
1910–1929			Frederick Banting (Nobel prize for discovering insulin 1923)	Nellie McClung (Famous Five) 1927 Persons Case	
1930–1949		FREE			
1950–1969				FREE	FREE
1970–1989	FREE	Brian Orser (Olympic figure skater)			
1990–2010			FREE		

FIGURE 3.6 Class Brainstorming Web (Sample)

of questions. Later, as students use the chart to develop their own questions, the chart becomes an assessment tool. It provides insight on students' understanding of question formation and acts as a talking point for student–teacher conferences as students conduct their research.

General Guidelines for Creating Assessment Tasks and Tools

An **assessment task** is what students do to demonstrate their learning. Teachers need to design instructional/assessment tasks that are challenging yet fun and relevant. The list in Table 3.12 indicates the wide variety of alternatives to a test, and each day brings new technological applications that can enhance them. Note that most of these tasks are generic and can

TABLE 3.11 That's a Good Question

Questions that ask you to . . .	Examples	My questions
Recall, remember facts (closed question; one right answer) Key words: label, name, what, when, who, list	When were you born? Who supported your cause? Where were you living when the bomb fell?	
Show understanding Key words: describe, compare, contrast, explain, summarize	Describe what it was like to ride the rails. How were women's lives different at that time compared to today? How was your life affected by your experience of war?	
Apply knowledge Key words: develop, plan, solve, make, design	What examples show that . . .? How would you solve the problem of . . .?	
Break down information to figure things out, to find evidence to support a claim, or to show connections between parts Key words: analyze, classify, prove, support	What is your analysis of the situation? What conclusion can you draw from this evidence? What details could support that opinion? How is this connected to that?	
Make a judgment or defend an opinion Key words: prove, justify, decide, evaluate	Which is better, A or B, and why? Do you agree with . . . and why? How would you rate . . .? Which is more important? What is the most important thing we should learn from your life? What is different about Canada because of you?	
Combine information and ideas in a new way Key words: create, imagine, predict, suppose	What would have happened if . . .? If you were alive today, what would you be doing? What could have been done to . . .? If you could do it all again, what would you do differently?	

Source: Adapted from EduPress (n.d.).

be applied to any subject depending on the purpose, curriculum expectations, and student interest. As well, they may be used as parts of or all of a rich performance assessment task.

An **assessment tool** captures and communicates information about performance during and after the task. The assessment tool sets out the judgment criteria; a student's work is assessed against these criteria, not in comparison to the work of other students. Thus, results may show a J curve of the "success-for-all" approach rather than the bell curve of "success for some" (see Figure 1.1).

TABLE 3.12 Examples of Assessment Tasks			
Book report	Survey	Video	Advertisement
Brochure	Interview	Song	Documentary
Essay	Speech	Musical instrument	Scale model
Role-play	Research project	Sculpture	Painting
Doll/puppet show	Web page	Scrapbook	Magazine/news article
Timeline	Quilt	Comic	Dance
Mock trial	Photo collage	Puzzle	Debate
Family tree	Experiment	Letter	Poster
Billboard	Review	Blog	Panel discussion
Demonstration	Book jacket	Diagram	Short story
Learning journal/log	Diary	Game	Poem
Annotated bibliography	Radio broadcast	Mural	Script
Glogster poster	Round table forum	Obituary	Multimedia presentation
Graphic novel	Prezi	Story board	

The teacher selects the tool most appropriate for the purpose. Lorna Earl and Stephen Katz (2006), two internationally recognized Canadian assessment experts, describe four overlapping categories of assessment tools. We have made additions to their list:

- For gathering information use questioning, observation, conversations, interviews, tests, learning logs, rich assessment tasks, projects and inquiry-based investigations, role-playing, performance, demonstration
- For interpreting information use rubrics, checkbrics, checklists, observation notes, student-conference notes, self-assessment, peer assessment, reflective journals, student blogs, class wikis
- For record keeping use anecdotal records, student profiles, portfolios, artifacts of student learning (video, photos), audio files
- For communicating use report cards, records of achievement, student–parent newsletters, class web page, student-led parent conferences, phone calls with parents

Most tools can be used in any subject area. Importantly, the choice of tool depends on the purpose and on the tool's fit to the task. For example, an observation checklist is appropriate for checking safe use of kitchen equipment, whereas rubrics are effective for assessing **performance tasks** that require more complex skills and higher-order thinking—a video documentary, for example. You have made a good choice of tool if you can answer "yes" to the questions below:

- Does the assessment tool match the assessment purpose?
- Does the assessment tool match the assessment task?
- Does the assessment tool provide valid and reliable information about student performance? (A valid tool measures what you intend to assess; a reliable tool

minimizes measurement error by providing precise performance indicators so that different scorers will come up with the same assessment judgment.)

- Does the assessment tool provide students with useful information and feedback to improve learning?

ASKING GOOD QUESTIONS

Elementary literacy assessment consultant Beth Charlton (2005), from Nova Scotia, reminds us that effective assessment can be informal. Ongoing AfL can be done through purposeful questioning and effective listening. Questioning is one of the key planks for AfL. Throughout this book a number of different ways to approach questioning are explored. Leslie Brien completed a doctorate on how questioning can make thinking visible. She learned that teachers ask mostly lower-level questions to find out what students know (Armbruster & Ostertag, 1989). Posing high-level, open-ended questions that invite responses that can range from simple to complex requires students to engage in higher-order thinking. Using frameworks to create and classify questions is useful. Brien recommends the revised Bloom's taxonomy (see Chapter 2) and *The Periodic Table of Learning* (Lew & Hardt, 2011).

Questions can also uncover student thinking. Brien advises teachers to use generic question stems as prompts for each type and level of thinking. Here are some examples (see also King, 1995):

- What do you already know about . . .?
- What is the difference between . . . and . . .?
- Why is . . . important?
- Do you agree with . . . and why?

Interpreting student responses requires deep subject knowledge, particularly if the responses are to open-ended questions (Bransford, Brown, & Cocking, 2000). Did the student give a description to a question seeking an evaluation? Were students unable to respond to a question asking for analysis? At what level did students answer? When teachers identify what level of knowledge or processing a student is using, they can pose questions that guide students from simpler to more complex understandings. For example, if a student does not know how to make inferences, the teacher can explicitly teach that student how to do so.

Brien notes that some teachers explicitly teach *students* to ask questions. In Chapter 4 you can see this happen in the Inquiry Hub (a twenty-first–century secondary school venture in Coquitlam, British Columbia) and also in Table 3.11 in this chapter. King (1995) provides students with generic prompts (stems) that elicit various kinds of questions and levels of difficulty. Some teachers use Hardt's "type of match" framework (Lew & Hardt, 2011).

EXPLORING RUBRICS

What Is a Rubric?

Rubrics can be one of the most versatile and effective assessment tools. A **rubric** is a scoring scale used to assess student work that is done in response to a specific task. It identifies the categories of criteria and describes performance at various levels of achievement.

Why Use a Rubric?

A rubric is best suited to complex performance tasks because it

- Provides a big picture view of the task beyond recall of facts to a more integrated application;
- Encourages a shared understanding among various stakeholders—teacher and colleagues, students, parents; and
- Encourages self-assessment and motivation, especially when it is accompanied by samples of work that demonstrate the rubric descriptors.

TYPES OF RUBRICS

An **analytic rubric** considers each criterion separately, allowing for more specific formative feedback. A **holistic rubric** considers criteria all together and assigns one overall mark or level or descriptor based on the combined criteria. Rubrics can be used analytically by category or holistically, depending on the purpose. The same rubric can be used analytically for formative assessment and then holistically to deliver a grade. See Table 3.13.

Often you can use a **generic rubric** for cross-curricular tasks such as a presentation, persuasive essay, or to assess cross-curricular skills like research. A generic rubric can be modified to suit specific content or a specific context. A **task-specific rubric** may be necessary for a particular assessment task. See Table 3.14.

TABLE 3.13 Comparing Analytic and Holistic Rubrics

Analytic	Holistic
Evaluates specific traits (e.g., use of conventions)	Makes judgment on overall quality
Advantage: good for providing specific feedback, recognizes strengths and weaknesses within the task (e.g., strong in content knowledge, weak in oral communication)	Advantage: good for "big picture" judgment

TABLE 3.14 Comparing Generic and Task-Specific Rubrics

Task-specific	Generic
Describes performance quality for a specific question/assignment	Describes performance for a generic task in general terms
Not transferable to another question/task	
Advantage: provides targeted feedback on one-time assessment events or specific tasks	Advantage: good for applying to generic tasks across subjects (e.g., oral presentation, supported opinion essay), which can support student understanding of criteria
Drawback: limited application; if the task is very specific, a checklist may be a better assessment tool	Drawback: may be too broad for useful feedback

TABLE 3.15 Analytic Scoring Rubric for a Venn Diagram Comparing Birds and Reptiles

Category	Level 1	Level 2	Level 3	Level 4
Knowledge	Identifies a few ways in which birds and reptiles are alike **or** different	Identifies a few ways in which birds and reptiles are alike **and** different	Identifies some ways in which birds and reptiles are alike **and** different	Identifies several ways in which birds and reptiles are alike **and** different
	Omits essential information and/or includes inaccurate information	Includes basic and accurate information	Includes essential and accurate information	Includes well-chosen and accurate information
Communication	Lacks evidence of organization	Shows limited evidence of organization (e.g., side-by-side placement of details)	Shows some evidence of organization (e.g., attempt to sequence details)	Shows clear evidence of organization (e.g., logical grouping and sequencing of details under subheadings, use of graphic features such as bullets)
	Includes inaccurate or vague vocabulary	Includes appropriate and accurate vocabulary	Includes accurate and descriptive vocabulary	Includes accurate, precise, and descriptive vocabulary
	Lacks labels or they are incomplete	Labels main parts of diagram	Labels all parts of diagram	Labels all parts of diagram clearly and effectively
	Lacks a title or title is incomplete	Includes a title	Includes a descriptive title	Includes a descriptive, eye-catching title

Let's say your students are learning content about birds and reptiles along with the skill of comparison. As an assessment task, you have asked students to represent their knowledge in a Venn diagram that will be assessed with a rubric. Tables 3.15 and 3.16 are generic rubrics for a Venn diagram that have been customized to this task by including specific details (about birds and reptiles) in the knowledge category. All other criteria could apply generically to a Venn diagram for any comparison. Table 3.15 is an analytic rubric while Table 3.16 is a holistic rubric.

CONSTRUCTING A RUBRIC

Identifying the Criteria

As with any assessment tool, you must be sure there is alignment among learning outcomes, the assessment task, and the assessment tool. Identify the categories for the criteria first, ensuring they are aligned with the outcomes. Criteria should do all of the following:

TABLE 3.16 Holistic Scoring Rubric for a Venn Diagram Comparing Birds and Reptiles

Criteria	Comments
Excellent	
The diagram includes well-chosen and accurate information to show several ways in which birds and reptiles are alike **and** different. There is clear evidence of organization in the logical grouping and sequencing of details under subheadings and/or the use of graphic features such as bullets. Vocabulary is accurate, precise, and descriptive. All parts of the diagram are clearly and effectively labelled. A descriptive, eye-catching title is used.	
Acceptable	
The diagram includes essential and accurate information to show some ways in which birds and reptiles are alike **and** different. There is some evidence of organization in the attempt to sequence details. Vocabulary is accurate and descriptive. All parts of the diagram are labelled. A descriptive title is used.	
Getting there	
The diagram includes basic, accurate information to show a few ways in which birds and reptiles are alike **and** different. There is limited evidence of organization in the attempt to place details side-by-side. Vocabulary is accurate and appropriate. The main parts of the diagram are labelled. A title is used.	
Getting started	
The diagram identifies a few ways in which birds and reptiles are alike or different. However, essential information may be missing or some information may be inaccurate. The diagram lacks evidence of organization. Some vocabulary is inaccurate or vague. Labels are missing or incomplete. A title is missing or incomplete.	

- Focus on the characteristics of the assessment task
- Exclude factors such as effort, initiative, or invested time
- Be measureable and teachable
- Address the product and the process of learning
- Be clearly worded
- Be manageable—perhaps three to five categories
- Focus on the important "big picture" aspects of your assessment task, especially for a generic rubric that you hope to use repeatedly

Writing the Descriptors

Usually, the descriptions of three to four levels of performance are sequenced across the top of the rubric. Some teachers think placing the top level of performance closest to the criteria will emphasize it, so the sequence moves right in descending quality; other teachers reverse the order. Either way, the sequence should indicate a sliding scale of quality. Some educators question the value of describing lower levels of performance. They prefer a more streamlined rubric that describes only proficient and above proficient performance. Often educators work with students on creating learning goals and success criteria to describe the requirements for success in detail.

The descriptors should be aligned with the stated criteria and make clear distinctions among levels. Consistency is important. The same criteria should be addressed in the same order at each level. For example, if the task requires students to cite research sources, the descriptors at all levels of performance should have a point about citing sources. If this is the first point for Level 1, then it should be the first point across all the levels. While such details may seem petty, they make a difference when students scan the rubric to compare descriptions and make plans for improvement.

Start by describing performance at the proficient level. What are you looking for in a performance that is at the expected standard? Then work down to the minimally acceptable level. Finally, describe the top level. Check your descriptions. Are there distinct differences between each level as you move up and down?

Wording in rubrics is challenging. Ideally, descriptors should be as specific, objective, and positive as possible. If the descriptors are too specific, the rubric becomes a detailed checklist that misses the KDB. On the other hand, using vague descriptors such as *poor, fair, good,* and *excellent* do not provide useful feedback. The student wonders what exactly was "poor" about the work. That is why students need to see samples of work that illustrate the descriptors, and why rubrics should always include commentary.

Finding the balance between precision and flexibility is at the centre of discussions about the pros and cons of rubrics (see Andrade, 2007/2008; Goodrich, 1996/1997; Popham, 1997; Tierney & Simon, 2004). Common descriptors include the following:

- Limited, some, considerable, thorough
- Little, some, sufficient, rich, detailed
- Superficial understanding, partial understanding, solid understanding, deep understanding
- Major errors and/or omissions, few major but several minor errors and/or omissions, few minor errors and/or omissions

What you do want to avoid is turning a rubric into a counting exercise (Cooper, 2010). A level should not be determined by the number of anything—not 1 or 5 or 7 or 10 examples of anything. Rather, the level needs to be determined by the quality. Take, for example, descriptive details in narrative writing. Level 1 should describe the minimal level of acceptable performance. A narrative with no descriptive details is not ready to be assessed and the descriptor "uses no descriptive details" should not be on the rubric for even the lowest level. Also, the criterion asked for *effective* use of descriptive details, not the number. The criterion is a good one, but determining effectiveness in the narrative by quality is what is important. Three rich descriptive details may be more effective than five bland ones.

Use the checklist below to assess the quality of your rubric. Does your rubric

- ✓ represent a range of performances?
- ✓ align with course expectations and provincial outcomes?
- ✓ describe the same features reading across levels?
- ✓ make incremental changes from level to level that are equal and appropriate for the grade?
- ✓ focus on the essential qualities of the task rather than those elements that are easy to measure?
- ✓ make it impossible for a student to produce an excellent piece of work yet receive a low level (or the reverse; a student receives a high mark if something is missing or overemphasized in the rubric)?

Who Should Create the Rubric?

Some educators believe that the expert, usually the teacher, should construct the rubric because the expert knows the criteria and the indicators of quality work best. Others take the opposite view—the students should construct it themselves or at least co-construct it with their teacher. Here, students extrapolate criteria from exemplars and describe levels by reviewing work samples. Cooper (2006) says it is too difficult for students to set criteria, but they can—and should—determine descriptors. Our position is that students should have input in the rubric, even if it is only to deconstruct it. Rubrics can demystify assessment criteria, especially when they are co-written with students.

Infusing the Spirit of AfL into Teaching and Learning

To enhance student learning, assessment needs to be integrated into the instruction. Planning should explicitly identify opportunities for AfL, but the teacher can only go so far in predetermining strategies that may be used. AfL is rooted in a philosophy about teaching and learning. For us, it is the spirit of AfL that needs to be infused into instruction and assessment—the spirit that prioritizes learning over grading.

As we stated at the beginning of this book, we believe that an RPAT is the secret to a rich, relevant curriculum. Infusing the spirit of AfL into everyday learning helps to enhance the learning, too.

SEAMLESSLY CONNECTING INSTRUCTION AND ASSESSMENT

Following these steps in backward design, you have seen how assessment is an integral part of the process. Many times the instructional activity is also the assessment task. Examples of AfL serving as both instructional strategy and assessment tool included the bingo card (Table 3.10), class brainstorming web (Figure 3.6), and the question template

(Table 3.11) for the history unit. As well, you have seen how a Venn diagram can be used in many different ways. Here we consider the development of conceptual knowledge and its relationship to instruction and assessment tasks and tools.

In an age of accountability, the teacher needs to implement evidence-based practice, which begins with gathering data from diagnostic assessment. Teachers continue to gather evidence of learning throughout the instructional period. Formative strategies illuminate student thinking. They use this information to target and adjust their instruction. When

Using Graphic Organizers to Instruct and Assess

One of the authors of this book, Joanne, was teaching a history class. The example here illustrates how an assessment tool can be used simultaneously as an instructional experience and an assessment task. Joanne was teaching the Big Idea of causation. Her Enduring Understandings were as follows:

- Many factors cause historical events (multiple causation).
- What these factors are and their degree of influence is a matter of interpretation, not absolute truth.
- The interpretation of history is always changing.

The skills that made up the Do component were

- Research
- Organization
- Analysis
- Evaluation

Joanne's instruction focused on analyzing generic graphic organizers such as concept webs, T-charts, and flow charts that can be found in most word-processing software. Students determined the pros and cons of each graphic organizer for various kinds of data and purposes. The concept of causation (cause and effect, single/multiple causation) was introduced using the example of a traffic accident. Once having acquired the concepts of graphic organizer and causation, the students tackled the instructional/assessment task.

The task was to select an appropriate graphic organizer and complete it to show the causes of World War II. Students researched the topic and chose or created a graphic organizer to demonstrate the Know. The completed organizer became an assessment tool that told Joanne what her students knew and how they were thinking about causation. Their choice of organizer indicated their level of higher-order thinking. A timeline showing a linear sequence showed less sophistication than an organizer that attempted to present immediate and background causes. A concept web that placed Hitler in the centre to show that the war could be attributed exclusively to the actions of this dictator showed less complexity and perhaps less research than a web or a mind map showing the interaction of several causes. Displaying and sharing the various graphic organizers provided opportunities for further instruction, nudging simplistic thinking to higher levels.

teachers embrace the spirit of AfL, they want to know how all their students are doing and how they can support continuing growth. Strategies for this abound, but remember, a strategy is only useful if it provides useful information and if that information is acted upon.

John Hattie (2009), in his synthesis of over 800 meta-analyses on the most important factors for learning, concluded that feedback to students was a very influential factor for student success. However, feedback to the teacher was also a key part of AfL. During his research he experienced the following "aha" moment:

> The mistake I was making was seeing feedback as something teachers provided to students—they typically did not, although they made claims that they did it all the time, and most of the feedback they did provide was social and behavioral. It was only when I discovered that feedback was most powerful when it is from the student to the teacher that I started to understand it better. When teachers seek, or at least are open to, feedback from students as to what students know, what they understand, where they make errors, when they have misconceptions, when they are not engaged—then teaching and learning can be synchronized and powerful. Feedback to teachers helps make learning visible (p. 73).

PEER AND SELF-ASSESSMENT

Teachers are sometimes leery of peer and self-assessment, but both offer huge benefits when they are seen as integral to the learning process. However, it is not advisable to use peer and self-assessment for grades. Indeed, some jurisdictions (like Ontario) prohibit it.

Effective peer and self-assessment depends on students having an understanding of assessment criteria and the characteristics of different levels of quality. In other words, like their teachers, students need to be assessment literate. The teacher might begin a lesson on descriptive writing by co-creating a rubric with students or "translating" the ministry rubric into student-friendly language. Students could apply the rubric to examples of different levels of work so that they recognize the indicators of success and different levels of quality.

Students need to be taught how to give feedback responsibly (Reynolds, 2009). In Wendy's (one of the authors of this text) school, teachers explicitly teach students appropriate ways to articulate feedback. Some learning communities post co-created anchor charts with appropriate sentence starters for comments, such as "I was confused when . . ." "I liked it when you . . ." "I was wondering why . . ." "Did you consider . . .?" The comments are supported by instructional rubrics.

When students can effectively assess their peers they are ultimately building their assessment literacy and their ability to self-assess. Self-assessment involves several interconnected parts: evaluation, reflection, metacognition, and goal setting (Ontario Ministry of Education, 2007). Evaluation is the actual act of assessing one's own work. Reflection is a necessary part of evaluation as one connects the work to learning outcomes and criteria. Metacognition involves thinking about thinking (Rolheiser, Bower, & Stevahn, 2000): "How do I learn best?" "What strategies should I apply to optimize my learning?" And goal setting involves determining what one needs to learn to be successful.

Self-assessment and metacognition are the pinnacle of assessment (Earl, 2003). This is AaL. When a student no longer needs a teacher, the real work has been done. It does not happen overnight; a teacher's role is to provide feedback, support, and opportunities for practice as the student becomes more skilled. Opportunities for self-assessment occur through the following activities:

- Journal or learning log
- Blogs
- Student–teacher or peer conference or interview
- Rubrics
- Checklists
- Audio–video recordings
- Exemplars
- Electronic portfolios

If students have been socialized in an educational environment that values grades over growth, they may balk or apply criteria haphazardly, too harshly, or too leniently. But with gentle persistence, time, and practice they will likely adopt the values of a learning culture and recognize that accurate, valid self-assessment is the ultimate goal. The Ontario Ministry of Education provides several ideas for implementing self-assessment strategies (see Ontario Ministry of Education, 2007).

LEARNING HOW TO INFUSE AfL INTO TEACHING AND LEARNING

Let's look at a real-world example of how to infuse AfL into teaching and learning from the experiences of one of the authors of this text. As a veteran teacher, Susan thought she knew about assessment: She gave useful feedback, assigned rich assessment tasks as well as tests, and used both peer and self -assessment. But she had not fully understood assessment as an interrelated system with the purpose of creating a culture of learning.

In addition, although she considered herself a constructivist teacher, she realized that she used a traditional Socratic style of questioning. She would pose a question, then try to wait the requisite three seconds for reflection. Then she asked a student with a hand up for the answer. If a student gave the right answer, she might ask if others understood. When students nodded (predictably), she moved on.

Susan knew there were flaws to this method. Quiet students rarely spoke. She really did not know what each student was thinking. Susan began to rethink the "how" and "what" of her questioning techniques.

Susan tried some of the Black and Wiliam (1998) strategies with her university students who were training to be teachers. She initiated a "no-hands" strategy, which meant instead of having students raise their hands she would call on any student at any time. She made sure that everyone had a chance to answer. At first, students disliked this approach. It meant that everyone had to be prepared and attentive. A few resented losing the opportunity to show off their knowledge, while others felt intimidated about being put on the spot. Once students understood that the class was a collaborative community for learning and that it was okay not to know something, tension abated. Students understood that Susan's goal was to enhance learning for all.

Susan needed to see every student's thinking. She provided each student with a white board and a dry eraser so that all students could display their answers simultaneously. Sometimes cellphone polls replaced whiteboards. Either method required short answers, so questions had to be carefully constructed ahead of class. Susan also implemented red, green, and yellow "traffic cards." Students displayed the colour that indicated their level of understanding: red meant "stop" while green meant "go ahead." Students completed exit cards after each lesson to indicate what they had learned and what confused them. These helped Susan plan and pace future lessons.

Initially, students were upset when Susan deviated from the pre-established course syllabus, but as they became more attuned to the idea of a learning culture they saw it as flexibility in response to learner needs.

Another AfL strategy is feedback only with no grades given. Will students work hard when they know their work is not going to be marked or will not "count"? Despite these reservations, research indicates that once students (and their parents) and teachers adopt a learning culture, as opposed to a mark-obsessed culture, students will put in effort to improve performance (Black et al., 2003; Fisher, Frey, & Pumpian, 2011; Pulfrey, Buchs, & Butera, 2011). Susan's students reluctantly accepted a no grade–feedback only policy. The question "what is this worth?" no longer held relevance. They came to understand that the feedback was important, but only if they acted upon it. It was the learning, not the grade that counted.

For Susan, the greatest measure of success was when her students adopted these same methods in their teaching placements and reported satisfaction with the results.

Closing the Loop in Curriculum Planning

The last step in backward design involves evaluating the effectiveness of your planning through consolidation and reflection during and after implementation. There are various ways to collect the reflective data to accomplish this task, such as ongoing student–teacher learning journals, reflections on daily lesson plans, and anecdotal observations of effective instructional strategies, rich performance assessment tasks, assessment tools, blog/web responses, and unit artifacts. In the spirit of backward design, it is important to always be thinking like an assessor, particularly when it is self-assessment. In the spirit of AfL, it is important to use assessment information to improve one's learning.

Conclusion

In this chapter, we outlined in detail the steps that a curriculum planner follows to design a relevant and accountable curriculum. The steps were presented in a linear manner, but in the real world they are iterative in nature. As well, there should always be spaces for the spontaneous teachable moments that are relevant but still coherent with the unit goals. The next two chapters will focus on creating curricula that illustrate the ideas of this chapter in a concrete way.

Professional Discussion Questions

1) Choose a curriculum document from one discipline, and choose one grade level to work with.

   a) Address the following questions in that document:
      - What does the introductory material tell you about the KDB?
      - Perform a vertical scan. What does this tell you about the KDB?
      - Unpack (deconstruct) selected broad-based curriculum outcomes in the vertical scan at your grade level. What does this tell you about the KDB?
      - Create appropriate learning goals for the outcomes you deconstructed. How do you decide on the success criteria for each goal?

   b) Create a KDB umbrella from your scan and cluster.
      - How would you teach and assess the Big Idea and Enduring Understanding?
      - How would you teach and assess the twenty-first–century skills? What would a rubric for one of these skills look like?
      - How would you teach and assess the Be?
      - Identify one or two Essential Questions.
      - Create a rich performance assessment task.
      - How would you assess this task?

   c) Create a rubric for the RPAT using the guidelines in this chapter.

   d) What might your daily instructional tasks/assessments be? How do they connect to outcomes? The RPAT? The KDB umbrella?

2) Was there anything that surprised you about Susan's story, presented in the section "Learning How to Infuse AfL into Teaching and Learning"? How would you infuse the spirit of AfL into your class?

4

Exploring Inquiry and Interdisciplinary Models

In this chapter you will learn about:

- A discipline-based inquiry approach
- A student-centred inquiry approach
- A rationale for integrated curriculum
- Different approaches for curriculum integration

In our conversations with twenty-first–century educators across Canada, we often heard about inquiry learning as a direction for the future. Inquiry-based planning uses backward design where the assessment process is interwoven with curriculum outcomes and assessment. In the first part of this chapter we will explore inquiry-based learning from a discipline-based teacher/expert design perspective by presenting several anecdotes from the real world. Then we shift to inquiry in which students themselves are the designers. In the second part of this chapter we will explore a continuum of integrated curriculum approaches. (We use the terms *interdisciplinary* and *integrated* interchangeably when we are talking in general terms about integrated curriculum.) Since integration may be more unfamiliar than inquiry, we offer a rationale for and description of different approaches. Many of the examples in the interdisciplinary section use the principles of inquiry learning. Again, all approaches use backward design, and curriculum, instruction, and assessment are interwoven.

Inquiry-Based Learning

Inquiry-based learning promotes creative problem solving. Students attempt to make sense of their world as they formulate questions and gather evidence to solve authentic, real-world problems.

DISCIPLINE-BASED INQUIRY

Well-designed discipline-based inquiry projects display characteristics somewhat akin to those we described in Chapter 3 for rich performance assessment tasks. However, several key components of inquiry projects set this approach apart. For example, the involvement of an expert reinforces the disciplinary perspective, while the requirement that students observe or work in the field and present their findings to an audience beyond their classroom provides an extra degree of authenticity and accountability. As part of discipline-based inquiry, students are required to engage in knowledge-building activities by building on each other's ideas to critique, innovate, provide evidence for, and compose compelling arguments to support their ideas. The inquiry approach influences not only the student product but also the process of the investigation. Ideally, an inquiry project demonstrates the characteristics described in Table 4.1.

Inquiry projects emphasize thinking like an expert in a specific discipline. Neil Stephenson was a teacher at the innovative Calgary Science School before he moved on to British Columbia to be an administrator in 2012. As a Canadian leader in inquiry learning, he has worked closely with the Galileo Educational Network (see the box on page 95). He emphasizes that richer, deeper learning occurs when we teach disciplinary ways of thinking. Disciplinary inquiry recognizes that scientists tackle inquiry differently than historians or artists do. The challenge is that not many educators actually know what

TABLE 4.1 Characteristics of Inquiry-Based Rich Performance Assessment Tasks

Designing inquiry projects

Characteristics necessary for designing curriculum	Descriptors
Authenticity	• Real-world issue or problem • Students work in a real-world setting • Students present findings to an authentic audience
Academic rigour	• Observe and question an expert in the field • Multiple paths • Risk taking as experts do • Scientific processes
Assessment	• Use criteria of an expert • AfL/AaL
Beyond the school	• Teamwork and collaboration • Involves work ethic
Appropriate uses of technology	• Use technologies that experts use
Active exploration	• Field work required • Students contribute data to expert database
Connecting with expertise	• Observe and work with experts in the field • Experts are involved in task design
Elaborated communication	• Student ideas matter • Student and teacher reflection informs the student design • Transparency of student and teacher work through documentation of the process • Students design and adjust their own hypotheses

Source: Adapted from Galileo Educational Network (2000–2013).

The Galileo Educational Network

The Galileo Educational Network (known simply as Galileo) is an independent charitable organization that creates, promotes, and researches innovative teaching and learning practices. Galileo has worked with educators in Quebec, Ontario, Saskatchewan, Alberta, and British Columbia as well as in the United States. Its mission is to improve teaching and learning for students, teachers, and leaders through the research and creation of twenty-first–century learning environments. The organization supports inquiry-based projects in which students use digital technologies in creative and thoughtful ways. The network promotes collaboration and hopes to transform education so that it is a new story. Projects are undertaken with collaborators from school districts, university partners, and community organizations and businesses.

disciplines require by way of thinking in a disciplinary way. That's one reason why teachers at the Calgary Science School, a school focused on inquiry, are subject specialists, not generalists, from Grades 4 and up. While Stephenson supports student voice and choice, the teacher as a subject expert must design the inquiry project. He uses the concept of "liberating constraints" to express the idea of freedom within a subject discipline.

The following sections provide two classroom-based examples of inquiry projects, starting with one from Neil Stephenson's Grade 6–7 history class.

The Cigar Box Project

Neil Stephenson and Galileo collaboratively designed and documented the award-winning cigar box project for his Grade 6–7 history class at the Calgary Science School. Stephenson was inspired by an online display of vintage wooden cigar boxes at the Canadian Museum of Civilization. Those boxes were extravagantly decorated with images depicting symbols and scenes of Canadian history. Stephenson's students built and illustrated their own boxes over the course of the school year. Each of the four side panels depicted a different time period, while the box top summarized a theme encompassing a "whole story" of Canada. The project was designed to allow students to answer a big inquiry question: What is my idea of Canadian history?

Students first designed a panel on paper, then collected historical images from digitized archives and cut and pasted them to remix the images. Their designs were affixed to wooden boxes they made themselves. Groups shared images and research, eventually expanding through Skype to include three other classes in other parts of Canada. A curator at the Museum of Civilization, the external expert, provided feedback through Skype.

The project developed historical thinking by requiring students to select images from primary sources and to arrange them in coherent, logical relationships that communicated a *thesis* (an overall main idea). As they worked, students questioned whether their work was plagiarism or a unique creation, and whether their work presented biased representations, perhaps even propaganda.

Technology was used creatively, but always in service of the learning. Stephenson cautions that too often students (and their teachers) spend too much time and effort on the aesthetics of the presentation (how good is this video?) and lose sight of the learning goals (how well does this video demonstrate deep understanding?). Skype, VoiceThread and Google Docs were used for collaboration, and Stephenson himself blogged regularly about the project's evolution (http://firesidelearning.ning.com/profile/NeilStephenson).

Assessment was ongoing, with heavy emphasis on peer and self-assessment. During and after the construction of each panel, students could choose to write or orally record a reflection justifying their choice of images and how the images communicated historical understanding. Summative assessment used a collaboratively designed rubric. The entire project work can be viewed online at www.galileo.org/initiatives/vmuseum/index.html.

The Mountain Project

Here is another disciplinary inquiry project—this time for a Grade 11 science class (see the entire project at http://galileo.org/classroom-examples/classroom-examples-high-school-science/ecological-field-study). By walking up mountain slopes and working with scientific experts, Grade 11 students in Alberta explored the Big Ideas of climate zones, transfer of energy, and the relationship between solar energy, climate, and biomes. Their guiding inquiry question was this: If knowing that going 300 metres up this mountain slope is like going 950 kilometres further north, what do our observations tell us about northern biomes as we walk up the slope?

The science teachers collaborated with Galileo, a biologist, and an environmental educator from the Biogeoscience Institute University of Calgary Field Station located in Kananaskis to design this project. Working alongside these experts, applying scientific inquiry research skills and using the same tools, students learned to think like scientists. As well, they learned how to collaborate.

Students first spent time in the mountain environment to become acclimatized. They studied exemplars of posters done by scientists and also observed and questioned the scientists working in this mountain environment. Students worked with the teacher to understand how to ensure that their own work was scientific, complex, and multidimensional.

On the first walk as a large group, students brainstormed questions:

- Does elevation affect forest density?
- Are there more animals at the top or bottom of the slope?
- How does altitude affect growth?
- How does slope affect height and dimension?

Students in small groups then designed testable research questions based on their observations. On the mountain slope the students collected data to explore their hypotheses. After the first round, the group assembled to discuss their results. The teachers asked questions to illuminate student thinking so that all the students could learn from each other.

Student teams went back two more times to different slopes to further investigate and collect data. They assembled each time to share knowledge and complete feedback loops. The teachers continually discussed among themselves ways to bridge the gaps in the student learning and help them refine their thinking. Finally, the students examined other research findings from this area and compared their results, then wrote a field report on the results of their research. This was followed by peer and teacher feedback. The students' final field report was submitted to the Biogeoscience Institute field station where it was added to the database at the station. The teachers reported that the students were engaged, asked thoughtful questions, and took risks as they completed their inquiry.

Moving Toward Student-Centred Inquiry Learning

Thus far we have discussed students as active participants in their own learning, but the curriculum design examples we have described have been teacher directed. There is a shift occurring where students are posing and pursuing their own questions. In Ontario, for example, there is a new framework for student questioning that includes text, personal, world, text/personal, personal/world, text/world, and dense questions (text/personal/world). Students then research their own questions (Literacy GAINS, 2013). These next curriculum examples show you how students can play an active role in the design of their own learning while still adhering to the rigour of the inquiry model.

INQUIRY LEARNING IN AN ELEMENTARY SCHOOL SETTING

Inquiry learning can begin in Kindergarten as play-based inquiry. For Ontario teacher Angie Harrison, inquiry learning means to "go where the kids' interests are." In her classroom, a picture of each student is posted on the wall with a think bubble containing the words "I am wondering . . ."; the individual inquiry question of each child completes the sentence. Harrison talks to students during play periods and gives them resources to help them address their "wonderings."

Technology plays a big role in Harrison's inquiry learning. For example, as she reads an informational text on leaves changing colour she shows video clips and Smartboard images of the colour-change process. Harrison's school board has a licence with Discovery Education Canada, an online resource centre (www.discoveryeducation.ca/Canada) that was the source of the videos. The changing images make the learning come alive.

For Harrison, technology allows for more **authentic assessment**. Harrison believes in giving immediate feedback by documenting the learning through audio recordings and photos that are then shown back to the students to help them understand the processes of their thinking. She uses the book *Windows on Learning: Documenting Young Children's Work* (Helm, Beneke, & Steinheimer, 2007) and *Worms, Shadows and Whirlpools: Science in the Early Childhood Classroom* (Worth & Grollman, 2003) to guide her.

Here's how inquiry works in Harrison's daily practice. During playtime the question arose as to whether a structure was a bridge or a ramp (Harrison, 2012). Harrison showed students different books and photos to illustrate the difference between the two. Students built structures that Harrison documented on an iPad. From these images she created a PicCollage (a simple app available at http://pic-collage.com) that included the children's questions with pictures of their products. The students participated in making the collage by choosing the photos to include and by giving Harrison the quotes. She is moving toward the students being able to create a PicCollage themselves.

Harrison has also taught Grade 3. She describes the use of technology for ongoing AfL in math for both Kindergarten and Grade 3. In Kindergarten, Harrison photographs student work and inserts the photos into her assessment notes and into the students' digital journal. She uses the document camera to magnify and project images on a large screen. Students use math manipulatives and discuss their thinking while the class watches, thanks to the document camera. Her Grade 3 students would bring their math problem-solving work to the document camera where it would be copied and inserted it into SMART Notebook (a collaborative learning software program). Students could write on the SMART Notebook page to explain their thinking while other students followed. The students' solutions to the same problem could also be compared. The final product or the process could then be printed out and used for portfolios. As well, solutions could be used as anchors for learning (a focus for anchoring instruction around an interesting topic or problem).

Like many other twenty-first–century educators, Harrison has a blog where she explores her own learning and that of her students. Her blog is called "Expanding Teaching, Exploring Technology" (http://techieang.edublogs.org/2012/10/23/what-can-you-see).

Snapshot of Student Inquiry

Bill Belsey from Alberta believes in developing the literacies needed in the twenty-first century. Inquiry, research, and communication were major elements in his Grade 5 project called "That's a good question." Asking a good question is the first step in inquiry and research—an important cross-curricular goal. The students chose the topic. Using the Internet, they researched to find the world's experts on the topic and emailed them asking for interviews. Each student developed three questions that were shared and critiqued by the class, after which the students prioritized the questions.

The goal was to learn good questioning techniques, but it was also a bit of a competition for the best questions. They hoped that the interviewee would say, "Wow! That's a good question." This is what happened when Nora Young, host of the CBC radio show *Spark*, was interviewed on Skype about the way technology was changing relationships. The students erupted in cheers. Bill concludes his story with the comment that technology is fine, but knowing how to ask good questions is one of the keys to relevant learning.

INQUIRY LEARNING IN A HIGH SCHOOL SETTING

An inspiring example of education with inquiry at the centre is the Inquiry Hub—a new twenty-first–century secondary school venture in Coquitlam British Columbia. The Inquiry Hub approach shifts emphasis to student-centred inquiry.

In September 2012, 33 students—mostly Grade 9s along with a few Grade 10s— entered the school. Since it is a high school, students need to get marks for individual subject credits. The Grade 9 students take math, science, social studies, and English, like other Grade 9 students in the province. But this is a school that promises to be different.

Inquiry Hub students are grouped into three cohorts according to three general interest domains: global/community, environmental sustainability, and media art/technology design. Students focus their course work in these areas. For example, for a student in the global/ community general interest domain, inquiry questions in science and ecology could focus on the health of a local stream, a grant for a community garden, or alternate forms of energy used in developing countries.

A unique aspect of the school curriculum is the inclusion of two "mandatory electives" called Digital Literacy and Inquiry Learning. These are both board-approved courses, which means that other teachers can choose to teach the courses in other schools. Information about this program can be found at www.inquiryhub.org.

The Inquiry Hub emphasizes seven key aspects across all subject areas:

- Inquiry: Students are encouraged to ask and explore their own questions through an in-depth inquiry.
- Student voice: Students share the results of deep learning with each other, the community, and/or online.
- Audience: Students craft their messages appropriately for an appropriate, authentic target audience.
- Community: Students collaborate with others outside their school on projects that matter.
- Leadership: Students are given opportunities to lead, such as being a buddy with a younger student.
- Play: Learning can be playful, and personal interest projects can be fun.
- Networks: The Inquiry Hub uses a hybrid model that blends community, classroom, and online experiences.

Inquiry Course

Stephen Whiffin is the district principal of Coquitlam Open Learning and the Inquiry Hub. Whiffin developed a stand-alone course on Inquiry that focuses on how to design rigorous inquiries. The goal is to move beyond the inquiry-based performance task that is teacher directed to one where students co-design with the teachers. In this way, students feel ownership for their tasks and also learn a twenty-first–century skill—design. Students transfer the knowledge and skills that they learn in this course to their disciplinary studies. Students learn the steps of inquiry by "playing" with each step in the process. Whiffin notes that students need to move from just following the steps as a procedure to deeply understanding inquiry in which one question can lead to 10 more. For teachers, the inquiry approach means creating an environment where students do not feel overwhelmed by pressure, but where they also accept the challenge of working beyond the superficial level.

For this course, Whiffin did not need to reinvent the wheel; rather, he needed to reframe inquiry learning. The Alberta Ministry of Education's *Focus on Inquiry: A Teacher's Guide to Implementing Inquiry-Based Learning* (2004) was a useful document. The Galileo Educational Network also provided a strong foundation for his thinking. Whiffin also adapted his approach using exemplary work from other schools, such as the Calgary Science School.

The design process begins with students learning about the big picture of inquiry process, shown in Figure 4.1.

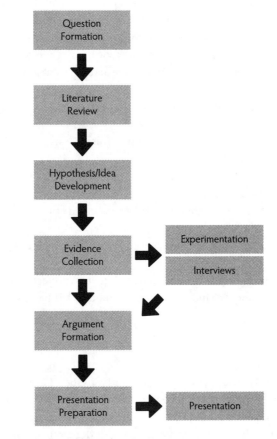

FIGURE 4.1 Inquiry Process Flow Chart
Source: Stephen Whiffin, Inquiry Hub

TABLE 4.2 Question Generation Worksheet

Initial Questions:	Who, what, where, why, when, how?
Question Stems	How is _____ related to _____?
	What is a new example of _____?
	What are some possible solutions for _____?
	Explain why.
	What do you think would happen if _____?
	Why is _____ important?
Perspective	How would experts in different disciplines ask the question?
Final Question	

Source: Adapted from Stephen Whiffin, Inquiry Hub

Next, students begin forming their questions, supported by the question generation worksheet shown in Table 4.2. (For another view of question formation, see the history unit presented in Chapter 3.)

Some of the inquiry questions students posted on their Wonder Wall included the following:

- What is the source of crime and what can we do to eliminate it?
- Why was the French Revolution important to the development of women's rights in Europe?
- At what point should people interfere with invasive species?
- Why hasn't Canada had a revolution like France and the United States?
- What is the role of politics in a politically charged issue such as climate change?

The questions that survive a vetting process require academic rigour and critical thinking. Some parents have wondered if these questions were more suited to university inquiry than Grade 9. Whiffin contends that these are the questions that matter in the real world and Grade 9 students can begin to address them.

As students follow through on their project design, they use an instructional rubric based on the characteristics in Table 4.1. This rubric is Whiffin's adaptation of the Galileo rubric that was originally created for teachers to assess their inquiry projects. The original teacher-directed rubric can be found at www.galileo.org/research/publications/rubric.pdf. The Inquiry Hub version is for the student as an inquiry designer.

Once the inquiry has been designed, students proceed with the project as outlined in the process flow chart (Figure 4.1). The completed project concludes with a reflection stage on next steps for learning and perhaps a reframing of the question or identifying a new question that emerged from the inquiry.

Digital Literacy Course

Whiffin's colleague David Truss developed the Digital Literacy course that focuses on one's digital footprint and the responsible use of the social network, personal learning environments and personal learning networks, digital presentations, and digital inquiry. For example, Truss teaches students how to use Creative Commons images (http://creativecommons. org/licenses/by-nc-sa/3.0). One assignment is about using one of the Creative Commons licences that describes the attribution, noncommercial use, and share-alike conditions for using images. In the performance demonstration task, students make a poster with a Creative Commons image and place the attribution on top of it. They are then expected to use this skill in their other courses.

In another assignment, students analyze and evaluate the effectiveness of an infographic, selecting one to improve. Truss (2013) points out that developing digital literacy skills takes practice, and sometimes past versions are better than current ones, and the transfer of skills to a new context is less successful. He writes, "Of course, assessment in a school of constantly changing questions and project iterations can't rely on a linear grading model. Learning outcomes are continuously re-examined to ensure that students are always improving. It takes a real shift in thinking to allow students to provide new opportunities for assessment of learning outcomes on a continuous basis. But ultimately, educators are there for their students, and that means that most courses really should allow this approach." For a deeper understanding of this program, follow Truss's blog: David Truss: Pair-a-dimes for Your Thoughts (http://pairadimes.davidtruss.com).

INQUIRY FOR CREATIVITY, K–12

Another example of student-centred inquiry is Genius Hour. This is a grassroots movement inspired by Daniel Pink's (2011) observation that employees were much more productive and creative when they were given free time to follow their own interests. Several Canadian teachers now implement a Genius Day theme. In Genius Hour/Day, teachers begin with student questions and use them to develop twenty-first–century skills such as independence, learning how to learn, and creativity through inquiry. There is no prescribed grade level and no curriculum documents specified. Students are given "free" time to follow their passion—often in 100-minute block times. Students also demonstrate presentation skills and relevant knowledge from the subject area that their inquiry falls into. The assessment is self-assessment.

Gallit Zvi, a Grade 6 and 7 teacher from British Columbia, is the co-moderator of the #geniushour chat that runs every first Wednesday of the month (http://geniushour. wikispaces.com). Zvi's students love Genius Hour. She gives them three, one-hour sessions to develop their inquiry question and then present what they have done to address the question. Zvi says, "Because of Genius Hour, I am a changed teacher forever. I no longer need to be in control of all the learning . . . it is okay and highly beneficial to step back and allow learning to happen" (innovative learning designs, 2012). Her students have created websites, learned about different countries, taken apart and built computers, and made movies.

Hugh McDonald (2012), another British Columbia teacher, describes his students' reaction when he implemented the Genius Hour in his Grade 7 class: "I love watching student engagement levels go through the roof." He began reviewing videos posted on Denise Krebs's (2011) blog of her students' creative work. His students then explored the questions that Krebs used with her students as starters for the Genius Day projects:

- What ideas do you want to explore?
- What do you want to try out?
- What skill can you master?
- What tool can you practice using?
- What tool could help you communicate better?

To get a good grasp on what creativity is, McDonald's class looked at the rubric that Denise Krebs's class created for creativity (see Table 4.3). Finally, students wrote their proposals on their blogs. The results of their first Genius Day were a hockey stick created from scratch, baked cookies and cakes, how-to videos, magnetic cards, a doll house made of popsicle sticks, movie trailers, an iMovie about the history of computers, novels, paintings, and Prezis on invented games, favourite foods, and people.

The final step was a reflection on the process. Students shared their learning on a classroom Twitter account. They completed the creativity self-assessment and wrote a letter for students participating in the next year's Genius Hour.

Interdisciplinary Learning

Interdisciplinary learning has a long history. The project-based method (Kilpatrick, 1918) is the precursor for inquiry learning and integrated curriculum that we describe in this chapter. Thus, these approaches are not new; they are grounded in deep philosophical perspectives from John Dewey, an instrumental leader in the progressive movement.

WHY?

For teachers who experienced the discipline-based approach of the old story as students (or maybe even taught under that approach), it is difficult, and a bit scary, to consider teaching from an interdisciplinary perspective. As we move further and further into the twenty-first century, however, there are more and more reasons to teach this way. In fact, in some ways it is hard to stay within the discrete disciplines of a subject area. We consider some of these reasons here.

IMPACT ON ACHIEVEMENT

How does an interdisciplinary approach impact achievement? It has been difficult to find quantitative research that focuses specifically on interdisciplinary programs. The Eight-Year Study conducted during the 1930s (described in the Snapshot box below) remains the only longitudinal quantitative study that affirmed integrated curriculum as a valuable pedagogy. In the

TABLE 4.3 Student-Created Rubric for Creativity, Denise Krebs's Class

Genius Hour Rubric

Genius = creating and producing. That's from the original meaning of the word

Quality	Yes, I have it! (5)	Where are you on the continuum between "Yes, I have it!" (5) and "Not yet!" (1)					Not yet! (1)
Ambiguity: I'm OK with a little confusion, knowing there is more than one way to do the job.	I don't need to ask the teacher a lot of questions. I can think for myself and get the job done.	5	4	3	2	1	I have to be told exactly how to do every job. There is only one right way to do the job.
Inquisitiveness: I ask questions and want answers.	I am curious and look up things that interest me. I'm a lifelong learner.	5	4	3	2	1	I don't ask questions just for the joy of learning, and I don't really want to learn new things.
Generating Ideas (brainstorming): I create lots of possible ideas.	I am able to fluently create a list of ideas. I use my imagination.	5	4	3	2	1	I cannot see beyond the obvious ideas. I am easily frustrated. I may be lazy.
Originality of Ideas: I create unique ideas!	I can think outside the box and I have a great imagination. I think of ideas that others never even thought of.	5	4	3	2	1	I can only think of ideas that others thought of first. I don't like the new ways of doing things. I just want to stick to the old way.
Flexibility/Adaptability: Mentally, I can bend easily any which way and not break.	I can think of new ways to do things when I get stuck. I can recognize other people's good ideas.	5	4	3	2	1	I am not willing to change my ideas or think of better ones.
Self-Reflection: I can look honestly at myself and evaluate my work.	I can honestly go through my work and know what's right or wrong.	5	4	3	2	1	I lie about my work. I can't or won't look honestly at the things I do well and the things that need more work.
Intrinsic Motivation: I want to do it. I know the purpose and it pleases me.	I want to try new things. I believe in myself.	5	4	3	2	1	I am not willing to try new things unless I get something for it.
Risk Taking: I'm not afraid to try something difficult for fear of failure. As Edison said, "I have not failed … I have succeeded in proving that 1000 ways will not work."	I'm not afraid to try anything, even if I don't do well at it. I keep trying and find a new way that might work.	5	4	3	2	1	I don't try new things for fear of failing. I try a couple of times and then give up altogether.
Expertise: I am proud and thankful to know a lot about one or more subjects. I am an expert.	I know I am good at one or more things, and I am not afraid to share my knowledge with others.	5	4	3	2	1	I don't try to be an expert at anything. Or I pretend to not know anything.

Snapshot of Real-World Interdisciplinary Problem Solving

One of your authors, Wendy, uses the story about the ill-fated Apollo 13 mission to show how complex problems are not solved using a single discipline. During the Apollo flight, a routine mixing of the second oxygen tank resulted in a series of short-circuits. The three astronauts were forced to abandon the command module and enter the lunar module, designed to hold only two men. The carbon dioxide level began to rise at an alarming rate. The crew did not have enough carbon dioxide filters for the lunar module, and the command module filters were the wrong shape.

On the ground at the Kennedy Space Center, a team was assembled to build a makeshift adapter that would fit the square command module filters into the round rescue ship's filter barrel. These NASA experts, each a specialist in a different field, could only use materials the Apollo 13 crew already had available. The team had little time to complete and test its prototypes and to write a manual for the astronauts to accompany each mock-up. Divergent thinking, creativity, and the convergence of several disciplines led to a successful outcome. Math, science (chemical and physical), and engineering skills were used to design the adapter. Strong communication skills were necessary to write the procedural manual and communicate the instructions to the crew orally. (For more information, see http://space.about.com/od/spaceexplorationhistory/a/apollo13.htm.)

late 1980s and early 1990s, integrated programs enjoyed a period of popularity. The movement generated a lot of literature that was largely anecdotal or qualitative in nature and resulted in its rejection by the research community. In any event, curriculum integration researchers Rennie, Venville, and Wallace (2012) claim that integrated curriculum can't be measured by the same measures as traditional curriculum because the outcomes of such curriculum can't be quantified. A general conclusion, however, of accumulated research was that students in integrated programs consistently demonstrated academic performance equal to or better than students in discipline-based programs (Drake, 2007; Smith & Tyler, 1942; Vars, 2001).

Importantly, in the twenty-first century we do have evidence of successful interdisciplinary learning. Some programs from the late 1900s in North America survived and have been subject to similar testing and accountability measures as other schools. Evidence that these programs consistently result in academic success and engagement in schools is listed below:

- Arts integration: Several rigorous studies have shown increased engagement and achievement for students from both high and low socioeconomic backgrounds (Vega, 2012a; Catterall, Dumais, & Hamden-Thompson, 2012; Walker, McFadden, Tabone, & Finkelstein, 2011; Upitis, 2011).
- **Project-based learning (PBL):** PBL practices are research supported (Vega, 2012b; Ravitz, 2009). The Buck Institute's 40 years of research (2009) demonstrate that

Snapshot from History

Were students educated in the constructivist progressive approach able to compete with their peers who had been educated in the traditional manner? The Eight-Year Study (Aikin, 1942) was a longitudinal study across the United States of 1475 pairs of students entering college. One partner educated in the traditional approach was matched to an equivalent partner educated in the constructivist approach. Colleges and universities dropped the typical standardized requirements for admission to allow access to students who had not taken the traditional standardized exams. Constructivist high schools were encouraged to use experience-based pedagogy because it motivated students and allowed for student choice and integrated subject matter.

In this study, students with a progressive background did somewhat better than the traditional students in all 18 variables. The more interdisciplinary the high school program had been, the better the students did in higher education. The results of this study were released right in the midst of World War II, and it is believed that the results were lost as the general culture returned to a more traditional position.

PBL is more effective than traditional teaching for academic success. The New Tech Network (www.newtechnetwork.org), a nonprofit organization dedicated to the PBL approach, is working successfully with 85 schools in 16 states to create innovative, hands-on learning environments.

- Challenge-based learning (CBL): CBL is a program promoted by Apple. CBL is PBL where the use of technology is mandatory. Six schools supported by the New Media Consortium showed academic success (Johnson, Smith, Smyth, & Varon, 2009).
- The Big Picture Learning Schools: These schools have grown to 120 in number since 1995. Graduation rates in these schools are 92% compared to 52% in traditional urban schools, and the college acceptance rate is 95% compared to 45% in traditional schools. (www.bigpicture.org). The snapshot of a transdisciplinary program on page 118 describes a Big Picture Learning School in Winnipeg.
- Expeditionary learning: This type of learning has been implemented in 165 schools across the United States. It focuses on academic learning expeditions, project work, case studies, and service learning with real-world issues. Research shows increased student engagement and academic achievement (Expeditionary Learning, 2013.)
- The Curriculum Project: Curriculum implementation following an interdisciplinary model of curriculum, instruction, and assessment developed by Curry and Samara offers several scholarly reports of success (Curry, Samara, & Connell, 2005; see also www.curriculumproject.com/knowledge_share_scholarly_reports.php for links to other scholarly reports).
- Social and emotional learning (SEL): Social and emotional learning includes self-awareness, self-management, social awareness, relationship skills, and responsible

decision making. Research shows that SEL promotes academic success (Vega & Tereda, 2012; see also Vega, 2012c, for an annotated bibliography of 29 additional studies).

Clearly, given this research, interdisciplinary approaches can no longer be dismissed.

LITERACY AND THE NEW LITERACIES

In the twenty-first century, a goal of education is literacy. Literacy includes the traditional three Rs as well as the new interdisciplinary literacies. The new literacies offer a natural fit for interdisciplinary approaches. The Saskatchewan Ministry of Education (2010) defines literacy in subject areas such as scientific literacy and historical literacy. It goes on to show how the new literacies, such as critical literacy and media literacy, are crucial to developing literacy in a subject area:

> Literacies provide many ways to interpret the world and express understanding of it. Being literate involves applying interrelated knowledge, skills, and strategies to learn and communicate with others. Communication in a globalized world is increasingly multimodal. Communication and meaning making, therefore, require the use and understanding of multiple modes of representation. Each area of study develops disciplinary literacies (e.g., scientific, economic, physical, health, linguistic, numeric, aesthetic, technological, cultural) and requires the understanding and application of multiple literacies (i.e., the ability to understand, critically evaluate, and communicate in multiple meaning making systems) in order for students to participate fully in a constantly changing world (p. 26).

These "new literacies" are referred to as *fluencies* by the 21st Century Fluency Project (http://fluency21.com) in British Columbia. Fluencies revolve around digital literacy and include information fluency, solution fluency, media fluency, collaboration fluency, and creative fluency. Fluencies are differentiated from literacies for a reason: "To be literate means to have knowledge or competence. To be fluent is something a little more; it is to demonstrate mastery and to do so unconsciously and smoothly" (21st Century Fluency Project, 2013, http://www.fluency21.com/fluencies.cfm). The project is facilitated by experienced educators and entrepreneurs. A curriculum integration kit is available at their website. Integrated units are provided to cultivate twenty-first–century fluencies and to foster engagement and adventure. This is a collaborative community where teachers share online.

For the Partnership for the 21st Century (www.p21.org)—a nonprofit organization in the United States—literacy includes civic literacy, health literacy, environmental literacy, information literacy, media literacy, information communications technology literacy, and financial, economic, business, and entrepreneurial literacy.

Canadian curriculum guidelines do acknowledge most of the literacies/fluencies mentioned above. In Ontario, for example, environmental literacy is to be infused into every grade in every subject, arts literacy is to be connected to other subject areas, a document on financial literacy was released in 2011, technological literacy is emphasized, and critical literacy and media literacy are required skills in English guidelines.

CURRICULUM DOCUMENTS

The Know, Do, and Be cut across disciplines and offer a good rationale for integrated or interdisciplinary curriculum. This is particularly obvious when the provincial K–12 curriculum has a unifying framework to show that all subjects share the same ultimate learning goals. Most Canadian curriculum documents describe some degree of integration and encourage making connections to the real world. In this section we provide a snapshot of some of these examples.

In British Columbia, the environmental theme is embedded into different subject areas. In Alberta, *Primary Programs Framework for Teaching and Learning* (2007) defines and promotes curriculum integration:

> Children in the primary grades see learning in a holistic way and not as separate subject areas. Organizing for instruction, using integrative approaches, therefore helps students make connections across subject areas. In planning for instruction, teachers purposefully draw together outcomes across the curriculum to develop a more powerful understanding of key ideas (p. 2).

The integrated approach to planning meaningful instruction across subject areas can be located in the introductory materials of the Saskatchewan and Ontario curriculum documents. The Prince Edward Island educational system has produced a Kindergarten integrated curriculum document to support early childhood education. The Quebec Ministry of Education has outlined cross-curricular competencies for inclusion in unit planning and focuses on an integrated project as a way to demonstrate learning.

One unique document is *The Ontario Curriculum, Grades 11 and 12: Interdisciplinary Studies* (Ontario Ministry of Education, 2002) policy document that allows students to combine all of the expectations from the interdisciplinary studies course with a relevant selection of expectations from two or more courses from the same grade or the grade immediately preceding or following. These courses may be offered as single credit or multicredit packages. In 2011, over 150 such programs were identified (Field & Kozak, 2011). The main integrating themes of such programs are environment, outdoor education, and citizenship. Other themes have been agriculture and horticulture, faith development, and technology.

To better reflect Ministry and school division directions in the province, the College of Education at the University of Saskatchewan has created a mandatory new course for pre-service students called "Pedagogies of Place: Context-Based Teaching." In the Saskatchewan Ministry of Education, three broad areas of learning represent the cross-curricular goals of K–12 education: lifelong learners; sense of self, community, and place; and engaged citizens. All subject areas need to be organized in relation to these competencies. "Pedagogies of Place" is aligned with these areas through an organizing focus on the "best place" for learning and an inquiry-based approach. Rather than beginning with a subject-based curriculum, it models integrating subject-specific content, such as language arts and science, into inquiry-based learning in relation to more diverse contexts of learning. This 13-week course is experiential and holistic in nature, with 50% of classes taking place outside of the classroom. The four contexts explored in the course are urban, land-based, virtual, and classroom-based learning. The course has a strong emphasis on social and ecological justice and Aboriginal pedagogy.

BREADTH OR DEPTH

One argument for integration is that a topic or issue can be studied in depth. "Google has given us the world at our fingertips, but speed and ubiquity are not the same as knowing something" (Cookson, 2009, p. 1). The Learning in Depth curriculum developed by curriculum theorist Kieran Egan (2010) from Simon Fraser University and co-director of the Imagination Research Group offers a good example of deep interdisciplinary learning. During the first week of school, Grade 1 students attend a ceremony where they are assigned the topic that they will become experts in over the next 12 years. Topics such as apples, dust, railways, and cats become multidimensional and experiential in nature with ties to students' emotional, historical, and cultural lives. Students work at their own pace for an hour each week to build a portfolio around their topics. Egan reports students increasingly work outside of school on their portfolios even though they are not assessed on them. The teachers are facilitators, not experts. The students as experts present their learning each year.

Growing from 30 children in two schools in 2008 to 2000 students in 2009, the Learning in Depth program went viral in 2010, reaching students in New Zealand, the United States, Romania, Australia, Japan, England, and Hungary. Egan believes the program is successful because it captures students' imaginations while it excites them about being experts and allows them to work independently at their own pace.

TIME AND EFFICIENCY

Interdisciplinary teaching can be a more efficient way to cover curriculum outcomes by reducing duplication. In elementary school, one teacher can assess skills for more than one subject at the same time. For example, if you are teaching science and language arts together, the blog entry in which the student writes about the environment can serve as a part of the communication grade in both subjects, while the science content can be assessed for science (Drake & Reid, 2010). A student does not need to be taught essay structure in history, English, and science—teach it in one department but apply it across subjects. Similarly, when departments share a generic rubric for common tasks, assessment becomes more streamlined and students develop a cross-curricular understanding of skills criteria.

SOLVING COMPLEX REAL-WORLD PROBLEMS

The key to an engaging curriculum is relevancy for students. An integrated approach where students work on complex problems is more motivating to students (Rennie, Venville, & Wallace, 2012). The traditional model can become mired in factual details, as one of your authors' experience exemplifies. Susan found herself hearing the same argument again and again over the question of whether the parts of the microscope should be on the Grade 9 science exam. On one side, science teachers answered that students would need this knowledge in Grade 11; on the other side, teachers didn't think it was important to memorize the parts—the important thing was to know how to operate a microscope. The disagreement was telling. The latter group of science teachers understood the importance of applying knowledge beyond simply knowing the facts. These were the teachers who took students out to the wetlands or measured water quality in local waterways. Inevitably, the learning from their students moved beyond the disciplinary boundaries because the real world was interdisciplinary.

Multifaceted problems like climate change and poverty require interdisciplinary outlooks (McMurtry, 2011). A rich interdisciplinary classroom environment provides the opportunity for students to look through multiple lenses to discuss current concerns:

> . . . social problems and issues transcend disciplinary boundaries . . . a major purpose of public schooling is preparing enlightened citizens who can make intelligent decisions about public problems; the curriculum, then, must provide opportunities for students to (connect), integrate and apply subject knowledge so they can understand and confront complex social problems (Wraga, 2009, p. 92).

Indeed, learners with interdisciplinary skills fare better as lifelong learners. Ken Bain (2012), an academic with a prestigious background in teaching and learning, conducted interviews with 100 remarkable lifelong learners. He distinguished between strategic learners who learned procedurally with the goal of high marks and deep learners who continually questioned everything and connected their learning across different domains. Later in life, the strategic learners could not problem solve effectively, whereas the deep learners connected what they had learned in different disciplines to imagine multiple solutions before they accepted a solution to a problem. Bain also noted that the successful lifelong learners used metacognitive strategies to explore how they had come up with an idea. Bain's research addresses both the strength of interdisciplinary perspectives for addressing complex problems and assessment as learning as ingredients for an extraordinary learner.

BRAIN RESEARCH AND PLASTICITY OF THE BRAIN

Looking at the shift from STEM to the ST²REAM model for learning illuminates how brain research can inform our educational practices. Our brain is plastic in nature; that is, we can alter our brains through learning (Willis, 2006, 2008, 2011; Doidge, 2007; Costa & Kallick, 2000; Sousa, 1998). This is good news for everyone, as it means we are not destined from birth to have fixed intelligence.

STEM is a movement that calls for the integration of science, technology, engineering, and math. Noting that Canadian students are not choosing science as a career and that Canada is falling behind in innovation, Barlow (2012) advocates that STEM be offered in schools. STEM can be serious fun—for example, when engineering is added to the mix and students create hockey helmets to prevent concussions or search for techniques that target and kill cancer cells without side effects rather than make baking soda and vinegar volcanoes. When Scofield Magnet Middle School adopted STEM principles to teach water quality, students did better academically and enjoyed school more (Drake, 2012).

ST²REAM is a model of connected learning that includes thematic instruction, reading/language arts, engineering, art (visual/spatial thinking), and STEM. Visual literacy is important as it allows students to describe, understand, or model a concept. The rationale for ST²REAM is based on brain research as described by esteemed neuroscientist Kenneth Wesson (2012). According to Wesson, the more parts of the brain involved, the deeper the learning:

> [W]hen we increase the number of neural pathways linking markedly different regions of the brain, we can make substantive changes to brain circuitry. . . . Instead of attempting to enhance student learning through the conventional delivery systems—subject-area isolation and memorization—ST²REAM helps achieve our learning goals via situated learning, where the content resembles the wafer-thin layers composing a hologram (p. 26).

What Is Interdisciplinary or Integrated Curriculum?

Defining integrated or interdisciplinary curriculum is challenging. Many different terms are used such as *cross-disciplinary, interdisciplinary,* or *integrated.* A dictionary defines *interdisciplinarity* as "research or study that integrates concepts from different disciplines resulting in a synthesized or co-ordinated coherent whole" (Harvey, 2004–2009). DeZure similarly describes interdisciplinarity as the "synthesis of two or more disciplines, establishing a new level of discourse and integration of knowledge" (1999, p. 3). Klein supports the above definitions, stating that "all interdisciplinary activities are rooted in the ideas of unity and synthesis, evoking a common epistemology of convergence" (Klein, 1990, p. 11).

The province of Alberta describes curriculum integration in *Primary Programs Framework for Teaching and Learning: Kindergarten to Grade 3* (Alberta Ministry of Education, 2007):

> Curriculum integration can be described as an approach to teaching and learning that is based on both philosophy and practicality. It can generally be defined as a curriculum approach that purposely draws together knowledge, skills, attitudes and values from within or across subject areas to develop a more powerful understanding of key ideas. Curriculum integration occurs when components of the curriculum are connected and related in meaningful ways (p. 2).

We agree that curriculum integration is about more than simply putting subjects together. Teachers who are attracted to these approaches tend to hold a constructivist philosophy and favour project-based learning and performance assessments; they believe their students learn when they are actively engaged in the learning and connect new knowledge to what they already know (Kuhlthau, Maniotes, & Caspari, 2007).

Researchers in the late 1980s and early 1990s described curriculum integration as occurring on a continuum according to the degree of integration and increasing complexity (Drake, 1993; Jacobs, 1989; Fogarty, 1991). Figure 4.2 shows these levels of increasing

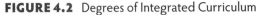

Disciplinary	Fusion	Multidisciplinary	Interdisciplinary	Transdisciplinary
No integration	Minimal integration	Increasing integration	Maximum integration

FIGURE 4.2 Degrees of Integrated Curriculum

integration. Rennie, Venville, and Wallace (2012) acknowledge a continuum but also suggest that it is best to consider integration from the "Worldly Perspective" (p. 99). This perspective includes both disciplinary and interdisciplinary, and both the global and local. Their research revealed that students learned disciplinary knowledge better by studying through disciplinary procedures. However, students learned twenty-first–century skills better through integrated approaches like problem solving.

FUSION

Fusion—the integration of one initiative into the general curriculum—requires the least degree of integration. For example, social justice is infused into the British Columbia curriculum at all grades and in all subjects. *Making Space: Teaching for Diversity and Social Justice throughout the K to 12 Curriculum* (British Columbia Ministry of Education, 2008) is a teacher resource that includes self-assessment tools, teaching strategies, and rubrics for classroom application to promote the achievement of social justice for all people and groups. Typically, topics explored across subject areas include bullying, recognizing whose voice is missing, challenging stereotypes, and helping students recognize oppression. The authors base the implementation strategies around the BC performance standards for social responsibility: contributing to classroom and community, solving problems in peaceful ways, valuing diversity and human rights, and exercising democratic rights and responsibilities. Full text for the social responsibility standards can be found at www.bced. gov.bc.ca/perf_stands/social_resp.htm.

MULTIDISCIPLINARY

The multidisciplinary approach maintains separate disciplinary boundaries (Figure 4.3). Disciplines are connected around a common theme or issue such as war and peace, urban life, or sustainable habitats.

In an elementary classroom, students may go to different learning centres to complete disciplinary activities. In high school, students may study the same theme in different subjects. Taking the multidisciplinary approach is not a guarantee of depth, however. Table 4.4 shows what learning centres in an elementary classroom might look like from a surface-level perspective, which uses the topic of polar bears, to a more substantive one that explores the Big Idea of sustainability and stewardship.

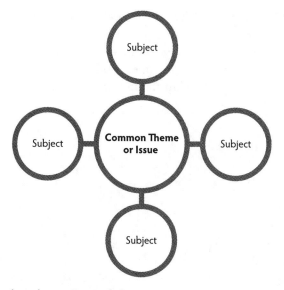

FIGURE 4.3 Multidisciplinary Curriculum

TABLE 4.4 Comparison Chart for Surface and Deep Learning at Multidisciplinary Learning Centres

Multidisciplinary Learning Centres		
	Surface learning	**Deep learning**
	Topic: Polar Bears	Big Idea: Sustainability and Stewardship
		Enduring Understanding: Living things have basic needs
Language	Read books about polar bears and list interesting facts.	Read current print and digital articles about the polar bear population. Categorize information using a graphic organizer of your choice. Create a poem using your information.
Science	Make a book about polar bears: Describe what they look like, what they eat, where they live, and their families.	Use the knowledge you have learned about polar bears to create a persuasive Prezi to post online regarding the decline of the polar bear population.
Math	Look at the map of where polar bears live. Create a bar graph that shows the number of bears at each location.	Study a variety of graphs about polar bears. Use your graphing skills to answer the following questions: What are the graphs telling you? How could you use this information? Create a graph predicting what will happen to the polar bear population if current trends continue.

Assessment in a multidisciplinary approach is likely similar to the disciplinary approach, since content is still taught in a disciplinary way even though it is focused on a common theme. A more integrated form of multidisciplinary curriculum occurs when a rich performance assessment task knits together the Know, Do, and Be across the disciplines, such as in the following example from Havergal College in Ontario.

Snapshot of a Multidisciplinary Approach

Havergal College sits on 22 acres of land that includes a lovely wooded area on a ravine called the Burke Brook. The STEM teacher who works with staff to implement an inquiry approach in science and the two Grade 6 teachers wanted students to create an ebook that would celebrate their understanding of biodiversity in Burke Brook.

After meeting with these three teachers, Havergal's curriculum director designed an extended, multidisciplinary project beginning with outcomes and aligning them with all the different parts of the unit's design. For the Know, the Big Idea was biodiversity and the Enduring Understanding was "Humans are the stewards of the Earth who impact biodiversity in both positive and negative ways." The Do included the twenty-first–century skills of research, communication, and media literacy. The Be was that students were to be environmentally responsible stewards. The Essential Questions were (a) Who are we on Earth and what are our responsibilities on Earth? (b) What do our actions say about who we are and what we value?

In each subject area, different outcomes were identified and used to plan the disciplinary task that would contribute to the final ebook. The plan included:

- Social studies: Research and communication, interviews, historical archives
- Science and technology: Biodiversity, scientific method, classification of local plants and animals
- Math: Data management and probability, chart and graph biodiversity data.
- Visual arts: Create images of Burke Brook for the ebook over the 36 weeks
- Religion: "What is stewardship?" reflection
- Language arts: Read information about Burke Brook, write reflections, create a job application for ebook publishers, and write a biography of Lisa Hardy (an environmental conservationist)
- Media literacy: Create media texts

Throughout the unit there was ongoing assessment for learning and assessment as learning for the tasks that led to the culminating RPAT.

INTERDISCIPLINARY

In the interdisciplinary approach, more than a common theme or issue connects subject areas. Planning follows backward design, and Big Ideas, Enduring Understandings, or twenty-first–century skills provide the common focal point of the curriculum (see Figure 4.4). *Edutopia* offers an excellent guide on creating interdisciplinary curriculum (available at www.edutopia.org/pdfs/integrated-curriculum-guide.pdf). Curriculum integration expert Heidi Hayes Jacobs outlines a step-by-step process in *Concept to Classroom* (go to www.thirteen.org/edonline/concept2class/index.html).

Aviva Dunsiger (2012), an Ontario Grade 6 teacher, connected math and language arts in an interdisciplinary unit that used technology in the RPAT. (Technology is used to enhance the learning but is not the main focus.) As always, Dunsiger began with curriculum outcomes. She wanted her students to learn "orders of operations" in math in a way that would engage them and help them to truly understand. In addition, Dunsiger's goal for the year was to enhance student communication in math, a need indicated by the provincial test results. Students began by looking at math expectations around number operations and at the achievement charts (assessment charts) in the math curriculum document. With Dunsiger, they developed their learning goals and their success criteria and decided that their rich performance assessment task would be to create a media text about the order of math operations. Thus, students had to consider media literacy expectations as well as writing outcomes. Students created digital storybooks, digital posters, movies, and PowerPoint presentations. The unit took longer than Dunsiger anticipated because her students were eager to revise their work according to the success criteria.

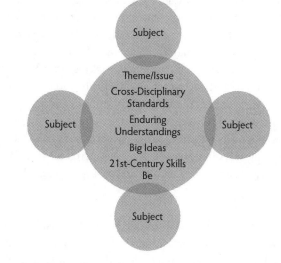

FIGURE 4.4 Interdisciplinary Curriculum

Snapshot of Interdisciplinarity in the Secondary Classroom

Interdisciplinary curriculum is well suited to the study of social justice and equity issues, a focus that can be seen in some classrooms—particularly with teachers who are passionate about these issues. Todd Bulmer from Ontario developed a full-day semester course that integrated four subject areas—politics, interdisciplinary studies, physical education (leadership), and philosophy. The Big Idea that bound these courses together was social justice. The rich performance assessment task for students in the program was to organize and carry out an activist campaign for a relevant social issue in the community. For example, one group of students organized a campaign for awareness of the homeless, another for environmental awareness. In Todd's class, the students were aware that "If we want to make a difference, we need to *be* the difference." Their tasks were assessed using rubrics they constructed themselves, making them reflect on their learning and ensuring that their priorities were considered in the evaluation of their work

Since 1995, one Ontario school board has offered a Grade 10 four-credit interdisciplinary program called Community Environmental Leadership Program (CELP). In 2006, a Grade 12 program called Headwaters: A Journey to the Source was started. Katie Gad, Janet Dalziel, and Joel Barr teach both programs (www.ugdsb.on.ca/celp/article.aspx?id=15446). In the Grade 10 program, students do a five-day canoe or winter camping trip for physical education, teach a Grade 5 program called "Earthkeepers" to younger students for interdisciplinary studies, bike around Guelph to learn about municipal functions for civics, and plan and make "Community Day" meals for their class as part of learning teamwork and group problem solving. The program concludes with a student-planned "Active Citizenship Day."

In Grade 12, students study outdoor education. They create moccasins for a six-night winter snowshoe trip, build a shelter for a night outdoors, and carve a paddle for a canoe trip. In environment and resource management, they focus on the Big Idea of sustainability and learn sustainable living skills such as making locavore meals for the class, growing an organic garden, and caring for chickens. For university English, they focus on ecocritical inquiry. They explore the field of ecocriticism and study literary genres that revolve around the themes of headwaters. Students research and interview citizens in the local community and publish a cultural journalism magazine called *Voices*. Throughout, students keep an ongoing reflective journal. The fourth credit is interdisciplinary studies, where students take on an aspect of "greening" and caring for their classroom or building.

TRANSDISCIPLINARY

Transdisciplinary means beyond the disciplines (see Figure 4.5). Planning begins with student interests and the real-world context rather than curriculum outcomes. Once a relevant theme, issue, or problem is established, the teacher and students decide which curriculum outcomes support the chosen focus. Since it has a real-world context, more than one subject area is involved. Students are encouraged to engage in the inquiry process and formulate their own questions.

Student Questions
Real-World Problems
Social Issues
Big Ideas
Enduring Understandings
21st-Century Skills

FIGURE 4.5 Transdisciplinary Curriculum

Curriculum theorist James Beane's work is foundational in curriculum integration, particularly for transdisciplinary curriculum design. Beane was deeply influenced by John Dewey and progressive education. Beane's goal is to promote a deep understanding of democracy. Beane (1993, 1997) believes that the very structure of school needs to radically change. For him, there are only two important questions to ask students to provide a relevant curriculum: (a) What questions or concerns do you have about yourself? (b) What questions or concerns do you have about the world? Students brainstorm around these questions to determine what they will study as a class. Beane believes that students will ask good questions worthy of study.

Although many schools have experimented with Beane's philosophy, it can be challenging to implement during an age of accountability—but it can be done. The Alpha program at Shelburne Community School in Shelburne, Vermont, has been applying this philosophy since 1972. In the school at large, there are three other more traditional groups, and students are randomly assigned to Alpha or one of the other groups.

Alpha is a multiage program from Grades 6 to 8. There are three teachers and 65 students. Students are divided into three groups, each facilitated by a teacher. They spend the first three or four weeks planning their study for the year. Students begin by brainstorming and selecting their questions. Initially, teachers show students how to ask deep questions, but over time the senior students model this. Each student generates 10 deep questions.

Then students work in small, multiage, mixed-gender groups to decide upon eight to 10 common questions. Next, they explore mandatory state documents for curriculum standards. Using backward design, students connect questions to standards and collaboratively plan curriculum with their facilitator teacher. Three transdisciplinary themes are determined each year. All subject outcomes are addressed, but math is done outside of the curriculum themes. Typical themes are "We the people" (government, careers, conflict resolution), earth science, cultural studies, and ecology.

Once a theme is determined, students decide on the relevant assessments and instructional activities that meet the standards. Differentiation is embedded in the instructional activities and happens organically as students plan. Today, technology is an integral part of the program. Self-assessment and peer assessment are prominent elements of the program. Each student sets weekly academic goals and completes reflections and self-assessments.

Students keep a portfolio organized according to Vermont's Vital Results, which comprises the twenty-first–century skills of communication, problem-solving, functioning independently, personal development, and civic and social responsibility. Students take state required tests, and their results are comparable or better than their peers in more traditional schools (Drake, 2012).

Snapshot of a Transdisciplinary Program

The Seven Oaks Met School in Winnipeg operates as a Big Picture Learning School within a school. (www.7oaks.org/school/themet/Pages/default.aspx). In 2010, the school won first place in the Ken Spencer Award for Innovation in Teaching and Learning. As of 2012, there are more than 120 such schools worldwide.

The school follows the guiding principles set in place in 1995, when the first Big Picture School opened in Rhode Island:

- Learning must be based on student needs and interests.
- Curriculum must be relevant and allow students to do real work in the real world.
- Assessment of student growth and abilities must be measured by the quality of the work and how students are changed by it.

The Canadian Met School has 50 students and four advisers. A teacher acts as an adviser for a group of 15 students. In addition, students have mentors who are people from their fields of interest. Parents are also involved as supporters. Students do core curriculum with defined goals and measurable outcomes. There is an emphasis on inquiry-based learning, cross-curricular projects, and community involvement in internships. Students have individualized learning plans that take them out of the school to explore their personal interests and passions through the world of meaningful work. Internships are two days a week. They involve 8 to 12 days at a business over two to three months.

This Met school follows the philosophy set out for Big Picture Learning Schools. Dennis Littky (2004), one of the original founders and teachers of the Met School, outlined the goals for students. Most important was the Be. Students were to be lifelong learners who were passionate risk takers. They were to be problem solvers and critical thinkers who were both ingenious and self-directed. Creative, preserving, and morally courageous, they were to be self-respecting and able to use the world around them well. These students would be both literate and numerate and would be able to truly enjoy life.

How do students acquire these attributes? The learning focused on five cross-disciplinary learning goals:

- Communication: How do I take in and present information?
- Social reasoning: How do other people see this?
- Quantitative reasoning: How do I measure this? How do I solve this problem? How do I think like a mathematician?
- Empirical reasoning: How do I prove it?
- Personal qualities (BE): What personal attributes do I bring to this endeavour?

Comparing Approaches

The boundaries determining multidisciplinary, interdisciplinary, and transdisciplinary curricula are fluid. This is particularly true when teachers are tied to curriculum documents and students need to take large-scale tests. A look at common teaching situations makes the differences among disciplinary and the three main approaches clearer.

The Hunger Games (Collins, 2008) is a popular novel used in many teaching contexts. The novel confronts many of the issues that we live with today, such as teenage angst, individuality, desensitization, survival, and the courage to stand up for one's convictions. Mariss Ferriolo, Steffany Kuhn, Robert Lambert, and Renee Mack from Ontario created a Grade 8 unit for language arts based on the novel. The purpose of the unit was for students to apply HOTS through reading responses focused on the main idea and themes of the book, and the students' own inferences and point of view. The culminating RPAT asked students to take the role of any main character and describe the overall effect of the Hunger Games on their character's life. Students could create a scrapbook, video, PowerPoint presentation, Photo Story, or news broadcast (or another approved activity of the student's choice). Students needed to include the following requirements:

- Three journal entries that demonstrate what their character's life was like
- An editorial that would have been published in a newspaper
- A news report on one of the events that occurred in the book
- An article on the effect of the turmoil on the District
- Two advertisements from a newspaper, magazine, or commercial depicting the types of clothing, weapons, food, shelter, and so on appropriate to the novel's time and place
- Various diary-type entries that demonstrate character change as a result of the turmoil experienced during the Hunger Games

From a multidisciplinary approach, two teachers in a secondary school could choose a common theme from *The Hunger Games* that would be taught in their separate classes. For example, an English class could explore the book as literature, while political, social, and economic structures could be examined in a history class. In technology class, students could create a Glogster poster about their learning and post it online. Educurious offers a lesson unit on these ideas at http://educurious.org/try/hungergameschallenge.

In an interdisciplinary situation, teachers work together to provide a curriculum that connects to outcomes. Teaching partners Mary Mobley and Michael Chambers began with curriculum standards to team-teach *The Hunger Games* over a three-week interdisciplinary unit at Manor High Tech in Texas (Nobori, 2012). This unit followed all the hallmarks of project-based learning. History standards revolved around causes of global depression, the rise of totalitarianism, and key world leaders in World War II. English standards included analyzing moral dilemmas across cultures in fiction, making complex inferences, and writing personal response essays. A rubric that defined all desired learning outcomes was created. As well as subject area outcomes, every project was assessed for the twenty-first–century skills of written and oral communication, collaboration, critical thinking, and technological literacy. (One project per semester must assess numeracy and global awareness/community engagement.)

Students were put into groups with each student having a contract outlining his or her role and responsibilities. As per **problem-based learning**, the students figured out how to research the problem. Teachers provided workshops depending on student needs. Students could also give workshops. Topics of student-led workshops were totalitarian leadership and a comparison of real and fictional moral dilemmas from events in history and events in the book. Students received ongoing assessment during the process. The rich performance assessment task was a multimedia presentation with audience participation about a moral dilemma faced by Nazi concentration camp survivors and a skit dramatizing the moral decision making of world leaders leading up to Pearl Harbour. Since teachers used AfL before the culminating assessment, there were few surprises on the final assessment. This study is described at www.edutopia.org/stw-project-based-learning-best-practices-guide.

In a transdisciplinary scenario, students begin with brainstorming their personal and social questions. Then they look collaboratively at the curriculum outcomes with their teachers. Together, they come up with the Essential Questions based on both student questions and curriculum outcomes from different subject areas. *The Hunger Games* could be a literary choice emerging from the students' interests as one of the instructional activities/ assessments to address their questions and also the relevant curriculum outcomes.

Conclusion

In this chapter, we have looked at inquiry learning and interdisciplinary learning. They have many elements in common and include approaches that are more disciplinary in nature and ones that transcend the disciplines. Yet for planners, the essentials are the same: backward design, curriculum comes first, and assessment is an integral part that is seamlessly connected to instruction.

Professional Discussion Questions

1) Which school or model presented in this chapter most appeals to you? Why?
2) How could your subject area benefit from a more focused inquiry approach? What are some possible inquiries?
3) Choose a theme or issue and describe how this theme could be addressed from the multidisciplinary, interdisciplinary, and transdisciplinary approach? How would you ensure that the lessons would be accountable?
4) Analyze the student-created rubric in Table 4.3 for its effectiveness using the guidelines for rubric creation in Chapter 3.

Integrating the Curriculum

In this chapter you will learn about:

- The five Ws of integrated curriculum
- How to create an integrated curriculum using backward design
- Assessment and integrated curriculum

In this chapter, we begin by considering some of the questions that often arise when integrating curriculum. We follow this by walking through the curriculum design process with an interdisciplinary lens. Finally, we consider assessment issues related to interdisciplinary curriculum.

The Five Ws of Curriculum Integration

There are many questions surrounding the actual process of designing an integrated unit. We address these questions based on our own experiences working with educators in many different contexts, both locally and internationally. Many years have passed since Susan Drake, one of the authors of this text, wrote *Planning Integrated Curriculum: The Call to Adventure* (1993). This small text described the process for Ontario teachers who were trying to implement the policy at that time—a mandated integrated curriculum for Grades 1 to 9. We find that the experiences of that past still ring true for many educators who are starting to design integrated units today.

WHO?

Who plans an integrated unit? Any educator or group of educators can plan an integrated unit. It should not be someone who is mandated to work this way, but rather a teacher who wants to use this approach. Integration is challenging work at first and requires the willingness of the curriculum writer. It is less complicated for an elementary school teacher who is teaching all the subjects (or many of them). With only one teacher, some excellent teaching and learning can happen with fewer obstacles.

Yet we have found that some of richest integrated units are designed collaboratively. The design process will not be conflict free—over seven in a group and it becomes too unwieldy with too many agendas. If members of a group are new to each other, they will go through a typical form – storm – norm – perform cycle. Typically, there may be territorial conflict about what knowledge and skills are front and centre. The backward design process facilitates a process where all collaborators can find a substantive place for their subject areas by providing a way to discover what is in common across them.

WHAT?

What does an integrated curriculum look like? In Chapter 4 we described examples of different types of integrated curriculum that ran across a spectrum. Some people venture into integration cautiously, beginning alone and fusing in an added dimension, or making changes in what they are doing already from a disciplinary perspective. Others begin at the other end of the spectrum by planning entirely from students' concerns or interests or from a pressing real-world issue, and finding a curriculum fit afterwards; this is the transdisciplinary approach.

Since our theme has been balancing relevance and accountability, we take an interdisciplinary approach in this chapter. The design begins with outcomes from different subject area curriculum documents (we used Ontario's) to shape an engaging learning experience around a significant and relevant issue, question or problem.

WHERE?

Scheduling for collaboration and implementation of integrated curriculum can be problematic. One of the issues that may arise revolves around space. How do students paint a mural about their science inquiry if they are constrained to the science lab? (Try the hallway.) How do students integrate technology if there is only one computer in the classroom? (Try using the one computer to Skype people from around the world where the class is the audience; ask students to bring their own personal devices for research purposes.) How do classes meet if each classroom only holds 36 students? (Try the library or cafeteria.) We have found that teachers who want to work together find creative solutions.

Many activities may take place outside of the classroom. Testing local water quality, interviewing community members, exploring the local art gallery or museum are all typical events in an integrated approach. If the curriculum has been generated in a real-world context, then there is usually a real-world context to visit and learn in. Place-based education is an approach that honours the local community as the primary source of learning (Sobel, 2004). The unique history, culture, environment, economy, art, and so on of the community are studied to give students a sense of place before explorations into the international or global world.

WHY?

Integrated curriculum has attracted teachers who want to increase relevance for students. In the twenty-first century, the rationale for integrating the curriculum seems even more compelling. When the curriculum begins with a complex problem to solve, it is less likely that it can be addressed within one subject area. The twenty-first–century skills are interdisciplinary. The Be cuts across disciplines. Importantly, research supports integrated learning as an effective way for students to reach learning goals (see Chapter 4). Regardless of academic achievement, students are more often engaged in this type of learning and enjoy school more. To us, it seems that the potential benefits are attractive enough to warrant the effort to design and implement integrated curriculum.

WHEN?

Time is important when planning and implementing an integrated curriculum. Teachers need blocks of time to plan—particularly when they are first starting out. Schools have addressed this concern by giving teachers similar schedules to have preparation time to work together. Sometimes creating this curriculum is the goal of a formal **professional learning community** (PLC). Each school needs to find its own solution depending on the unique needs of the students, teachers, school, and community.

THE BOTTOM LINE

We have found that where there is a will there is a way. Witness the many examples of innovative practices throughout this book of educators who work in a context of accountability (and there are many more in Chapter 6). When teachers first design and implement an integrated unit, they often say, "This is the most exhausting work I've ever done, but also the most exciting and rewarding!" For these teachers, the boundaries between subjects have become fluid; they claim it is hard now to think of teaching within strictly defined boundaries of distinct subjects.

What is the relationship between disciplinary approaches and interdisciplinary ones in the new story? Teaching with a disciplinary focus allows for a deep understanding of the subject matter and the disciplinary procedures. To be able to think like a historian, artist, writer, or mathematician is valuable and is learned in a disciplinary setting. At the same time, we can see a place for integrated approaches. One can bring the perspectives of the historian, artist, writer, and mathematician to the complex problem solving needed for the twenty-first century. Thus, we reiterate the stance we took in Chapter 4: There is a best time and place for both approaches, and they can complement one another (Rennie, Venville, & Wallace, 2012).

Designing a Sample Interdisciplinary Unit

In essence, the process of designing an interdisciplinary curriculum echoes the disciplinary one that we walked through for a Grade 10 history unit in Chapter 3, except for two additional steps to allow for connections among subject areas: an initial brainstorming for connections as a pre-step and an Essential Questions web before determining the daily instructional activities/assessments. There are three preliminary steps and three actual stages to the backward design process. The steps are reviewed in Figure 5.1. Remember that although we present this as linear step-by-step process, it is actually an iterative process that can feel very messy and might be frustrating at times. Eventually the pieces fall together like the pieces of a large jigsaw puzzle, and you will most likely find yourself as delighted with the results as other teachers have.

This chapter offers an example using a Grade 4 called "We're all in this together". The unit is teacher directed with a focus on inquiry and is "interdisciplinary" as defined by the definitions provided in Chapter 4. Again, we did not choose Grade 4 for any special reason. We provide the planning process as an example of how to do it for any grade level.

Pre-Steps
- Know your curriculum document (introductory material)
- Know your students
- Brainstorm for possible connections

Stage 1
- Choose a relevant topic
- Curriculum scan and cluster (vertical and horizontal across relevant subject areas)
- Curriculum unpacking chart
- KDB umbrella
- Exploratory web

Stage 2
- Create a rich performance assessment task
- Create reliable and valid assessment tools to assess the RPAT

Stage 3
- Create Essential Questions web
- Create daily instruction and assessment tasks and tools

FIGURE 5.1 Stages in Interdisciplinary Backward Design

KNOW YOUR CURRICULUM

A starting point is to review the introductory material for each subject as shown in Table 5.1. This is done in conjunction with the unifying framework across subject areas in K–12. Here you use a wide-angle lens to see the big picture. What is considered to be the critical learning from K–12? What is the KDB for your subject area? How does it align with the unifying framework? Remember that this is interpretive work, although many of the documents are explicit about what students are expected to learn across the curriculum.

TABLE 5.1 Looking at the Introductory Material for the Know, Do, and Be, K–12

Horizontal Introductory Material Review

	Social Studies	Science	The Arts	Language Arts
Know	Systems and structures Interactions and interdependence Environment Change and continuity Culture Power and governance	Systems and interactions Sustainability and stewardship Matter Energy Structure and functions Change and continuity	Culture/cultural identity Social justice Procedural knowledge for critique and creativity	Understand a wide variety of texts, language conventions Procedural knowledge for writing, speaking, listening
Do	Inquiry Communication Mapping	Scientific inquiry Technological problem solving Research Communication	Create Problem solve Connect Communicate	Reading Writing Listening Speaking
Be	Informed citizens in a culturally diverse and interdependent world who participate and compete in a global economy	Scientifically and technologically literate	Reach their potential by being full participants in their community and society as a whole	Literate Media literate Critically literate

KNOW YOUR STUDENTS

This unit was designed for a Grade 4 class in southwestern Ontario. The school's semi-rural community is economically depressed. Most manufacturing jobs have disappeared, and farm families struggle to make their crops cover expenses. One thing the region does have is plenty of wind; the exploitation of this resource has stirred up strong community feelings that have been expressed at kitchen tables, on the street, and in the local papers—and not always in a friendly fashion. Not all adults have been positive role models when it comes to exchanging differences of opinion. The teacher felt it was important that students learn how to disagree respectfully. In addition, he kept in mind the multiple intelligences and learning preferences of his students in his different activities and assessments.

BRAINSTORM FOR CONNECTIONS

As a preliminary step, it is a good idea to brainstorm for possible connections. If you are creating the curriculum alone, you can do this by yourself. If you are working collaboratively, you will do this together. To do this, you need some sense of the curriculum outcomes at both the big picture and grade level. Experienced teachers who are familiar with the curriculum can have a general conversation around what topics, Big Ideas, or 21st-century skills they might teach that connect applicable subject areas. Those who are not that familiar with curriculum outcomes may do this brainstorming after they have looked at curriculum documents. This step is only to get some initial ideas of how to work together. It is important to have a sense of connection with each other and relevant subject areas to be motivated to move forward to actual curriculum design.

There is one caveat to this brainstorming conversation: A common trap is to begin with integrated activities that teachers could do and move right into implementation without thought to backward design or alignment. This may result in a curriculum that students find engaging, but the learning does not have a purpose and does not meet curriculum mandates. Following the process in this chapter, the curriculum can be both engaging and accountable.

BACKWARD DESIGN: STAGE 1

Choose a Relevant Topic

This step was probably done in the initial conversation of brainstorming for connections. The issue chosen was one of local concern prompted by the possibility of bringing wind turbines to the region to deal with economic issues.

Curriculum Scan and Cluster

This step of the process is more complex than the disciplinary design because there is more than one subject and often more than one person involved. Figure 5.2 outlines the funnelling process that occurs during the scan and cluster.

As in the disciplinary scan and cluster, there are two steps to this procedure. First, you scan relevant outcomes for meaning. Second, you cluster the outcomes into bundles to represent key learnings. This scan involves scanning reams and reams of hard copy pages of curriculum documents or pages online. To cluster, some people cut up the outcomes with scissors and paste them in bundles onto a big sheet of paper; some cut and paste electronically. Others put groups of clustered outcomes into small plastic baggies and label the baggies with the Big Idea/Enduring Understanding or twenty-first–century skill. Still others prefer to highlight outcomes and colour code the groupings, either on hard copy or electronically. *The purpose is to group relevant outcomes into a meaningful pattern to guide the curriculum design. The intent is not to cover all of the outcomes, as not all outcomes are created equal.* If you are addressing the overall outcomes, you are on the right track. Having said this, most outcomes will fit in one cluster or another

The vertical scan involves two grades below the target grade (to see what students should have learned already) and one grade above (to see what they are expected to learn after your class). Bundle outcomes together to create meaningful clusters to represent the critical learning or KDB. This bundling is informed by the big picture in Table 5.2 and is still at the exploration stage—*you are not trying to determine what to teach but to see what KDB are embedded in the outcomes.* Once you have created this chart, you can also look horizontally at the bundles of outcomes you created across the four subjects. In looking at Table 5.2, you can see that in some subjects, such as language arts and social studies, the outcomes are identical every year. This is the spiralling curriculum. Each year the learning is the same but is expected to be more sophisticated and more complex.

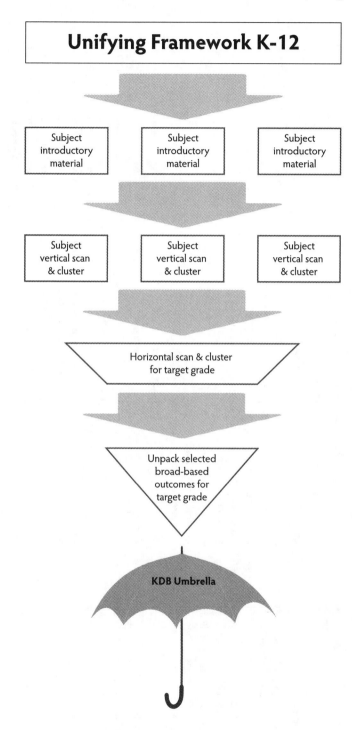

Unifying Framework K-12

Subject introductory material | Subject introductory material | Subject introductory material

Subject vertical scan & cluster | Subject vertical scan & cluster | Subject vertical scan & cluster

Horizontal scan & cluster for target grade

Unpack selected broad-based outcomes for target grade

KDB Umbrella

FIGURE 5.2 Funnelling Process to Determine the KDB

TABLE 5.2 Vertical Scan and Cluster for a Grade 4 Unit

Scan and Cluster of Relevant Outcomes across Four Grades

KNOW
Big Idea: Interdependence

Science

Grade 2	Grade 3	Grade 4	Grade 5
Assess ways in which the actions of humans have an impact on the quality of air and water, and ways in which the quality of air and water has an impact on living things.	Assess ways in which plants have an impact on society and the environment and ways in which human activity has an impact on plants and animals	Investigate the interdependence of plants and animals with specific habitats and communities	Identify the interrelationships between bodily systems
Describe ways in which living things, including humans, depend on air and water.	Identify examples of environmental conditions that may threaten the environment		

Social Studies

Grade 2	Grade 3	Grade 4	Grade 5
Explain how the environment affects people's lives and the ways in which their needs are met	Explain how communities interact with each other and the environment to meet human needs	Identify relationships, in a variety of fields that link Ontario and the other provinces and territories (e.g. in art, literature, music, dance, technology, heritage, tourism, sports)	Research and report on how the three levels of government work together to meet challenges or perform tasks
			Explain how two or more early civilizations shaped and used the environment to meet their physical needs

KNOW

Big Idea: Cause and effect

Science

Grade 2	Grade 3	Grade 4	Grade 5
Identify positive and negative impacts that animals have on humans Identify positive and negative effects that human activity can have on animals.	Assess the impact of different human activities on plants and list personal actions to minimize harmful effects and enhance good effects	Analyze the effects of human activities on habitats and communities Analyze the positive and negative effects of human interactions with natural habitats and communities taking different perspectives into account and evaluate ways of minimizing the negative impact.	Assess the effects of social and environmental factors on human health, and propose ways in which individuals can reduce the harmful effects of these factors and take advantage of those that are beneficial

Social Studies

Grade 2	Grade 3	Grade 4	Grade 5
Identify an area of concern (e.g., littering) and suggest changes in rules and responsibilities	Compare and contrast tools and technologies used by early settlers and/or First Nations peoples with present-day tools and technologies	Identify and describe a cause-and-effect relationship between the environment and the economy Relate the physical environment with the economic and cultural activities in various provinces and territories.	Report on the relevance to modern society of selected scientific and technological discoveries made by early civilizations

KNOW

Big Idea: System

Science

Grade 2	Grade 3	Grade 4	Grade 5
Assess ways in which animals have an impact on society and the environment and ways in which humans have an impact on animals and the places where they live	Assess ways in which plants have an impact on society and the environment and ways in which human activity has an impact on plants and plant habitats	Demonstrate an understanding of habitats and communities and the relationships among the plants and animals that live there.	Demonstrate an understanding of the structure and function of the human body systems and interactions within and between systems.

(Continued)

TABLE 5.2 (Continued)

Scan and Cluster of Relevant Outcomes across Four Grades

DO
Mapping

Social Studies

Grade 2	Grade 3	Grade 4	Grade 5
Use a variety of resources and tools to gather, process, and communicate geographic information about the countries studied	Use a variety of resources and tools to gather, process, and communicate geographic information about urban and rural communities	Use a variety of resources and tools to determine the influence of physical factors on the economies and cultures of Ontario and other provinces and territories	Use a variety of resources and tools to gather and analyze information about government processes, the rights of groups and individuals, and the responsibilities of citizenship in Canada, including participation in the electoral college

DO
Inquiry

Science

Grade 2	Grade 3	Grade 4	Grade 5
Use scientific inquiry/experimentation skills to investigate the basic needs, characteristics, behaviour, and adaptations of an animal of their choice	Use scientific inquiry/ experimentation skills to investigate a variety of ways in which plants meet their needs	Use scientific inquiry/research skills to investigate ways in which plants and animals in a community depend on features in their habitat to meet important needs	Use scientific inquiry/ experimentation skills to investigate changes in body systems

Social Studies

Grades 2 to 5

Formulate questions, research information, interpret data, and present findings (media works, oral presentation, notes and descriptions, drawings, tables and graphs.)

Language Arts

Grades 2 to 5

Develop ideas for writing for a purpose and audience, research ideas by gathering information to support them, sort and classify ideas in a variety of ways, organize with main ideas and supporting detail, review.

DO
Communication across subjects

Grades 2 to 5

Read and demonstrate an understanding of how a variety of literacy, graphic, and informational texts use a range of strategies to construct meaning **(language arts)**

Use a variety of forms to communicate with different audiences for a variety of purposes **(science, language arts)**

Use appropriate vocabulary **(science, language arts, social studies)**

Presentation: Use speaking skills and strategies

Use media works, oral presentation, notes and descriptions, drawings, tables and graphs to identify and communicate **(social studies, language arts, social studies)**

Creating and presenting: Apply the creative process to produce a variety of two- and three-dimensional art words using elements, principles, and techniques of visual arts to communicate feelings, ideas, and understandings **(visual arts)**

Creating and presenting: Apply the creative process to a dramatic play using the elements and conventions of drama to communicate feelings, ideas, and stories **(drama)**

BE
Stewardship

Science

Grade 2	Grade 3	Grade 4	Grade 5
Suggest ways that negative impacts animals and humans have on each other can be minimized	Suggest ways humans can protect plants. List personal actions to minimize the harmful effects and enhance the good effects	Evaluate ways of minimizing the negative impacts. Propose possible actions for preventing such depletions or extinctions from happening	Assess the effects of social and environmental factors on human health and propose ways individuals can reduce the harmful effects and take advantage of beneficial ones

Social Studies

Grade 2	Grade 3	Grade 4	Grade 5
Explain how the environment affects people's lives and the ways in which their needs are met	Explain how early settlers valued, used, and looked after natural resources	Make connections between social or environmental concerns of medieval times and similar concerns today	Identify concrete examples of how government plays a role in society and how the rights of groups and individuals, and the responsibilities of citizenship, apply to their own lives

As you continue in this funnelling process as shown in Figure 5.2, you will focus on the horizontal scan and cluster for Grade 4—your target grade. This step has essentially been done in the cross-classification matrix in Table 5.2. We focus on the outcomes for the KDB in Grade 4 in Table 5.3. This chart identifies the KDB embedded in Grade 4 outcomes. You will choose the KDB for your unit from this chart.

TABLE 5.3 Horizontal Scan and Cluster for a Grade 4 Unit

Grade 4 Horizontal Clusters	
KNOW—Big Idea: **Interdependence**	**Science**
	Investigate the interdependence of plants and animals with specific habitats and communities.
	Social Studies
	Use a variety of resources and tools to determine the influence of physical factors on the economies and cultures of Ontario and other provinces and territories.
KNOW—Big Idea: **Systems**	**Science**
	Demonstrate an understanding of habitats and communities and the relationships among the plants and animals that live there.
	Social Studies
	Explain the concept of a region.
	Identify, analyze, and describe economic and cultural relationships that link communities and regions within Ontario and across Canada.
	Relate the physical environment with the economic and cultural activities in various provinces and territories.
KNOW—Big Idea: **Cause and Effect**	**Science**
	Analyze positive and negative effects of human interactions with natural habitats and communities.
	Social Studies
	Identify and describe a cause-and-effect relationship between the environment and the economy.
	Use a variety of resources and tools to determine the influence of physical factors on the economies and cultures of Ontario and other provinces and territories.
DO: **Inquiry**	**Science**
	Use scientific inquiry/research skills to investigate ways in which plants and animals in a community depend on features in their habitat to meet important needs.
	Social Studies
	Formulate questions, research information, interpret data, and present findings (media works, oral presentation, notes and descriptions, drawings, tables and graphs).
	Language Arts
	Develop ideas for writing for a purpose and audience, research ideas by gathering information to support them, sort and classify ideas in a variety of ways, organize with main ideas and supporting detail, review.

DO: **Communication**	Read and demonstrate an understanding of how a variety of literacy, graphic, and informational texts use a range of strategies to construct meaning. (language arts)
	Use a variety of forms to communicate with different audiences for a variety of purposes. (science, language arts)
	Use appropriate vocabulary. (science, language arts, social studies)
	Presentation: written, oral, media (language arts, science, social studies)
BE: **Informed** **Environmental** **Stewards**	**Social Studies** Informed citizens in a culturally diverse and interdependent world. **Science** Propose possible actions for preventing such depletions or extinctions from happening

Curriculum Unpacking Chart

At this point, you have some idea of what your curriculum might look like. To unpack the curriculum outcomes, review the horizontal scan and choose the key broad-based ones to build your unit. Less is more: however, all the key outcomes you select need to be addressed and assessed. Table 5.4 shows an unpacking chart where the Know is italicized (nouns) and

TABLE 5.4 Unpacking the KDB from Selected Broad-Based Outcomes

Selected Broad-Based Outcomes from a Horizontal Scan and Cluster for Curriculum Unpacking

Broad-Based Outcomes	KNOW	DO	BE
Analyze the *positive and negative effects of human interactions with natural habitats and communities* **taking different perspectives** into account, and **evaluate** *ways of minimizing the negative impact.* (science)	Cause and effect Habitats Communities Positive and negative effect of human activities How to minimize negative effects	Analyze Evaluate Create (HOTS)	Environmental steward
Identify and **describe** *a cause-and-effect relationship between the environment and the economy in a province or territory.* (social studies)	Cause and effect Economy Community (region)	Analyze (HOTS)	Informed citizen
Use *a variety of forms to communicate with different audiences for a variety of purposes.* (science, language arts)	Different forms of communication Procedural knowledge about communication skills	Communicate Create	Good communicator
Formulate *questions,* **collect** *research information,* **interpret** *data,* and **present** *findings* (media works, oral presentation, notes and descriptions, drawings, tables and graphs). (social studies, science. language arts)	Procedural knowledge on research skills (similarities between science and social studies)	Inquiry/research	Researcher

the Do is in bold (verbs). The Be is often implicit and may need to be interpreted—but the Know and the Do should be unpacked exactly as they appear in the outcome.

KDB Umbrella

This KDB umbrella represents critical learning across several subject areas (Figure 5.3). Again, an important thing to remember is that less is more on the KDB umbrella. Limit yourself to no more than three in each of the categories: Know (Big ideas, Enduring Understandings), Do (21st-century skills) and Be (attitudes and behaviours). With lots of space on the KDB umbrella, you will find it easier to create a meaningful curriculum that still is aligned and accountable. Essential Questions emerge from the selection of the KDB. Similarly, one to three interesting Essential Questions are much better for planning and motivating students than a long laundry list coming straight from the curriculum outcomes.

Exploratory Web

Now that you have a good connection to the outcomes, you can brainstorm more knowledgably about possible connections to instructional and assessment tasks. Often designers choose to brainstorm possibilities by discipline, as done in Figure 5.4. Sometimes this step is done earlier in the process to help generate ideas and to see that an interdisciplinary

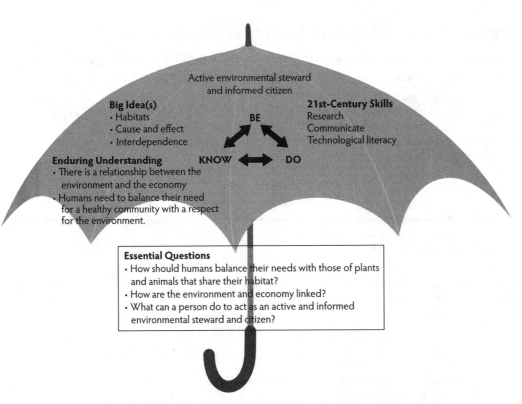

FIGURE 5.3 The KDB Umbrella for the "We're All in This Together" Unit

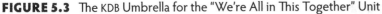

FIGURE 5.4 Grade 4 Exploratory Web

---

curriculum is possible. It is important to understand that this web is exploratory only and the final product may look very differently. In Step 3, another web will be created that shifts the brainstorming organizer to Essential Questions.

BACKWARD DESIGN: STAGE 2

In stage 2 of backward design, you create an RPAT that allows students to demonstrate that they have learned the KDB. The RPAT created for the Grade 4 unit is a town hall meeting (details are in the box on the next page).

The Town Hall Meeting

An important Town Hall meeting will take place on December 9 to decide how to use a piece of land that has been donated to the town. The land is located at the town boundary and is close to a main transportation route. The land was the former pioneer homestead farm of the Brown family but has been unoccupied for the last 10 years. The original log cabin and the 102-year-old brick home are still standing. The barn has been taken down.

You will be one member of a group that will support a proposal describing how the land should be used. Four proposals have been submitted:

1) An economic development group would like to build a community centre and shopping mall on the land.
2) An environmental group would like to preserve the land as a natural habitat. It could be used for non-motorized recreation such as hiking and bird watching.
3) The Heritage Society would like to restore the cabin and home and turn the farm into a working pioneer farm for tourists.
4) An alternative energy company would like to build a wind farm on the land.

You will be a member of the _____ group.

We will take a field trip to the donated land. At the site, your group will take research notes to add to your research study. Your notes will include the following:

1) Describe the current habitat, including how the plants and animals are adapted to their environment and how they are dependent on each other.
2) Include a map or sketches of the land and any notable landmarks, including human-built structures. (hand drawn, iPad sketch, photos, video)

At the meeting, your group will deliver a PowerPoint presentation supporting your proposal to the other groups and three city council members (our local mayor and two city council members have been invited to view and respond to the presentations). You will need to be prepared to answer questions from your classmates and our visitors.

The PowerPoint presentation will explain the following:

1) The possible positive and negative effects of your proposal on the habitat and the local human community. Consider the environmental and the economic advantages and disadvantages of your plan.
2) How you can minimize any negative impact of your plan on the environment.
3) The reasons why you think the town council should accept your plan. Include a map, pictures, and images to support your argument.

Your responsibilities include equal presentation time for each person presenting the slides. You will also observe and listen to your classmates. You will ask them questions after their presentations. The city council members will offer feedback. They, along with your classmates, will vote on a final decision for the land usage.

You will assess your individual contribution and participation using the class-generated instructional rubric. There will be a teacher evaluation of all parts of the task. The presentations will be videoed and uploaded to our class website. We will ask members of the public to offer feedback.

You will write two pieces to be posted on our class website:

1) Write a news report of the meeting (who, what, why, when, where, and a summary of the discussion).
2) Write a letter to the editor on whether you agree/disagree with the council's decision.

Create Valid and Reliable Assessment Tools to Assess the Rich Performance Assessment Task

Once the task has been determined, the assessment tools for it need to be created. We have included a rubric that addresses some components of the Know and the Do (Table 5.5).

The Be is assessed separately through an electronic journal that students write about their experiences in the unit. The first entry is an "envirography"—an autobiography about themselves as environmental stewards. The student will continue to submit entries throughout the unit. The final entry will be a new envirography, coupled with a self-assessment reflection on their environmental literacy/stewardship. There is no grading for this. Students are provided with anecdotal comments in their electronic journal.

BACKWARD DESIGN: STAGE 3

Essential Question(s) Web

Now it is time to create daily learning tasks and assessment tools. But first you need to ensure that your activities and assessments are aligned with the KDB, prepare students for the RPAT, and also answer the Essential Question(s). A good step here is to brainstorm again for activities that address an Essential Question rather than the different subject areas (as was done in Figure 5.4). This can be done through an Essential Questions web. Figure 5.5 shows the web for three Essential Questions for this integrated Grade 4 unit.

Daily Instructional Strategies/Assessments

This integrated unit has been divided into three mini-units, all of which lead to students being able to demonstrate the KDB through the RPAT. Here we flesh out two mini-units based on two of the questions as examples of the process. Different learning goals are established for each mini-unit based on outcomes, but they are written in student-friendly language. Table 5.6 shows the planning chart for mini-unit 1. Note that activities and assessments are considered in the first column, as well as differentiation for students. The outcomes being met are in the second column. The third column contains the way in which this strategy is aligned to the KDB and how it prepares students for the RPAT. The first mini-unit explores habitats and human impact on habitats.

TABLE 5.5   Rubric for the Grade 4 Rich Performance Assessment Task

Big Ideas	4	3	2	1
	Accomplished	Competent	Developing	Beginning
Cause and effect; Interdependence (blog)	The blog thoroughly described cause-and-effect and interdependent relationships among plants, animals, humans, and the economy.	The blog adequately described cause-and-effect and interdependent relationships among plants, animals, humans, and the economy.	The blog somewhat described cause-and-effect and interdependent relationships among plants, animals, humans, and the economy.	The blog showed limited understanding of the cause-and-effect and interdependent relationships among plants, animals, humans, and the economy.
Inquiry/ Research	All steps of the research were done thoroughly. Deep questions were addressed in the proposal.	All steps of the research were done competently. Good questions were addressed in the proposal.	All steps of the research were done adequately. Questions were adequately addressed in the proposal.	The student created a plan with limited effectiveness. Questions were of limited use.
	The student accurately articulated possible impacts and solutions with a high degree of relevance.	The student accurately articulated possible impacts and solutions with considerable relevance.	The student articulated possible impacts and solutions with some relevance.	The student articulated possible impacts and solutions with limited relevance.
Communication	The PowerPoint presentation was very engaging and very informative.	The PowerPoint presentation was engaging and informative.	The PowerPoint presentation was quite engaging and informative.	The PowerPoint presentation was somewhat engaging and informative.
	The student maintained focus in his or her role through body language, movement, and gesture, and sustained belief in the character throughout.	The student largely maintained focus in his or her role through body language, movement, and gestures, and sustained belief in the character most of the time.	The student moved in and out of focus in his or her role with inconsistent body language, movement, and gestures, a sustained belief in the character some of the time.	The student showed little focus in his or her role with limited effort to adopt body language, movement, and gestures, and it was hard to believe in the character.

Suggestions for upgrades:

Essential Question:

How can humans balance their needs with those of plants and animals that share a habitat?

- Post-it pileup as an AfL to assess prior knowledge
- Ongoing electronic journal
- Sociograms (local habitats, interdependence)
- Current stories of natural disaster
- Fiction (cause and effect)
- Videos (presentation skills)

We're all in this together

Essential Question:

How can a person act as an active and informed environmental steward and citizen?

- Schoolyard garden design (class action plan)
- Model research process as a class
- Obstacles? Land use? Space? (good and poor websites)
- Double-entry journal
- Interviews with stakeholders (create interview questions; analyze and interpret findings)
- Create class plan
- Research for Town Hall proposal (create points for proposal)
- Role-play presentation of proposal to town council
- Write and edit summary of meeting and letter to editor
- Envirography electronic journal

Essential Question:

What is the link between the economy and the environment?

- Field trip (mapping, photos, drawing, note taking)
- Debate (homes vs. habitats)
- News search linking economy and environment (class brainstorming web)
- School trash audit (inside and outside; campaign to clean up)
- Cost of packaging vs. reusable containers
- Where does garbage go (web research landfill sites)
- Investigate land use for landfill vs. other uses
- Investigate recycling programs in school/town; write a letter to town council
- Investigate and create a plan for composting, a greenhouse, and a garden (food and plants)

FIGURE 5.5 Essential Questions Web

TABLE 5.6 Planning Chart for Mini-Unit 1

Mini-Unit 1

Essential Question: How can humans balance their needs with those of plants and animals that share a habitat?

Learning Goals

I can analyze the positive and negative effects of human interactions with the plants and animals in their natural habitats.

I can consider different perspectives and evaluate ways of minimizing the negative impact of humans.

Daily instructional tasks/assessments

Daily Instruction/Assessments	Outcomes	Connection to KDB and RPAT
A pileup of post-its strategy to determine class understanding of habitats. *AfL: diagnostic assessment*		
Ongoing electronic journal: First and last entry is an envirography—a reflection on personal environmental stewardship. *AaL: teacher feedback, no grade* *Differentiation/Personalization*	Identify the topic and purpose for a variety of writing forms (Establishing a personal voice in writing)	Environmental Stewardship Communication
Investigate a variety of habitats. Examine structure (schoolyard, local community), components (plants and animals, including people), and interactions (food chain, food web). Construct a sociogram based on analysis of a habitat. Display sociograms in gallery walk. *AfL: sociograms; gallery walk: peer assessment* *AaL: electronic journal*	Investigate the interdependence of plants and animals with specific habitats and communities.	Interdependence Inquiry
View videos (e.g., Severn Suzuki's presentation on the environment to the United Nations when she was 12 years old). Students determine ways humans have used communication and presentation skills to impact the environment. *AfL: students create anchor chart on communication and presentation skills* *Differentiation/Personalization: students who are having difficulty communicating in writing can use a voice recorder on an iPod Touch and send voice file to teacher.*	Use a variety of forms to communicate with different audiences for a variety of purposes. (science, language arts)	Need to present their own research proposal at Town Hall meeting. Communication (presentation)

The second mini-unit begins with a teacher-directed series of activities/assessments to learn how to develop a research proposal (Table 5.7). Then the students develop their own proposals to present at the town hall meeting.

Create Assessment Tools for Daily Instructional Activities/Assessments

Students use Table 5.8 as they move through the research process in the second mini-unit. As with all rubrics, the descriptors help students recognize levels of performance for self-assessment.

TABLE 5.7 Planning Chart for Mini-Unit 2

Mini-Unit 2

Essential Question: How can a person act as an active and informed environmental steward and citizen?

Learning Goals

I can ask questions about the relationship between plants and animals in a habitat, and do research to find out the answers.

I can communicate my research findings effectively in different ways.

Daily Instructional Tasks/Assessments

Daily Instruction/Assessments	Outcomes	Connection to KDB and RPAT
Model research inquiry process. Create a written proposal for designing a garden in the schoolyard. *AfL: exemplars of proposals, anchor chart* Brainstorm possible sources of information (e.g., the schoolyard habitat, land use, possible issues). Tech literacy: reliable and unreliable websites. *AfL: parents, volunteers, and the school community for peer assessment* Note taking (double entry journal, point form, Google Forms, Google Docs, Word doc on iPad). *AfL: self-assessment, teacher observation* *Differentiation/Personalization through use of support with Google Forms and strategic small groups* Develop effective questions for interviews re: schoolyard habitat, land use, possible issues. *AfL tool: Q-chart* Brainstorm possible stakeholders with differing points of view (e.g., students, custodian, teachers, gardeners, etc.). Conduct face-to-face and Skype interviews with the stakeholders. Take notes. *AfL: observation, rubric for notes* Investigate different methods of citation for various sources of information. *AfL: anchor chart* Create citation cards in their personal electronic folders. Together, analyze and interpret findings from the class research example. *AfL: observation* Create a class plan of action for the garden. *AfL: discussion*	Formulate questions, collect information (primary and secondary sources), interpret data (graphs, graphic organizers), and present findings (media works, oral presentation, notes and descriptions, drawings, tables and graphs). (social studies, science, language arts) Use scientific research skills	Inquiry/Research Model inquiry Create a class proposal Walk through steps needed to do their own research and proposal for culminating assessment Students will keep an electronic record of the research process to use as a model as they complete the rich culminating task.

(Continued)

TABLE 5.7   (Continued)

Daily Instruction/Assessments	Outcomes	Connection to KDB and RPAT
Research and create points for a proposal for Town Hall meeting. Create PowerPoint. *AfL: checklist, submit for feedback* *Differentiation/Personalization: Mixed ability/learning style groupings*	Formulate questions, collect information (primary and secondary sources), interpret data (graphs, graphic organizers), and present findings (media works, oral presentation, notes and descriptions, drawings, tables and graphs). (social studies)	Inquiry skills Technological literacy
Review drama techniques for role-playing. In groups, rehearse role-play of presentation to town council panel. *AfL: peer assessment with rubric* *Differentiation: Mixed ability/learning style groupings* ** Kim & Sandy—pair* ** Joseph alone* ** Ira, Judy, Tina with education assistant (EA)*	Use a variety of forms to communicate with different audiences for a variety of purposes. (science, language arts) Apply the creative process to a dramatic play using the elements and conventions of drama to communicate feelings, ideas, and stories. (drama)	Role-play Oral presentation Creativity Need to role-play for rich culminating performance task
Write and use editing process: 1. Summary of Town Hall meeting 2. Letter to the editor *AfL: feedback from teacher and peers; revision*	Use a variety of forms to communicate with different audiences for a variety of purposes. (science, language arts) Editing process (language arts, writing)	Need to send two letters at end of Town Hall meeting
Envirography electronic journal (*AaL*)	Identify the topic and purpose for a variety of writing forms. (establishing a personal voice in writing)	Environmental stewardship

TABLE 5.8 Rubric for Research Process

Criteria	Accomplished	Competent	Developing	Beginning
Plan research approach (Thinking)	The student: • Brainstormed ways to answer the knowledge-based questions (who, what, where, when) • Independently developed a graphic organizer that allowed him or her to gather and organize all the information in a logical way	The student: • Brainstormed ways to answer the knowledge-based questions (who, what, where, when) • Chose a class graphic organizer that allowed him or her to gather and organize all the information in a logical way	The student: • Described ways to answer the knowledge-based questions (who, what, where, when) • Used a teacher-developed graphic organizer to organize his or her information	The student: • Made a brainstorming web and added information to it during the research process
Search a variety of sources	• Used a variety of sources (book, article, website, blog, podcast, video, etc.) to answer each of the questions in the research plan	• Used a variety of sources (book, article, website, blog, podcast, video, etc.) to answer most of the questions in the research plan	• Found information to answer some of the questions	• Found some information related to the topic
Cite Resources	• Cited all sources correctly according to the classroom-determined format	• Cited most sources according to the classroom-determined format with few errors	• Recorded the title and author of each source and where it came from (book, website, etc.) • Attempted to use the classroom-determined format	• Recorded the title and author of each source on a teacher-created table
Note taking	• Used an effective and personally created format to record and organize information	• Used a classroom-created format to record and organize information	• Used a list to record and organize information	• Recorded information in random order
Analysis and interpretation of findings	• Forms logical conclusions based on insightful analysis and interpretation of relevant data	• Forms appropriate conclusions based on analysis and interpretation of gathered data	• With help, forms a conclusion based on some gathered information	• With help, attempts to form a conclusion based on limited data

Suggestions for upgrade:

TABLE 5.9 A Q-Chart

	is/are was/were	do/does did	can could	will would
What?				
Where?				
When?				
Who?				
Why?				
How?				

Source: Original source unknown; found at a social studies wiki on a YouTube video featuring Joe Ribera; www.youtube.com/watch?v=Uy44J7p2E04

The cross-curricular skill of question formation is a component of the unit's focus on inquiry. A Q-chart is useful to scaffold and strengthen this skill. In the Q-chart, students create different questions in each box using the question starter and the verbs in the corresponding boxes (Table 5.9). The questions generated with "why" and "how" as starters often require HOTS. Question formation can be made into a game. Students are challenged to create good questions and also to answer them. Questions can also form the basis for research and inquiry. See www.youtube.com/watch?v=Uy44J7p2E04 for more details about the Q-chart strategy.

A Checkbric for Your Curriculum Design

As you can see, to create a relevant and accountable integrated curriculum involves a comprehensive understanding of curriculum, instruction, teaching, learning, and assessment. Table 5.10 offers a checkbric as a way to reflect on the curriculum development process. A *checkbric* is a cross between a rubric and a checklist. The far right column is reserved for qualitative comments and insights. This checkbric can be used for a disciplinary curriculum in most categories.

Thinking about Assessment

As you design and implement an integrated unit, there are some assessment questions unique to this type of curriculum. The principles that we have encouraged throughout this book still apply. Assessment needs to fair, reliable, and valid; AfL should be embedded into instruction seamlessly. Indeed, we have shown you samples of how an assessment tool can be used for both instruction and assessment in the Grade 4 unit above. The Q-chart, and the rubric for the research process are used for instructional purposes and help the students to know exactly what is expected for success; they also offer information for the teacher on where students are in their understanding and acquisition of skills and what the next steps might be.

Learning goals from different subjects are included in each mini-unit. Thus, the expectations for the student are made transparent. Indeed, as mentioned before, many teachers work with students to create the learning goals and then the success criteria that follow.

TABLE 5.10 A Checkbric for Reflection on Designing an Integrated Unit

		Comments
Know your curriculum	Have I considered the unifying framework for my province (if there is one)?	
	Have I scanned the introduction of the curriculum documents of the subjects involved?	
Know your students	Have learning preferences been considered? multiple intelligences?	
	Is there variety in both instructional strategies and assessment?	
	Have I differentiated or personalized curriculum in appropriate places?	
Preliminary planning brain-storming	Have I brainstormed for possible places where I might make connections with other subjects? teachers? possible experts in my community/globally?	
Scan and cluster	Have I done a vertical scan of two grades below and one grade above the target grade for each subject?	
	Have I clustered these outcomes into bundles that represent critical learning (the KDB)?	
	After reviewing the target grade in the horizontal scan, have I selected broad-based outcomes for the KDB?	
Unit focus	Is my focus for the unit age-appropriate and relevant?	
	Does my unit address the outcomes?	
Unpacking curriculum outcomes	Have I unpacked relevant broad-based curriculum outcomes selected in the scan and cluster?	
	Have I created a chart to identify the Know (nouns), Do (verbs), and Be?	
KDB umbrella **Essential Questions**	Have I been selective in refining the KDB so that I can realistically teach and assess it?	
	Have I created Essential Questions to guide planning that are connected to the KDB?	
	Do my Essential Questions encourage inquiry and have the potential for complex answers?	
Exploratory web	Have I brainstormed for activities/assessments that are linked to outcomes and the KDB umbrella in an exploratory web?	
Rich performance assessment task	Have I clearly described an RPAT that will engage and challenge students?	
	Do students need to demonstrate the KDB? Is the Essential Question addressed?	
Assessment tools	Have I developed assessment tools to accompany the rich performance assessment task?	
	Are rubrics created with explicit, meaningful, and relevant descriptors?	

(Continued)

TABLE 5.10 (Continued)

		Comments
Essential Question web	Have I created a new web to brainstorm for each of the Essential Questions?	
	Have I revisited my instructional strategies/assessments so that they address the Essential Questions?	
	Are all the instructional strategies aligned with KDB and the RPAT?	
Daily instructional activities/ assessments	Have I created daily instructional activities/assessments that lead to the RPAT?	
	Are students receiving instruction in all aspects of the task that they need to demonstrate?	
	Have I created tools for instruction and AfL?	
	Is assessment as learning included?	
	Have I considered differentiation? personalization?	
	Are students active learners?	
Alignment check	Have I gone back to ensure that my curriculum is aligned?	

Just as students often have a hard time differentiating among subject areas in an integrated task, so do teachers. How do you make a distinction between social studies and science, for example, when teaching the concept of cause and effect? For many teachers the answer is that they do not differentiate. Rather they gave the same "mark" for concept development in both science and social studies. Similarly, when a generic rubric is used for a cross-disciplinary task such as research, the grade for research can be counted for more than one subject area. For example, a presentation of science and social studies content can be assessed for communication in English, science, and social studies. This practice actually makes assessment more time efficient. What is important is that whatever is to be

Snapshot of Classroom-Based Interdisciplinary Assessment Practice

What is different about interdisciplinary assessment? Melissa Dixon from Ontario has found an effective way to grade when she is teaching an integrated curriculum on her own. She creates a marking sheet of all the outcomes from selected subject areas on one page in her assessment book. When a student meets an outcome in any subject area, she records the level of achievement for that outcome. When she needs to come up with a grade for one subject area, Melissa reviews the levels that the student has achieved for that subject's outcomes, taking into account the level of difficulty of the task. She then translates this into a letter grade, which is needed for the report card.

evaluated needs to have been taught explicitly to the students. If students are using drama as part of the culminating presentation and drama skills will be part of the assessment, then these skills either need to be taught or reviewed. Similarly, student use of technology effectively should not be taken for granted, especially if the skills are needed for successful completion of an assessment task such as a PowerPoint presentation. It is only fair that those skills are taught before they are assessed.

A concern around integrated learning is that teachers may find themselves outside their comfort zone. For some it is a refreshing challenge to learn and teach new material in a different subject while others prefer to stay within their areas of "expertise." This issue can be especially challenging when it comes to grading. In a science essay, for example, should the English teacher be considered a valid assessor of the science content? One solution is to collaborate: The science teacher marks the science content and the English teacher marks the same essay for style and structure.

The Australian Science and Mathematics school in Adelaide, Australia, has long had an integrated program and explored different methods of assessment (Drake, 2012). Teachers tend to assess more than one subject in their assessment tasks. In one interdisciplinary unit the students investigated the historical, scientific, and technological perspectives of a technological invention as the major research task. The resulting essay on the impact of technology on society had rubrics for history, technology, and English, depending on a student's choice of approach. The English teacher marked all the essays, the technology teacher marked the technology essays, and the history specialist marked the history essays.

In another science assignment, students wrote letters to various audiences. The letter writing satisfied a component of the English curriculum. All the Australian teachers on the team were involved in the assessment. The English teacher gave the science teachers "lessons" on what to look for and tips for teaching what was being assessed. At the same

Snapshot of Authentic Interdisciplinary Assessment

Ontario teacher Donna Stewart's students were involved in something that really mattered. A local bird, the piping plover, was in danger of losing its habitat at a local beach. The expansion of the beach to promote tourism impacted the bird population. It was an environmental issue that touched the local community. The children wrote a nonfiction information piece on the issue. Although their written work was evaluated by the teacher for English and science, a more authentic assessment came from the community. The students' work was published and distributed through the tourist information centre in the community. A local environmental group obtained Trillium funding to pay for the publication of the students' efforts. Even a few years later, the students from that unit still talk about it today. They also continued to learn about it on their own after the school year ended.

time, the science and technology teachers guided the English teacher on the science and technology content. On yet another assignment, the team invited experts from the community to evaluate the students' knowledge and skills. The teachers trained the experts on the use of a comprehensive assessment tool.

The Australian team is very attentive to assessment; they know that credibility is crucial to the ongoing success of this integrated program. They meet regularly to plan curriculum and assessment. They develop, review, and revise assessment tools like rubrics according to teacher and student responses. There is ongoing discussion and moderated marking. They make their expectations to students transparent in a variety of ways.

Conclusion

In this chapter we have explored how to create an integrated curriculum. We have considered some of the issues that can complicate the planning and implementation process. Then we walked through the creation of an actual unit. Finally, we looked at assessment and the particular issues that can arise when using an interdisciplinary approach.

Professional Discussion Questions

1) Choose two or more subjects that you think would integrate effectively. Collaboration with colleagues from different subject areas would enrich the conversation. Read the introductory material of the curriculum documents for each subject area.
2) Create a vertical and horizontal scan and cluster for your grade level. Choose the outcomes for an integrated unit of study.
3) Complete the KDB unpacking chart and umbrella.
4) Design an RPAT. What might an assessment tool look like for your students?
5) What instructional strategies might you use?
6) How does your work match up against the checkbric (Table 5.10)?

The Twenty-First–Century Teacher

In this chapter you will learn about:

- The personal, cultural, and global frame of the Story Model
- The twenty-first–century teacher
- Living contradictions
- Technology and a new culture of learning
- New pedagogy and deep learning
- Global connections
- Teaching the Be
- Teacher as change agent
- My story—how I fit into the new story
- Personal learning goals and success criteria

Revisiting the Story Model

We began this book with an exploration of the evolving story of education in North America. As a collective, across the globe, educators work and live in an emerging new environment, whether we welcome it or not. Indeed, our students "are *in* the twenty-first century, and are waiting for the education system to catch up," says twenty-first–century researcher Heidi Hayes Jacobs (2010, p. 211). Collectively, we as educators have the power to embed our values and beliefs in our practice to shape the new story.

In this final chapter, we apply the Story Model to explore the concept of the twenty-first–century teacher as it relates to you personally.

The Personal Story

The inner ring of the Story Model is the personal story frame. Teachers first make meaning of their profession and their own practice through the lens of their personal experiences, their present values and beliefs, and their future aspirations. The old adage is that teachers teach the way that they were taught. But in the twenty-first century this no longer works for the many reasons addressed in this book.

The ability to be a **reflective practitioner** (Schön, 1983) is more important than ever. For John Dewey (1910), without reflection there can be no growth. Reflection is an important part of the learning cycle and helps us move forward to more effective ways of doing

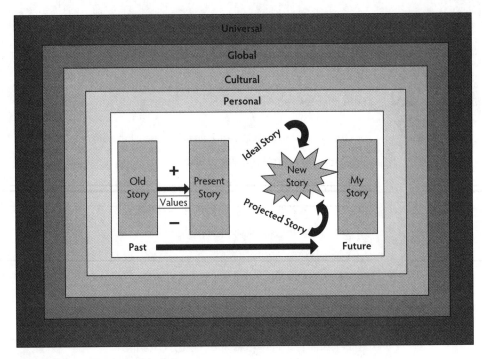

FIGURE 6.1 The Story Model

things in changing times. It requires a process of learning—unlearning—relearning, and thus involves a certain amount of ambiguity, tension, and discomfort. It involves personal introspection of one's own values and whether they are being lived out in practice. It also involves uncertainty and tension.

Reading this chapter, we ask you to be reflective. What are your values? How do they align with research and best practices? Are you living out your values in your teaching practice? A Canadian Education Association study called *Teaching the Way We Aspire to Teach: Now and in the Future* (2012) asked teachers what they valued. The teachers identified the following:

- Passion for teaching and learning
- Caring and commitment for students
- Creativity, flexibility, and willingness to take risks
- Knowledge and drive for self-improvement
- Energy, enthusiasm, and engagement
- Trust, collaboration, and connectedness

Sadly, although most teachers had actually experienced teaching the way they had hoped to teach, it did not happen on a consistent and system-wide basis. As a complementary view, when asked what engaged them, 220 students wanted teachers who loved their work, who believed in students, and who acted like human beings (Wolpert-Gawron, 2012). In short, a close match existed between how teachers aspired to Be and how students wanted their teachers to Be. (Students also appreciated teaching strategies that included working with peers and with technology and that provided choice, variety, and connection to the real world/project-based learning.)

The teachers who felt their practice did not reflect their aspirations experienced what Jack Whitehead (2012) identifies as "living contradiction." A **living contradiction** is the tension experienced when your practice does not fit your values. The teachers may have felt caught between traditions of the old story and elements of the emerging new story. For example, the requirement to provide grades may contradict teachers' commitment to AfL; a policy to exclude effort from grades or a policy against late-mark deduction may contradict the importance teachers place on teaching students the value of effort and punctuality.

We hope that much or some of the content of this book has made you pause and reflect. There may be places in the emerging new story that do not feel right to you. Perhaps, for example, you find yourself predominately lecturing when you believe in inquiry learning. Or you are resisting using technology because there is such a steep learning curve. For Whitehead, every practitioner needs to ask "How will I live out my espoused values in my teaching practice given the system that I teach in?" or "How will I close the gap between my espoused values and my practice"?

To resolve the potential contradiction, we need to find ways to reconcile or synthesize the seeming opposites of the old and the new stories. Caring about our students and finding joy in their growth, and striving to improve our professional work are age-old markers of a good educator.

LIVING CONTRADICTIONS IN PERSONAL STORIES

Helen Pereira-Raso from Ontario describes her living contradiction in her struggle to balance the need to scaffold learning to meet student needs while also challenging students to discover things independently:

> The transition to project-based teaching and learning was not easy. I now realize that I did not understand the roots of project-based learning. As a result, the first time I constructed a project-based unit of study I did not scaffold the learning for my students. What I did was take an assignment and turn it into a project. I did not align the teaching and the assessment components of the project into a learning experience. It was a difficult moment for me as a teacher. I had a bit of success in the classroom engaging my students, but not as much as I wanted to. The students had no sense of what they were supposed to be learning. They were also frustrated with the long process and the fact that much of it was independent. Students were unsure what I was going to evaluate them on. They only knew that they needed to do a seminar presentation to the class and their parents.
>
> The students were confused; I was confused. I was unsure of my purpose, and really this was where it became very clear to me as a professional that passion isn't enough. You have to start all your learning with a clear purpose. I identified with Rudy Crewe (2011) when he writes about being a first-year teacher in *I Used to Think . . . And Now I Think*. He

Snapshot of a Living Contradiction

PEI teacher David Costello (2012) explores a living contradiction through an action research project that he used to explore his own teaching of reading to a Grade 1/2 split classroom. He resolved his conflict by discovering that his teaching can be practised with a both/and solution:

> *I came into this research thinking that my reading instruction was based on decisions made by people outside my classroom and that my students' needs were not being considered. I was neglecting the idea that I was the classroom teacher and that I made countless instructional decisions each day. I could use the initiatives set forth by Mainstream Elementary's literacy program while at the same time meet the needs of my students with complementary strategies for instruction and assessment. It was up to me to use the knowledge of my students and teaching practices to assist students in their reading development (p. 58).*

writes that "passion and the love of children had fallen short of being enough. I learned that purpose, planning, strategy, and skill were the next chapters in my growth—that without them I was a surgeon using hope as my only tool" (p. 20).

Like Crewe, my first efforts at project-based learning made me reflect on my teaching. I asked what do the students really need to learn—what matters? What are we doing, why are we doing it, and how are we doing it? What was the balance between scaffolding learning and letting them discover it themselves?

Shelley Wright (2012) from Saskatchewan blogs about how she has shifted her understandings since she began teaching. These shifts in thinking presumably were the result of resolving her personal living contradictions. She concludes, "I'm becoming a better teacher by giving up a lot of what I used to think." Shelley's thoughts are summarized in Table 6.1.

TABLE 6.1 Shelley Wright's Shifts in Thinking over Her Teaching Career

I used to think . . .	Now I think . . .
Compliant, well-behaved students were the ideal.	I'm afraid for kids who think a 90% is preparing them for life.
Teaching reading was someone else's job.	All teachers are responsible for teaching reading.
Some kids were lazy, unmotivated, and not cut out for school.	It's the school that is not cut out for some kids. Kids love to learn, but they may not be buying what I am selling.
Kids are passive learners—empty vessels for me to fill with knowledge.	Students are reflexive learners who are capable of change and teaching me.
I need to transmit the learning.	Students are capable of co-designing curriculum—from choosing curriculum outcomes to creating units and assignments to co-constructing assessment criteria.

TABLE 6.1 (Continued)

I used to think . . .	Now I think . . .
Content is most important to transmit through lecture.	The most important thing to learn and for me to model is skills (e.g., collaboration, critical thinking, information management).
Homework is very important to show I am in control.	Homework does little to enrich learning.
Marks are important.	Marks don't mean much. I wish we had feedback only.
Technology was for searching for resources.	Technology is infused into every step of the learning process.
The current K–12 organizational system made sense. Some kids just can't succeed in it.	All kids want to succeed. It's my job to help them find ways to do that. Students are capable of showing me what they need, if only I take the time to listen and ask authentic questions.
Exams are vital to know what students have learned.	Learning needs to be captured in multiple formats.

The Cultural and Global Story

To explore the cultural/global story in the new story, we return to Michael Fullan's (2013) framework for twenty-first–century learning described in Chapter 1. The cultural and global story are collapsed into one frame because technology allows for global interaction. There are three interconnected ingredients in this story:

1) Technology to accelerate learning
2) A new pedagogy to teach deep learning that includes twenty-first–century skills
3) A teacher who acts as a change agent

PROFILE OF A TWENTY-FIRST–CENTURY TEACHER

We spoke to many front-runner educators who share certain traits. These twenty-first–century educators always begin planning with curriculum outcomes and classroom assessment before choosing instructional outcomes. Relevancy and accountability go hand in hand. These educators often use technology as a way to enhance learning and allow for deeper assessment for learning. But technology is used thoughtfully and always comes second to pedagogy. They have strong belief systems grounded in constructivist philosophy that are played out in their classrooms. They use traditional methods when they are appropriate and are conscious of the need to differentiate and personalize the curriculum for students.

The twenty-first–century educators open their classrooms to the world; they often have a class website accessible to parents—indeed, to anyone. They take risks and put their practice under the microscope by writing reflective blogs so that they can improve. They strive to develop strong relationships with their students. They collaborate with their colleagues and engage in personalized professional development. At the heart of their practice is caring about their students and being a catalyst for their growth as a whole person. These teachers want to make a difference.

TECHNOLOGY

Students are often described as digital natives—those who grew up using technology and take it for granted (Prensky, 2001). Older people can learn the language but will always be digital immigrants. Indeed, technology is so much a part of young people's lives that the brains of digital natives are evolving differently because constant exposure to digital media affects the neural pathways (Small & Vorgan, 2008). Prensky (2013) goes further:

> Technology, rather, is an extension of our brains; it's a new way of thinking. It's the solution we humans have created to deal with our difficult new context of variability, uncertainty, complexity, and ambiguity. The human mind, as powerful as it is, is no longer powerful enough for our world; the old "tried and true" human capabilities just aren't enough. Technology provides us with the new and enhanced capabilities we need. So technology isn't something we need *in addition* to mental activity; technology is now *part* of mental activity (p. 22).

Digital Citizens

The original Web was about transmitting information. Web 2.0 is interactive, characterized by social networks where people share information and create new knowledge. By itself, Web 2.0 is value neutral, but put in the hands of people it can be both a positive and negative force.

In her first placement, Ontario pre-service education student Amber Botelho created a Social Networking unit for a Grade 11 media studies class. Amber's goal was for each student to have a deeper understanding of the risks and benefits of social networking, how to keep safe on a variety of networks, and how their actions online could affect them in their everyday lives. Amber suspected that these students used social media more than she did; thus, she gave a diagnostic assessment to find out what they knew. All the students had access to computers and 95% were on at least one social network such as Facebook, Twitter, or Tumblr. But few had read the privacy policy of their social network.

Amber used the Jigsaw strategy. She created four different "expert" groups, each assigned to a social network site (either Tumblr, Twitter, YouTube, or Pinterest; Amber used Facebook as the example in class discussions). Students created individual accounts on their assigned social networks. Topics covered included privacy, ethics, cyberbullying, netiquette, and current issues. Students investigated their assigned network for such things as its privacy policy and

Snapshot of Teaching Digital Citizenship

It is crucial we teach our students how to handle the Internet in both its positive and negative aspects. For example, social networking can be used as a powerful learning tool, but it can also be a tool for cyberbullying. Bill Belsey from Alberta is the creator of antibullying.com. His work has received a lot of attention internationally. Through Belsey, teachers can take online courses to train themselves on how to recognize cyberbullying and how to deal with it once it is recognized. Learning to be a good digital citizen can be taught.

how the site responded to offensive posts and common forms of cyberbullying. After students consulted within their expert groups and recorded what they learned on chart papers, they reassembled into instructional groups made up of one expert from each social network group.

The culminating rich performance assessment task was to create an awareness campaign. Students could choose any topic and any communication form they liked (commercial, poster, pamphlet, online advertisement). They formed their own groups with someone represented from each expert group. They had to decide on a target audience and justify their choice as well as how and where to present the information in the campaign.

Technology and Change

Knowing the fast and furious pace of change, we hesitate to predict how technology will be used in schools even in the next few years. Delivery methods are changing, with various versions of blended learning or hybrid learning being tried in some K–12 schools (Horn, 2013). Even the physical design of new schools is changing to provide spaces for Internet access and small group learning; classrooms are interactive and mirror workplaces (Ash, 2013).

Predicting what educational apps will take precedence tomorrow amounts to a hazardous guess. Some categories of apps have proven to be transformational to educators thus far, including the following:

- Videoconferencing through Skype or Google Hangout in the classroom
- Open online curriculum such as the Khan Academy
- Learning management systems (LMS) such as Edmodo and Schoology that offer an array of tools like gradebooks and a space for online discussions
- Social media such as Twitter, Facebook, Instagram, and Pinterest
- Google Apps for Education for its influence on student work, collaboration, differentiated instruction, and communication (Della Vedova, 2013)

Snapshot of Professional Learning and Technology

Jennifer Burke, a curriculum consultant, uses technology to support teachers across Nova Scotia. Some teachers may be the only ones teaching a particular course in their school. Jennifer uses Via, a videoconferencing system, to bring together teachers from different geographical areas. Jennifer works with museums to assist them in designing learning programs that align with curriculum outcomes. The museum websites are linked to Moodle (https://moodle.org). She uses Moodle, a virtual learning environment, to house resources for teachers to use for social studies. Teachers also use Moodle to share their ideas, resources, and student exemplars with Burke and with their colleagues across the province. Burke finds that more and more teachers are beginning to use technology in professional learning sessions and during the implementation process in their practice to share their learning.

Despite our enthusiasm for the potential of technology to transform education, we do agree with Ontario teacher Tom Freure, who told us that technology is only valuable when it enhances learning. For now, Tom uses a Smartboard and a document camera for a variety of purposes in his Grade 4/5 classroom. Students show their work to the class and discuss their own thinking for AfL; peers add to the discussion for peer assessment, which Tom facilitates. He uses iPads to differentiate instruction and assessment; one strategy is to give individual students appropriate apps at different levels of difficulty. This strategy is particularly useful when teaching a split grade, as Tom does. He cautions that the iPad is not a tool that should be viewed as a teaching platform for teachers. The teacher's role when using an iPad is to facilitate and guide rather than directly instruct. With an iPad's multiple tools and student-specific apps and options, students can self-differentiate as well as consume, explore, create, collaborate, and communicate. Technology works best when it facilitates learning and activities that would occur without the technology by extending the time, place, or pace of the learning (Naidu, 2008).

One valid concern is that not all students or schools will have equal access to technology or the Internet. The teachers in this book do not all have 1:1 laptops, Smartboards, or the latest gadgets. However, they commented that it was possible to do a great deal in a classroom with one or two computers. As long as they had access to the Internet, they had access to Skype and other ways to connect with experts and gather information. As well, a growing number of school districts have policies and the technological infrastructure to support students bringing their own devices to school (BYOD). Perhaps surprisingly, almost every student has a digital device in his or her pocket, particularly the older students. If someone does not have one, teachers have found that usually other students have more than one or there are extra ones that can be shared. Another concern is that teachers are uncomfortable embracing technology-rich teaching because they know less about it than their students. Roles are reversed when students teach their peers and their teachers. Fortunately, this role reversal often results in a collaborative and reciprocal learning community; thus, teachers can relax and work toward this positive result (Mishra & Keohler, 2006).

The New Culture of Learning

Technology is allowing people to learn differently. Two seemingly opposite experiences are emerging. One is that people are learning in a group and, paradoxically, this has facilitated a very personalized approach to learning. What do these two opposite but complementary experiences mean for us?

In *A New Culture of Learning*, Thomas and Brown (2011) suggest we are moving toward people learning primarily in a collective, but the "collective" is distinguished from a "classroom" by its voluntary and diverse membership. People join a collective because they share a passion for the topic, so learning in a collective is intrinsically motivating. People move in and out of the collective as needed. New media such as blogs or social networks replace books, teachers, or classrooms. Learning in the digital world values play, questioning, imagination, peer interaction, tacit knowledge, and the fluid and impermanent nature of the collective membership. It is highly democratic; both students and teachers are involved in learning through the collective.

Passion-based learning (Maiers, 2011; Maiers & Sanvold, 2010) is an approach that has gained traction in the twenty-first century. Passion-based learning is possible because of technology, which in turn allows for collective learning and personalization. The Genius Hour discussed in Chapter 4 is an example of passion-based learning. P.S. 188 The Island School in Manhattan offers an example of a passion-based elementary school (see details at http://schools.nyc.gov/schoolportals/01/m188/default.htm).

In the new culture of learning, **intrinsic motivation** is a key concept—doing something for the pleasure that it gives you rather than for an external reward. A principle of AfL, for example, is that students learn for the sake of learning—not for the **extrinsic motivation** of the grade. Given open-source access, people are intrinsically motivated to collaborate and offer their services for free. In Web 2.0, people work together to co-construct knowledge and meaning. For example, people contribute, edit, and critique content in Wikipedia rather than refer to a static encyclopedia written by an expert (Pink, 2009). Teachers who blog or Twitter for professional reasons contribute without being paid—they choose to develop professionally because they are motivated to do so by the pleasure of the task.

Personal Learning Networks as Professional Development

As we talked to educators across Canada, we heard over and over about their **personal learning networks (PLN)**. The PLN has all the characteristics of the collective and has its roots in professional learning communities (PLC). PLCs are well recognized in school systems as an effective way to bring about change (Kanoid, 2011; Dufour & Marzano, 2011). PLCs involve people from school systems who work together in small groups for a common purpose. For example, the teachers in one division in an elementary school may work

Snapshot of Technology-Rich Deep Learning

Kathy Cassidy is a multiple award-winning Grade 1 teacher in Saskatchewan who writes a number of blogs that feature her innovative practice with primary students. She is very aware of her impact on students and uses technology to make her practice public for students, parents, and other educators. She shares classroom happenings through pictures and videos to show what students are learning. All of her six- and seven-year-old students have their own blogs, which are digital portfolios showcasing their learning in reading, writing, math, science, social studies, and health. Students use drawings, podcasts, screencasts, and videos to present their ideas. They use wikis and Google Docs to collect information and connect online to experts, other classrooms, or friends with Skype. Kathy is also transparent about assessment. The students' blogs are the focus of student-led conferences. With a bit of guidance, Kathy's students choose which artifacts from their blog will be the focus of the conference (Cassidy, 2013a). They share with their parents what they have done well and what they want to get better at. Kathy's first book, *Connected from the Start: Global Learning in Primary Grades* (2013b) details how to use global connections to meet curricular outcomes in a primary (or any) classroom.

together to plan for implementing AfL in their classrooms (Miller, 2005). A PLN is very different from a PLC. A PLN is a community created by and for educators to explore areas of personal but also professional interest. A PLN comes to life through a social network.

Increasingly, teachers are taking professional development into their own hands. The professional growth of Michelle Metcalfe, whom you met in Chapter 1, has changed over the past few years. She learned about her storytelling method TPRS for teaching language through blogging and connecting with a global learning community. During the past two years, Michelle describes her work as a "constant state of collaboration" with her fellow Spanish-teaching colleague. They have an enriching professional relationship. But her most powerful learning experience has been online sharing and learning with other professionals. She is participating in webinars with other people interested in the same topics. Together, these colleagues in Europe, Russia, and the United States have formed a community of learners with a common purpose.

The teachers who are implementing Genius Hour (described in Chapter 4) are a PLN that meets through a Twitter chat. Any educator who is interested in the Genuis Hour can participate by logging into Twitter and searching for hashtag #geniushour. "Members" move in and out of this group as needed, sharing challenges and the excitement of students. Every first Wednesday of the month at 6:00 p.m. Pacific Standard Time, they hold a chat that is open to anyone. In addition, many of these educators have personal blogs or class websites where student work is posted and shared with others in the PLN.

Open-Source Curriculum Resources

In the new culture of learning, open-source K–12 resources for education enable professional collaboration and inspiration among educators. Discovery Education Canada is a site for administrators, teachers, parents, and students. It offers "award winning digital content, interactive lessons, real time assessment, virtual experiences with some of Discovery's greatest talents, classroom contests & challenges, professional development and more—Discovery is leading the way in transforming classrooms and inspiring learning" (www.discoveryeducation.ca).

Canada's Cube for Teachers is an interactive database that originated in Ontario for teachers to share their work (www.cubeforteachers.com/#6). Educators from the field—professors, administrators, educators, and faculty students (from the tech savvy to technophobics) provide ongoing testing and feedback to the site. All voices are equally important.

Curriki is a K–12 global community for teachers, students, and parents to create, share, and find open learning resources (www.curriki.org/welcome). According to the website, near the end of 2012 there had been 7.6 million users of Curriki.

The Khan Academy is another popular open-source resource (www.khanacademy. org). Videos available from the Khan Academy are often used for the flipped classroom-students study the material to be taught in class online before class and do hands-on work in the classroom based on the concepts learned. Salman Khan—a businessman, not a trained teacher—makes YouTube videos that explain mathematics, science, finance, and history concepts in a way that is easy to understand. These are low-tech, mini-lectures featuring voiceover commentary and a hand scribbling on an electronic whiteboard. The website includes over 2400 videos. The Khan Academy also provides ongoing feedback. The data are private, but students can get hard data on how well they are reaching their goals. All videos are free and can be accessed by students at any time from any place and can be watched as many times as needed. There are 2 million users a month who watch over 100 to 200,000 videos a day. The Khan Academy is now exploring partnering with public districts of education.

NEW PEDAGOGY

As mentioned in Chapter 1, the new pedagogy revolves around the twenty-first–century skills with four necessary characteristics of instructional activities and embedded assessments:

- Irresistibly engaging
- Elegantly efficient—learning is easier and more interesting
- Technologically ubiquitous—24/7
- Steeped in real-world problem solving (Fullan, 2013, p. 33)

For us, Chapters 2 to 5 in this book describe the new pedagogy in depth and how to ensure it is accountable. Now we explore the new pedagogy through the lens of the lived experiences of our twenty-first–century teachers. You will see that Fullan's four requirements are often in place, but there are also practical elements of the traditional story that these teachers bring with them to their practices.

Deep Learning in a Classroom

Pierre Poulin's Grade 6 classroom illustrates how a teacher can implement the new pedagogy for deep learning. Poulin has developed iClasse, an innovative program built on constructivist and twenty-first–century education principles. By 2012, five Quebec classrooms from Grades 3 to 6 in Poulin's school were implementing iClasse. (Websites for these classrooms are www.ppoulin.com and www.hyperclasse.com.) The program involves Pierre-François Bourdon and principal Isabelle Massé.

To create the warm and inviting classroom environment that iClasse requires, a student council is created with a president and several appointed ministers, such as a Minister of Environment. These roles rotate among students over time. Together with the teachers, the council votes on the most engaging activities for learning. Students, for example, voted to be able to work toward learning goals when they wanted to during class time.

To work toward twenty-first–century skills such as communication, collaborative teamwork, and creation, the classroom features round tables for groups of three students. It is a 1:1 laptop school, where digital literacy is an important goal. Students use social media to communicate. The Internet is used for research, and there are no textbooks. Homework is done online. Students engage in challenge-based learning (CBL), "a new teaching model that incorporates the best aspects of problem-based learning, project-based learning and contextual teaching while focusing on real problems faced in the real world" (Johnson,

Smith, Symth, & Varon, 2009, p. 7). Technology is an integral part of CBL. For example, once a week Poulin's students help seniors use computers and multimedia tools.

Student-created electronic portfolios capture varied and informative assessment information. Technology is used to reach even students who considered themselves to be failing. For example, a group of five boys built a school in Minecraft (a computer game where you use Lego-style blocks to build anything you can imagine in a virtual world). The students invited Poulin into the 3-D world and showed him how they calculated measurements such as perimeter and volume in the indoor pool. Poulin could see and hear their thinking processes in ways that were inaccessible through more traditional methods.

Technology has also provided an authentic audience. Poulin's school was the first one in Quebec to post short French podcasts on iTunes. His students wrote the text and he gave feedback. Then students could choose to read the podcast themselves or have someone else read it. The quality of French writing escalated when students knew they had an international audience. Often, relatives from many different countries who heard the podcasts reported back how proud they were.

Deep Learning through Assessment

One of the characteristics of the new pedagogy is that it is steeped in real-world problem solving. We asked teacher education students and practising educators to recall their best assessment experiences over the course of their lifetime and why the experience was a "best" (Drake, Reid, & Beckett, 2010). Many of the stories involved RPATs that were remembered later because as students they had learned so much. The RPAT experiences had been challenging but fun (irresistibly engaging) and motivating (elegantly efficient) because they were interesting. The one thing that these experiences were not was high tech. These RPATs show us that not everything has to be high tech all of the time. The list below outlines some of the tasks we heard about:

- Student-created test: Students in pairs create a test and exchange it with another pair. The task is not to actually take the test but to assess it for completeness, quality of questions, and so on.
- Simulations such as a mock trial or sugar babies: Bags of sugar represent the babies. Student couples must carry the baby-bags everywhere or find a babysitter, as well as figure out how to meet the responsibilities of household budgeting. One student reflected that, "Inside every Grade 11 student there was a Kindergartner who just wanted to play house, and in doing so, realized just how complicated 'house' can be."
- Mock documents such as a newspaper (Elizabethan Times), diaries (students in role keep journals projecting themselves into historical events/events in novels), lost sketchbook (students in role of actual artists create a posthumously discovered sketchbook reflecting the artistic growth of the inspiring artist)
- Public performance/competition: Examples included *Iron Chef* competitions and a *Romeo and Juliet* performance. Rehearsals are perfect opportunities for AfL.

AaL: Students Learn to Be Assessment Literate

Kristen Clarke (2013) of Ontario initiated an action research project to increase student engagement through developing student assessment literacy. She wanted her students to be more aware of feedback and to increase their metacognition. She and her students discussed what AoL, AfL, and AaL meant. Then she had students track their own assessment journeys. The process was simple and frequent. Students had an organizer where they identified details about different assessments, such as who was the assessor, what was the feedback, and what was the grade (if any). Kristen kept data on the assessments, too. Most students responded positively to the concept of assessment literacy. At report card time, students reviewed typical comments for parents, looked at the language in the achievement charts, and practised writing parent-friendly comments. Peers gave feedback on their comments. Kristen's students had taken responsibility for monitoring their own achievement. Now their report card comments were personal and meaningful.

An intergenerational aspect to a good performance task can make it richer and take it out of the boundaries of a classroom (Fullan, 2013). Poulin incorporated intergenerational learning when his students worked with seniors. Bill Belsey created a similar task when he designed a "Generations Can Connect" project during the International Year of the Elderly. Bill's students interviewed seniors and photographed each of them with an item that represented their lives. Then students built web pages about the seniors and taught them how to use the Internet. In turn, the seniors taught the students about budgeting and mortgages by managing dummy bank accounts. (Other great examples are on Bill's website for his Grade 5 class, www.coolclass.ca.)

Deep Learning through Global Connections

Talking to teachers from across the country, we were surprised by how often they were connecting their students to others across the globe. This might happen through a formal connection like iEARN (the world's largest and longest running K–12 global learning network) or through teachers who inspired each other or through connections in a PLN.

Jeff Whipple, a technology learning mentor working with K–12 schools in New Brunswick, has organized the Global Collaborative Projects—an example of an ongoing commitment to global connections (http://jwhipple.wikispaces.com/Global+Collaborative+Projects). Students in Fredericton participated in a French-language collaborative project with students from the International School of Bombay in Mumbai. All students were learning French; the Big Idea was community. Students in Canada and India decided what important landmarks would help describe their own communities to each other. They each chose an ambassador: Canadian students chose a small stuffed black bear and the students in Mumbai chose a small toy snake. Students took the ambassador to local landmarks such as the hockey arena, the local mall, and city hall. They created stories from the perspective of the ambassador at that locale and told the story—using their evolving French skills—asynchronously through images and videos and then synchronously through Skype. During the project, students sent information to each other in French through a variety of texts, images, and videos that were posted to a public wikispace. Most students either talked themselves or used an avatar and created a video. Others created a web page. There was a cluster map on the wiki so students could see who visited their space and where they came from.

This authentic audience allowed for embedded assessment of French. The activity culminated with a Skype call. Whipple recalls that the students from New Brunswick came to school at 6 a.m. to Skype with their counterparts in Mumbai. Near the end of the 90-minute connection, three of the boys in India began to play music and dance the Macarena. Immediately, a small group of girls in Canada jumped up and danced with them in an "international sock hop." There might have been more learning in the last 15 minutes of less structured time than the previous hour.

French as a second language teachers will attest to the fact that motivating middle school students to speak French is difficult, but the students in this project were motivated by the opportunity to connect with students in Mumbai. Most were more than willing to put their emerging skills to the test and to connect with new friends across the world.

Global Connections through Nonprofit Organizations

Other teachers connect with formal organizations that facilitate global connections. Ontario teachers Mali Bickley and Jim Carleton discovered iEARN and now coordinate its Canadian branch (www.iearn-canada.org). Ongoing projects involving Canadian students include Learning Circles, My Hero Learning, the Teddy Bear Project, and the Public Art Project. There is an international conference each year.

Mali starts with the Ministry curriculum when she chooses her projects. Most of the projects are cross-curricular and have a social justice focus. Mali's students have engaged in a variety of projects, such as helping child soldiers in Sierra Leone, learning how to make solar cookers with students in the United States, creating a book for children in Afghanistan, testing local water quality and reporting the results on their blog, and interviewing an astronaut from NASA.

In her classroom, Mali has three computers, four video cameras, a Smartboard, and a data projector. The students collaborate in groups and share the technology. She believes it is not the type or number of tools that matters; it is about the students using the technology to learn how to think, create, and communicate. For her, the students are engaged and learn more because the work is relevant and they have choices in how they will demonstrate their learning. We see Mali as a pioneer in her district as she continues to focus on creating a caring and responsive learning environment that promotes critical thinking, technological literacy, and global responsibility.

Teaching Students to Be

Teachers want to be caring people who connect with their students. In fact, when we talked to teachers about the KDB, they often commented that the Be is the most important thing for them as teachers. The titles of recent books indicate the importance of the Be: *Teach Your Children Well: Why Values and Coping Skills Matter More than Grades, Trophies or "Fat Envelopes"* (Levine, 2012); *Resilience: The Science of Mastering Life's Greatest Challenges* (Southwick & Charney, 2012). Author and classroom educator Kevin Washburn (2010) recommends that we explicitly teach students how effort empowers learning. Stories about people struggling through to eventual success need to be intentionally and frequently showcased (Washburn, 2012). Every subject area has struggle-and-success stories: Timothy Eaton, Emily Stowe, Thomas Edison, Harriet Tubman, James Bartleman, Terry Fox. We can do this in our AfL feedback by using the Carol Dweck's concept of a growth mindset discussed in Chapter 1.

Educators have embraced psychologist Paul Tough's vision of educational reform that de-emphasizes testing and academic achievement. Rather, students need to be taught non-cognitive skills such as persistence, grit, curiosity, self-control, delayed gratification, and conscientiousness if we want to make a difference in their lives. Tough describes research that followed children from early childhood education to college in *How Kids Succeed: Grit, Curiosity and the Hidden Power of Character* (2012). The brain development of students experiencing adversity is actually altered, and adversity can be experienced at any socioeconomic level. His conclusions were that it was not intelligence that determined how well students did in school, but resilience and other strong positive character traits. Students who had had character education and coping skills intervention courses in the early childhood years were the ones who succeeded in college against all odds. For Tough, what was important was that resilience could be taught.

From another perspective, faculties of education are responding to the need for attention to the Be. At Cape Breton University, Catherine O'Brien has developed a course cross-listed in education and communication on sustainable happiness. Sustainable happiness "contributes to individual, community and/or global well-being and does not exploit other people, the environment, or future generations" (www.sustainablehappiness.ca). The Big Ideas in this course revolve around concepts of sustainability (well-being for self, others, and the planet), accountability (wealth consumption, choices), and genuine happiness (intentionality, giving back, appreciation). Students study academic concepts and engage in happiness inquiries by interviewing people (O'Brien, 2011). An online version of this course integrates sustainable happiness with the FosterHicks model (http://fosterhicks.com) and is available for the general public at a low cost (www.sustainablehappinesscourse.com).

Teaching for Social Justice: Being the Change

One way that teachers demonstrate their own passion and ignite passion in their students is by teaching for social justice. Such teaching is also about character education and change. "Be the change you want to see in the world" is the mantra in many classrooms—a saying attributed to Mahatma Gandhi.

For many teachers the commitment to social justice is about transformation through action and making a difference—not just critical literacy. They connect with influential Brazilian educator Paulo Freire, who you first met in Chapter 1. This call to action has been effectively taken up by the Me to We activist campaign (www.metowe.com). Founded by Marc and Craig Kielburger, this well-organized global business/charity works with Free The Children (an international charity) to empower and enable youth to be agents of change. Schools get involved by fundraising to build a school, taking class trips to locations such as Ecuador, Ghana, or India, and establishing activist groups involved with local and global issues.

Tracy Dinsmore is an Ontario Grade 5 French Immersion teacher. She teaches the Big Idea of human rights as part of the social studies curriculum. Through research about the rights and freedoms of children around the world, her students became aware of injustices and wanted to share their learning with others. Using their oral language skills, Tracy's students presented—in French—to other junior grade students. The group also joined in the Me to We Vow of Silence to raise awareness about those children who do not have a voice to speak for themselves. Typically, the students take part in a school fundraiser each year with prizes or small toys awarded to students according to the amount of money raised. This year, students decided they wanted to present an alternate plan to the school community council. The students proposed that they not take the prizes and instead ask for a dollar donation from the school community council for each magazine sold. The proposal was accepted and the money raised was donated to building a school in the Republic of Sierra Leone, West Africa. Each child who raised money had his or her name printed on a paper brick. A wall of the paper bricks was built at the students' Ontario school to symbolize their project. The small class of 19 students raised $600 in the first year. The students said at the end of the unit that they learned about needs versus wants and how to make a change in the world.

Snapshot of Social Justice in a Classroom

Saskatchewan teacher Shelley Wright tells the following inspirational story:

Our Schools for Schools campaign was conceived and driven entirely by the initiative of students. There were three or four adults on the margins helping when necessary. The goal was to raise $20,000 for the campaign. I have seen my students do amazing things. They've worked hard. Stretched. Gone far beyond their comfort zones. Last week we held a barbecue at the school to raise money. The students cooked, took orders, and dealt with the money. Unfortunately, it was also minus 20 degrees Celsius. Out of two barbecues, they had half a barbecue that worked. But in the end, we cooked almost 200 hamburgers and hot dogs. It took two-and-a-half hours.

Next, we held a dinner and auction. I expected that one of our more outgoing students would canvass local businesses for donations. Instead, one of the quietest and shyest male students in our class volunteered. He went to almost 50 businesses, and found a beautiful array of donations. Amazing.

CHAB, a local radio station and one of our biggest supporters, began asking people to donate as we had raised a little over $15,000 dollars and we were short of our goal. People went online to donate or came into the school. By 9:30, we were at $19,000.

Meanwhile, some of my students were watching a live stream of the wrap-up celebration in San Diego of the charity Invisible Children. The students and one of our teachers communicated with the people in San Diego through Facebook. A call went out, via the live stream, to donate to our school so that we could reach our goal. These were people we had never met. I wonder how many of them had heard of Moose Jaw, population 35,000. More people began to donate. And as the total went higher, the people in San Diego chanted, "Moose Jaw! Moose Jaw!" When we finally hit $20,000, the crowd in San Diego went wild. They burst into "O Canada." Our final total: $22,824. Wow.

TEACHER AS CHANGE AGENT/TEACHER AS ACTIVATOR

For Michael Fullan (2013), who has researched educational change for decades, it is not enough to adopt the new pedagogy and use technology to accelerate learning. The twenty-first–century teacher has to be an agent of positive change. "The new pedagogy involves helping students find purpose, passion, and experimental doing in a domain that stokes their desire to learn and keep on learning" (Fullan, 2013, p. 24).

For John Hattie, passionate and inspired teaching isn't just about being passionate about one's subject matter, it is a characteristic of being an expert rather than an average teacher. For Hattie (2012), the teacher as change agent is a "teacher as activator," and it is the major role for educators. In his meta-studies he found that a teacher as facilitator is not as effective as a teacher as activist. The teacher as facilitator facilitates problem-based learning or discovery learning but does not provide scaffolding for learning (see Helen Pereira-Raso's story earlier in this chapter). Expert teachers have a deep understanding of their subject, facilitate both surface and deep learning outcomes, give constructive feedback while monitoring learning, recognize and attend to the Be (e.g., through motivation and self-efficacy), and constantly evaluate the impact of their actions on student learning.

Teachers as Activators

Teachers are initiating innovative ways of learning that go beyond the classroom walls. Angie Harrison from Chapter 4 is a teacher as activator. She wanted her students to know more about classrooms around the world. Her primary students created an iBook of what was outside their own window, converting digital photos of sites like the pond in the schoolyard into PDFs and a QuickTime movie. She invited other teachers to join her. A class in Alaska showed them volcanoes in their schoolyard, which amazed the Ontario students. Other classrooms in North America took up Harrison's invitation and created similar books. Classroom walls came down as students saw what was real in other contexts. There is a now an entire website dedicated to the "We Can See" project (http://wecanseeprojectsharingspace.blogspot.ca).

The Global Read Aloud (www.globalreadaloud.com) is a popular program created by an American teacher as activator, Pernille Ripp. Any teacher can join. Aviva Dunsiger and Denise Krebs from Chapter 4 both participate. Students around the world read the same book, connecting by Twitter, email, or Skype. Two books that have been read, for example, are *Tall Flat Stanley* and *Charlotte's Web*.

British Columbia teacher Sarah Johnson's class and three other intermediate classes in her school were working with the inquiry question "How can we use technology to enhance students' reading skills?" (Johnson, 2012). They decided to participate in the Global Read Aloud. The October 2012 Global Read Aloud featured *The One and Only Ivan* by Katherine Applegate. Johnson's students participated in in-depth meaningful discussions of events, themes, and characters and made connections to the text, themselves, and the world. First they studied the book in their own classroom. They posted their questions on Kidsblog, a safe site for students to blog (http://kidblog.org/home); they were motivated by the sight of other students' questions from around the world. Applegate spoke about the process of writing the book and addressed the questions of many of the students; her talk can be seen in a video available on YouTube (www.youtube.com/watch?v=OqbyWN4f4OM). In addition, students were motivated by speaking to the author and were much more enthusiastic about reading. Teachers also liked the program because it fulfills curriculum requirements at the same time as it helps students care about something bigger than themselves by seeing and connecting with children in other countries.

Making Professional Learning Public

Most of the teachers in this book are very aware of Hattie's "know thy impact" on student learning. They are intrinsically motivated to reach even the most difficult student. They do this by creating irresistibly engaging instructional activities with embedded assessments. They make their expectations transparent to students in a variety of ways. They are conscious of the impact of their ongoing feedback. And they are constantly seeking new ways to engage their students.

One of the ways that they make their practice transparent is by writing ongoing blogs that describe their thoughts about teaching in detail and also show the students' work—both ongoing and final products—through YouTube, video, or still photographs. For them, students, parents, and teachers are partners in learning. They invite feedback from whoever reads their blogs. When they get feedback from other teachers, it is authentic peer feedback (Davidson, 2011).

These twenty-first–century teachers understand Jeff Whipple of New Brunswick's concern that both students and teachers need to create a personal digital brand. They model what students most need to know as twenty-first–century learners. They use social media responsibly and show students how to manage their own digital footprints so that they do not send the wrong message about themselves.

Snapshot of a Twenty-First–Century School

How does an administrator as activist lead a twenty-first–century school? Ontario principal Brian Harrison's school reflects the twenty-first–century philosophy—one that is guided first by what is good for the students. As a twenty-first–century leader, he makes his practice transparent in his blog (http://brian-harrison.net). He posts ongoing school events that demonstrate the "3-I" school improvement plan of *inclusion, inquiry,* and *innovation:*

- *I* for *inclusion*: Staff, students, and parents recognize and value diversity.
- *I* for *inquiry*: Powerful questions are at the root of teacher and student learning and a move toward deep learning. Teachers work in teams of four to eight to develop and refine questions about their own teaching and learning. With a whole-school focus, for example, teachers are asking, "What do I need to know to teach math in the twenty-first century?" "What are ways that students learn?" "How can we use iPads as teaching and learning tools?" Harrison (2012a, 2012b) blogs about, for example, the school's journey, "mathematizing" rather than memorizing, and celebrating a teacher's successful problem-solving unit that used student-led analysis of proofs.
- *I* for *innovation*: The school's focus is integrating technology into curriculum and assessment. For example, AfL is enhanced when a video captures a student presentation or a still of student work on an iPhone; these snapshots provide immediate feedback to both students and parents. The school is also exploring new learning management systems such as Edmodo and Moodle.

Twenty-first century teachers' blogs are worth following (you can get one regularly through an RSS feed). You can find the blogs by educators in this book by googling their names or looking for them on Twitter. Follow, for example, Shelley Wright, Heidi Siwak, Bill Belsey, Kathy Cassidy, Angie Harrison, Aviva Dunsiger, David Truss, Brian Harrison, or Neil Stephenson.

Pathways to Change

In this era of rapid change, change will come from the margins (Horn, 2013). Indeed we will learn from those who already have twenty-first–century practices that are both engaging and accountable (Fullan, 2013). Like the students who need to see models of people moving from struggle to success, we too need models of teachers who stepped outside the mainstream and succeeded. We can learn from big picture thinkers like Ron Canuel from the Canadian Education Association and the pan-Canadian studies on student engagement and teachers trying to be the way they aspire to be. We can learn from the focused picture of the individual teachers in this book who have resolved their living contradictions enough to move forward to unknown and exciting territory. Regardless of the struggles these educators will encounter in the future, they will risk navigating the tensions of uncertainty because implementing the new story fits their values and beliefs.

My Story?

As we close this book it is time to look at My Story—My Action. For without commitment to action the new story can never be fully realized. Perhaps you are feeling a bit overwhelmed by all there is to learn ahead. Perhaps you have living contradictions to resolve. The way forward is one step at a time.

Regardless of your feelings about twenty-first–century learning, there is still an important place for you in the classroom. Award-winning innovative Ontario teacher Heidi Siwak is a twenty-first–century teacher who is widely recognized for developing new models of learning. Her students, for example, designed apps for the iPhone and hosted the first student-led global Twitter chat on the novel *Hana's Suitcase* (www.hanassuitcase.ca). Siwak reminds us that our students may no longer need us to teach content, but they do need us to do the following:

- Teach thinking, critical literacy, and media literacy
- Ensure a strong foundation in math, science, and technology
- Help them recognize the impact and consequences of their decisions, articulate ideas to be participants in a global conversation, use modern forms of communication, and develop strategies for learning
- Ask probing questions
- Provide opportunities to explore ideas through the arts
- Provide opportunities to collaborate
- Provide real-world opportunities to make meaningful contributions to society
- Connect with parents of struggling students

Siwak jokes that teachers are still needed to collect money for field trips and pizza days, but her list clearly shows a broad and deep need for the human teacher in the digital age (Siwak, 2011).

MY STORY—MY ACTION

We take to heart Hattie's advice "know thy impact." As educators, we need to do this by seeing the learning through the eyes of the students. We end this book by offering learning goals as described in Chapter 3. The success criteria for these goals are identified throughout the previous pages of this book.

- I am learning through the eyes of my students.
- I know my impact on students.
- I provide a safe and caring environment.
- I plan using backward design.
- I use integrative thinking—seeing both the big picture and the focused picture.
- I interweave and align curriculum, instruction, and assessment.
- I use the introductory material of curriculum documents to guide me.

- I plan with outcomes.
- I teach to Big Ideas and twenty-first–century skills.
- I teach the whole person.
- I teach for both surface and deep learning.
- I make learning interesting.
- I embed technology into curriculum to enrich sound pedagogy.
- I make learning expectations transparent.
- I use learning goals and success criteria.
- I create RPATs that are engaging.
- I co-create assessment tools/tasks (even curriculum) with students.
- I only assess what has been taught.
- I ask of students "Where are you going? How will you get there? What are the next steps?"
- I have high expectations for all.
- I use student feedback to adjust my teaching to fit student needs.
- I know when and how to differentiate/personalize the curriculum.
- I use variety in my instruction/assessment tasks.
- I help students realize that personal effort is the key to success.
- I welcome mistakes/errors and see them as opportunities.
- I teach to develop grit and resilience.
- I show my passion for my teaching and learning.
- I am a positive change agent.
- I collaborate with my peers.
- I take risks and am excited to learn,
- I am a twenty-first–century teacher.

Conclusion—Both/And

The old story in education is undergoing transformation. The future is impossible to predict other than that change will probably continue at an ever-increasing pace. How can we best manage the changes? How can we be the best teachers we aspire to be? How can we resolve our living contradictions?

The title of a blog perhaps says it best: *Tailoring the classroom of the future with the fabric of the past* (Walsh, 2012). In this guest post, high school chemistry teacher and apps creator Matt Myers writes about his practice. How do we keep students engaged in learning? For Myers, the answer is simple: Teachers keep students engaged the same way they did before technology. Myers recommends we "make schoolwork as addicting as Facebook, Twitter and YouTube" while engaging in sound pedagogy.

We hope that this book has provided you with many ways to make learning addictive for you and your students. We know that the new story is inevitable. You have just met many teachers who are making the new story a reality by taking risks and trying new ideas at the same time as they apply the basics of good teaching and learning. Interweaving curriculum, instruction, and assessment is the path that they have followed, and it is a path that will allow you to tailor the classroom of your future with the best of the past.

Professional Learning Questions

1) What is your personal response to the cultural and global story? Do elements of the stories provoke living contradictions for you? Are there ways that you can resolve the gap between what you value and how you may be expected to practise?

2) Follow the blog of a Canadian educator. Analyze how well the educator fits into Fullan's three-pronged twenty-first–century framework of creating a technology-rich classroom, implementing a new pedagogy, and being a change agent? (We have suggested a few possibilities in this chapter and elsewhere.)

3) Look at the learning goals we have provided as a conclusion to this chapter. Which ones resonate with you? Which ones surprise you? Which ones do you resist? Why?

4) What are the success criteria for these learning goals?

Glossary

analytic philosophy A philosophy that focuses on logically precise language to describe phenomena. Mandated curriculum outcomes reflect this idea.

analytic rubric A rubric that describes characteristics of performance at various levels for specific aspects of the assessment task. A grade/score/level is given for each criterion.

assessment Assessment is considered classroom-based and includes diagnostic and formative feedback during the instructional period to improve learning.

assessment as learning (AaL) Strategies and tasks that support student metacognition. By involving students in the assessment process, students learn to self-assess. They monitor their own learning by setting targets and planning, implementing, and adjusting their learning strategies.

assessment criteria The characteristics of performance against which a student's work will be judged.

assessment for learning (AfL) An ongoing process of gathering and interpreting evidence of student learning for the purpose of determining where students are in their learning, where they need to go, and how best to get there. The information gathered is used by teachers to provide feedback and adjust instruction and by students to focus their learning. Assessment for learning is a high-yield instructional strategy that takes place while the student is still learning and serves to promote learning. (Ontario Ministry of Education, 2010b, p. 143)

assessment of learning (AoL) The process of collecting and interpreting evidence for the purpose of summarizing learning at a given point in time, to make judgments about the quality of student learning on the basis of established criteria, and to assign a value to represent that quality. It occurs at or near the end of a cycle of learning. (Ontario Ministry of Education, 2010b, p. 143)

assessment task An activity that the student does to demonstrate his or her learning. The task usually occurs at the end of a learning period. Common forms include an exam or a culminating project. In AfL assessment, tasks are seamlessly embedded in instructional strategies.

assessment tool The mechanism by which information about performance is captured and communicated. Common forms include a rubric, a checklist, or a scoring guide.

authentic assessment Authentic assessment occurs when the assessment task presents a real-world challenge and when students construct their own responses rather than choosing from provided options. For example, an authentic assessment task in a history course would require students to act like real historians; they would have to identify a question, formulate a tentative hypothesis, conduct research, evaluate sources of information, and come to their own conclusions. Some performance tasks and demonstrations can be considered authentic either because the task is oriented to the real world or because the assessor is not the teacher but rather a real-world expert.

backward design process Backward design is a curriculum design process that is based on three sequential steps:
1) The designer identifies the learning goals. These are the curriculum standards/outcomes/expectations.
2) The designer determines what will be the evidence that the goals have been accomplished. This is the assessment task—what the student does to demonstrate learning.
3) The designer plans the instructional activities that students need to acquire the knowledge and skills to be successful on the assessment task.

bell curve A graphic representation of distribution that shows the majority clustered around the median and gradually fewer and fewer at the two margins. In education assessment, the bell curve would show that while a few students are very unsuccessful and a few students are very successful, most are clustered around the middle. Bell curve grading can determine the distribution of grades in advance by establishing the number of students who will receive a grade for each interval (e.g., only 10% of the class can get an A, 20% can get a B, and so on). This is in contrast to the J curve.

Big Idea   A Big Idea is a concept made up of one or two words. Big Ideas are broad-based, abstract, and do not change over time (Erickson, 2005).

Bloom's revised taxonomy   Several revisions of Bloom's taxonomy exist. One rejects the hierarchy and describes the thinking skills as operating as a holistic interdependent system. Another retains the hierarchical structure of the three lower-thinking levels but places the upper three on an equal plane. Lorin Anderson proposed a revised framework in the 1990s to address a twenty-first–century context. The revised model places "creating" at the top level.

Bloom's taxonomy   First proposed in 1965 by a committee of educators under Benjamin Bloom's leadership, the taxonomy was a framework of learning objectives in six classifications: Knowledge, Comprehension, Application, Analysis, Synthesis, and Evaluation. Each category was associated with particular verbs that describe what students do. For example, Knowledge is associated with the verbs state, list, or name, while Evaluation is associated with verbs such as judge or defend. Interpretations of the taxonomy have tended to rank the categories into levels with Knowledge at the lowest and Evaluation at the highest order of thinking. This hierarchy, as well as the notion of categorization itself, have been critiqued and revised.

both/and approach   A both/and approach is an alternative to either/or thinking. Both/and incorporates elements of two seemingly contradictory ideas. For example, a both/and approach would say that students construct meaning for themselves based on their experiences, and they also benefit from direct instruction from experts.

competencies   Some jurisdictions call the knowledge and skills that students are expected to learn *competencies*. Similar terms are *expectations* and *outcomes*. It is also used in descriptions of twenty-first–century education to describe skills or ways of being. *Fluency* touches on a similar idea. Competencies can include collaboration, critical thinking, and communication.

concept attainment model   Students develop conceptual understanding by figuring out the characteristics of a group or category. The students compare examples, deciding which do and which do not contain the characteristics. The process clarifies the attributes of the concept.

constructivist approach   A theory of learning based on the idea that knowledge is constructed by an active, meaning-seeking learner. Meaning is constantly changing in light of the learner's new experiences and multiple perspectives. Knowledge is internal and uniquely constructed by the individual. By contrast, objectivism situates knowledge outside the learner.

co-operative learning   Students work together in small groups. Each group member's success depends on the success of the group as a whole. The premise is co-operative interdependence rather than competition.

critical pedagogy (theory of)   A philosophy of education that raises consciousness of the taken-for-granted assumptions about the power structures of society. Questioning these assumptions leads to an "unlearning" and "relearning" and a perspective that fosters social justice.

diagnostic assessment   Assessment that provides information about what students already know and can do, their preferred learning styles, and their general interests. The assessment happens before instruction and is considered to be one of the two planks of assessment for learning, the other being formative assessment.

differentiated instruction (DI)   An approach that modifies instruction or assessment to suit the learning needs (e.g., readiness, interest, prior knowledge, and learning preferences) of individual or small groups of students.

empirical research   Research conducted to reach a conclusion or solution based on observable evidence, often derived through experimentation.

Enduring Understandings   Generalizations, principles, or essential learnings that stay with students long after the lesson or grade is completed.

Essential Questions   Rich, complex questions with no single right answer and that require higher-order thinking to address it.

evaluation   Summative assessment conducted at the end of an instructional period to measure achieved learning.

expectations   Curriculum outcomes (sometimes called prescribed learning outcomes or standards) that are identified in curriculum documents as what is to be taught.

extrinsic motivation   Motivation that is driven by external rewards (grades, money) or punishments (loss of privileges).

factory model   A metaphoric, usually pejorative if not entirely accurate, way to describe public education as a representation of the nineteenth-century factory. The model is characterized by an emphasis on large-scale efficiency, sequential age-grade progress (assembly line) toward an end product (graduate), a top-down authority structure, and standards-based quality control (grades, testing).

fairness   With regard to assessment, fairness means that all students have an equal opportunity to succeed regardless of gender, prior knowledge, teacher bias, or any other factor unrelated to what was taught and is being assessed.

formative assessment   Assessment feedback, often informal and anecdotal, that occurs as part of instruction. Like AfL, its purpose is to support improvement during the learning period.

generic rubric   A rubric that describes the general characteristics of work at different levels of performance on an assessment task that is used more than once. Such tasks include a supported opinion essay, a lab report, or a reflective blog post.

guided discovery model   A constructivist approach to instruction. The teacher acts as a facilitator, using questions and activities rather than direct instruction to lead students toward their own new knowledge.

Hoberman sphere   A Hoberman sphere is a polyhedron structure invented by Chuck Hoberman. Opened, it resembles a globe, but thanks to the scissor-like action of its moveable joints, it can fold in on itself to a fraction of its opened size (www.youtube.com/watch?v=sZb27h-aF1g&NR=1).

holistic curriculum   A philosophy of education that seeks to address the whole person. A holistic curriculum integrates the physical, emotional, spiritual, and cognitive.

holistic rubric   Unlike an analytic rubric, a holistic rubric gives one grade/score/level based on the performance as a whole.

HOTS (higher-order thinking skills)   Cognitive skills such as analysis, evaluation, creative thinking and critical thinking. HOTS are at the higher levels of Bloom's taxonomy.

inquiry learning   A method of curriculum planning and instruction in which students investigate and resolve a problem, issue, or claim and in doing so come to new learning. This is similar to problem-based learning.

integrative thinking   A term coined by Roger Martin, meaning the ability to constructively face the tensions of opposing models, and instead of choosing one at the expense of the other, generate a creative solution of the tensions in the form of a new model that contains elements of the individual models but is superior to each. http://rogerlmartin.com/devotions/integrative-thinking

intrinsic motivation   Motivation that exists within the person—doing something for the pleasure that it gives you rather than for an external reward. The "rewards" include pleasure or a sense of satisfaction.

J curve   A graphic representation of a distribution that shows a dip or flat line for some but a pronounced increase for most. In education assessment, the J curve would show that while a few students are not successful, most have achieved the learning goals. This is in contrast to the bell curve.

KDB framework   The term used to express the content (Know), the skills (Do), and the learner's traits (Be) that are explicitly or implicitly expressed in curriculum documents.

learning goals   Statements that break down and express the curriculum outcomes for the learner. They are often posed as "I can" statements. For example, "I can structure an expository essay using an introduction, three supporting body paragraphs, and a conclusion."

learning styles   A theory about learning that is based on the premise that people learn best through certain modalities. A common model is to categorize learners as visual, auditory, or kinesthetic (hands on). While some applaud this approach as a way to differentiate learning effectively, others criticize it for its lack of supporting empirical evidence.

living contradiction   A term used by Jack Whitehead (2012) to describe the tensions that teachers hold when their practice does not align with their values. For example, a teacher may believe in constructivist teaching but primarily teaches and gives tests to evaluate the learning. Ideally a teacher can close the gap between their values and their practice.

mastery learning   Learning is broken down into small, incremental, sequentially ordered units. Students must demonstrate competence in one unit before moving on to the next. Curriculum planning requires well-defined learning objectives. Valid assessment must be focused on the objectives of that unit. Instructional methods vary widely, ranging from teacher-led direct instruction to self-paced, individualized computer delivery.

moderated marking   A process to develop a common understanding and application of assessment criteria and standards within a division, across classes, and across schools. Teachers examine student work together and share assessment decisions against a common set of criteria.

motivation   Goal-directed behaviour or a drive to do something.

multiple intelligences   a theory of intelligence based on the work of Howard Gardner. The theory proposes that there are domains of human intelligence. Education has used Gardner's framework as a way to differentiate instruction by appealing to students' strengths.

outcome   Curriculum outcomes (sometimes called prescribed learning outcomes, expectations, competencies, or standards) that are identified in curriculum documents as what is to be taught.

passion-based learning   An approach to instruction that is driven by student interest and commitment. Thus, curriculum becomes personalized and relevant.

performance task   An assessment task in which students demonstrate their learning by doing something such as creating a website, role-playing an interview with a historical figure, or writing an essay.

personal learning network (PLN)   An informal (so far) way in which people connect to share ideas about a common topic of interest. Often PLNs are developed online through social media. Membership is flexible and dynamic; learners do not have to know each other personally and often never meet face to face. Nevertheless, affiliations can be strong and highly emotional.

prescribed learning outcomes   Curriculum outcomes (sometimes called expectations or standards) that are identified in curriculum documents as what is to be taught.

problem-based learning   Problem-based learning begins with a real-world problem that is usually open ended and ambiguous (i.e., there is more than one solution). Students need to gain the content knowledge to address the problem. As its focus, the problem may have a dilemma to be confronted, a decision to be made, an issue to be resolved, a policy to be debated, or a new product or service to be developed.

professional learning communities (PLC)   Associated with Richard Dufour, a PLC is a formalized, usually school-based collaboration of educators who meet to participate in activities and reflection intended to improve practices, improve their students' learning, and improve their schools.

progressive education   The term "progressive" has been used since the early twentieth century to distinguish itself from the rote learning associated with "traditional" forms of education. Characteristics of progressive education include experiential learning, collaborative projects and performance tasks, and integrated curriculum, among others.

project-based learning   Learning that begins with the students' own interests and questions. Learning activities are long term, interdisciplinary, and student-centred and are integrated with real-world issues and practices. Students are involved in making decisions about how they will find answers and solve problems. (Alberta Ministry of Education, 2004)

reflective practitioner   This term is associated with philosopher and education theorist Donald Schön (1930–1997) whose work explored the thinking processes of professionals as they work. Schön proposed that a combination of reflection-in-action (thinking on one's feet) and reflection-on-action (retrospective review of actions and situations) allows the practitioner to make sense of his or her practice. This deeper understanding informs action.

reliability   The degree of consistency of the assessment results. A reliable assessment produces consistent results no matter when or where it occurs or who scores it.

rich performance assessment task (RPAT) Tasks are rich when they require students to apply deep knowledge and complex skills to an activity, demonstration, problem, or challenge. A task is described as "a performance" when it requires students to *show* what they know and can do.

rubric A rubric describes the characteristics of work at different levels of performance. The descriptions can be holistic or broken out into particular components or aspects (analytic).

scientific method According to the scientific method, acquiring knowledge is based on systematic, empirical inquiry (experimentation to confirm or refute a hypothesis). Conclusions are supported by rational, measureable evidence.

social reconstruction A view of education that seeks to redress socioeconomic and political inequities by raising consciousness about them. In twenty-first–century education, this awareness takes both a local and global perspective and fosters the recognition of the rights and responsibilities of citizenship.

standards As an element of curriculum design, *standards* is another term for learning outcomes or expectations. These are what provincial curriculum documents articulate as the things students must learn. *Standards* in assessment refers to the levels of proficiency of student work. For example, Level 3 of an achievement chart in Ontario is considered the provincial standard of acceptable achievement.

success criteria Descriptors that explicitly outline the "look fors" to achieve the learning goal. The success criteria are written in student-friendly language and make learning and successful achievement transparent and attainable. Teachers co-construct success criteria with students to promote student ownership of the learning.

task-specific rubric Unlike a generic rubric, a task-specific rubric describes the particular characteristics of work at different levels of performance on an assessment task that is used only once. Often a task-specific rubric is a customized version of a generic rubric.

teaching precision through reading and storytelling (TPRS) Just as young children acquire their first language, the TPRS method of teaching a second language immerses students in listening then speaking; reading and writing are taught after, which arise from an oral base. Storytelling and active role-playing are prominent features.

traditional approach A term used to describe education based on the so-called factory model. The traditional model is characterized by transmission of knowledge by teachers to passive students, limited social interaction, standardized testing and grading, large group age-grade settings, and sequential promotion. The traditional model is often described in contrast to the progressive model.

triarchic intelligences A theory of intelligence based on the work of Robert Sternberg (1988, 1997). Students all have three intelligences—analytic, practical, and creative—and use them to different degrees.

twenty-first–century skills Various frameworks define the skills (sometimes called competencies) considered necessary for life in the twenty-first century. These skills include complex interdisciplinary skills such as communication, higher-order thinking skills, design and construction (creativity), as well as disciplinary literacies and new literacies (e.g., technological literacy).

unifying framework A model or an organizational structure that shows the convergent relationship among components. Provinces have developed unifying frameworks to convey their overarching philosophical visions for education.

validity The degree to which an interpretation or conclusion based on assessment data is appropriate and meaningful. For example, a multiple-choice test on the rules of the road may be a valid assessment of a person's knowledge, but would not be a valid assessment of his or her actual driving skills.

References

Action Canada. (2013). *Future tense: Adapting Canadian education systems for the 21st Century*. Retrieved from www.actioncanada.ca/en/wp-content/uploads/2013/02/TF2-Report_Future-Tense_EN.pdf

Adams, C. (2013, February 27). Character education seen as student achievement tool. *Eduweek.org*. Retrieved from www.edweek.org/ew/articles/2013/02/27/22character.h32.html?r=1927265351

Aikin, W. (1942). *The story of the eight-year study*. New York, NY: Harper.

Airasian, P., Engemann, J., & Gallagher, T. (2012). *Classroom assessment: Concepts and applications*. Toronto, ON: McGraw-Hill Ryerson.

Alberta Ministry of Education. (2004). *Focus on inquiry: A teacher's guide to implementing inquiry-based learning*. Edmonton, AB: Alberta Learning: Learning and Teaching Resources. Retrieved from http://education.alberta.ca/media/313361/focusoninquiry.pdf

Alberta Ministry of Education. (2007). *Primary programs framework for teaching and learning: Kindergarten to Grade 3*. Retrieved from http://education.alberta.ca/teachers/program/ecs/ppp.aspx

Alberta Ministry of Education. (2010). *Inspiring action on education*. Retrieved from http://ideas.education.alberta.ca/media/2905/inspiringaction%20eng.pdf

Amnesty International. (2012). *Becoming a human rights friendly school: a guide for schools around the world*. Retrieved from http://amnesty.org/en/library/info/POL32/001/2012/en

Anderson, L., Airasian, P., Cruikshank, K., Krathwohl, D., Mayer, R., & Wittrock, M. C. (2001). *A taxonomy for learning, teaching and assessing: A revision of Bloom's taxonomy of educational objectives*. Boston, MA: Allyn and Bacon. Pearson Education.

Andrade, H. (2007/2008). Self-assessment through rubrics. *Educational Leadership, 65*(4), 60–63.

Armbruster, B., & Ostertag, J. (1989). Questions in elementary science and social studies textbooks. *Center for the Study of Reading Technical Report No. 463*. Retrieved from www.ideals.illinois.edu/bitstream/handle/2142/17741/ctrstreadtechrepv01989i00463_opt.pdf

Ash, K. (2013, March 11). Digital learning priorities influence school building designs. *Education Week*. Retrieved from www.edweek.org/ew/articles/2013/03/14/25newlook.h32.html?tkn=NOLFcJLiUbXysT%-2F0HobTHOF1Yhv3Pw%2BvXm-5X&cmp=ENL-DD-NEWS1

Assembly of First Nations. (2010). *Transforming the relationship: Sustainable fiscal transfers for First Nations*. Retrieved from www.afn.ca/misc/PBS-2010.pdf

Assessment Reform Group. (2002). *Assessment for learning: 10 principles. Researched-based principles to guide classroom practice*. Retrieved from http://assessmentreformgroup.files.wordpress.com/2012/01/10principles_english.pdf

Atlantic Provinces Education Foundation. (2001). *Atlantic Canada framework for essential graduation learnings in schools*. Retrieved from www.ednet.ns.ca/files/reports/essential_grad_learnings.pdf

Auditor General of Canada. (2011). Chapter four: Programs for First Nations on reserves. *June Status Report of the Auditor General of Canada*. Retrieved from www.oag-bvg.gc.ca/internet/English/parl_oag_201106_04_e_35372.html

Bain, K. (2012). *What the best college students do*. Cambridge, MA: Harvard University Press.

Barbar, M., Donnelly, K., & Rizvi, S. (2012). *Oceans of innovation.* London, UK: Institute for Public Policy Research (IPRR). Retrieved from www.ippr.org/publication/55/9543/oceans-of-innovation-the-atlantic-the-pacific-global-leadership-and-the-future-of-education

Barlow, R. (2012, November). Addressing Canada's declining youth STEM engagement: An urgent and important change. Retrieved from http://doc.mediaplanet.com/all_projects/11379.pdf

Beane, J. (1993). *A middle school curriculum: From rhetoric to reality* (2nd ed.). Columbus, OH: National Middle School Association.

Beane, J. (1997). *Curriculum integration: Designing the core of democratic education*. New York, NY: Teachers College Press.

Bereiter, C. (2002). *Education and mind in the knowledge age*. Hillsdale, NJ: Lawrence Earlbaum & Associates.

Berkowitz, M. W., & Bier, M. C. (2004). Research-based character education. *Annals of the American Academy of Political and Social Science, 591*, 72–85.

Black, P., Harrison, C., Lee, C., Marshall, B., & Wiliam, D. (2003). *Assessment for learning: putting it into practice*. New York, NY: Open University Press.

Black, P., & Wiliam, D. (1998). Inside the black box: Raising standards through classroom assessment. *Phi Delta Kappan, 80*(2), 139–148.

Black, P. & Wiliam, D. (2004). The formative purpose: Assessment must first promote learning. *Yearbook of the National Society for the Study of Education, 103*(2), 20–50.

Bloom, B. (1956). *Taxonomy of educational objectives: The classification of educational goals. Handbook 1: Cognitive domain*. New York, NY: David McKay Co. Inc.

Boss, S. (2013, April 4). Shoe design offers a Trojan horse for problem solving with design thinking. *Edutopia.* Retrieved from www.edutopia.org/blog/design-thinking-opportunity-problem-solving-suzie-boss

Bransford, J., Brown, A., & Cocking, R. (2000). *How people learn: Brain, mind, experience, and school.* Committee on Learning Research in the Science of Learning, National Research Council. Washington, DC: National Academy Press. Retrieved from www.nap.edu/openbook.php?record_id=9853&page=R1

British Columbia Ministry of Education. (2008). *Making spaces: Teaching for diversity and social justice throughout the K to 12 curriculum.* Retrieved from www.bced.gov.bc.ca/irp/pdfs/making_space/mkg_spc_intr.pdf

Brookhart, S. (2004). Classroom assessment: Tensions and intersections in theory and practice. *Teachers College Record, 106*(3), 429–458.

Brookhart, S. (2011). Starting the conversation about grading. *Educational Leadership, 69*(3), 10–14.

Brookhart, S., Moss, C., & Long, B. (2008). Formative assessment that empowers. *Educational Leadership, 66*(3), 52–57.

Brown, G. (2011). Self-regulation of assessment beliefs and attitudes: A review of the students' conceptions of assessment inventory. *Educational Psychology, 31*(6), 731–748.

Buck Institute for Education. (2009). Does PBL work? *Project-Based Learning for the 21st Century.* Retrieved from www.bie.org/research/study/does_pbl_work

C21 Canada. (2012). *Shifting minds: A 21st century vision of public education for Canada.* Retrieved from www.c21canada.org/wp-content/uploads/2012/10/Summit-design-English-version-Sept.-26.pdf

Canadian Education Association. (2012, July). *Teaching the way we aspire to teach: Now and in the future.* Toronto, ON: Author. Retrieved from www.cea-ace.ca/sites/cea-ace.ca/files/cea-2012-aspirations.pdf

Cassidy, K. (2013a, March 24). Whose conference is it anyhow? *Primary preoccupation* [Web log message]. Retrieved from http://kathycassidy.com/2013/03/24/whose-conference-is-it-anyhow

Cassidy, K. (2013b). *Connected from the start: Global learning in primary grades.* Available at http://plpnetwork.com/connectedkids.

Catterall, J., Dumais, S., & Hamden-Thompson, G. (2012). *The arts and achievement in at-risk youth: Findings from four longitudinal studies, Research Report 55.* Retrieved from www.nea.gov/research/arts-at-risk-youth.pdf

Charlton, B. (2005). *Informal assessment strategies.* Markham, ON: Pembroke.

Clandinin, D., & Connelly, F. (1992). Teacher as curriculum maker. In P. W. Jackson (Ed.), *Handbook of research on curriculum* (pp. 363–401). New York, NY: Macmillan.

Clarke, K. (2013, Spring). Assessment intelligence: Student engagement in their growth. *The Trillium: Ontario ASCD,* 1–2.

Clausen, K., & Drake, S. (2010). Interdisciplinary practices in Ontario: Past, present and future. *Issues in Integrative Studies, 28,* 69–108.

Collins, S. (2008). *The hunger games.* New York, NY: Scholastic Inc.

Cookson, P. (2009). What would Socrates say? Teaching for the 21st century. *Educational Leadership. 67*(1), 8–14.

Cooper, D. (2006). *Talk about assessment: Strategies and tools to improve teaching and learning.* Toronto, ON: Thomson Nelson.

Cooper, D. (2010). *Talk about assessment: High school strategies and tools.* Toronto, ON: Nelson Education.

Cooper, D. (2011). *Redefining fair: How to plan, assess, and grade for excellence in mixed ability classrooms.* Bloomington, IN: Solution Tree.

Costa, A., & Kallick, B. (2000). *Describing 16 habits of the mind.* Alexandria, VA: Association for Supervision and Curriculum Development.

Costello, D. (2012). Why am I teaching this? Investigating the tension

between mandated curriculum and teacher autonomy. *Canadian Journal of Action Research, 13*(2), 51–59.

Crewe, R. (2011). Passion versus purpose. In R. Elmore (Ed.), *I used to think . . . And now I think* (pp. 19–24). Cambridge MA: Harvard University Press.

Crossman, J., (2007). The role of relationships and emotions in student perceptions of learning and assessment, *Higher Education Research Development, 26*(3), 313–327.

Curry, J., Samara, J., & Connell, R. (2005). *The Curry/Samara Model*®: *Curriculum, Instruction, & Assessment.* Retrieved from www.roell.k12.il.us/GES%20Stuff/Day%205/Models%20Packet.pdf

Davidson, C. (2011). *Now you see it: How the brain science of attention will transform how you learn.* New York, NY: Viking.

Davidson, M. (2012, April). *OECD international assessment of problem-solving skills.* Presented at Educating for Innovative Societies. Paris, France. Retrieved from www.oecd.org/edu/ceri/50435683.pptx

Dean, C., Hubbell, E., Pitler, H., & Stone, B. (2012). *Classroom instruction that works* (2nd ed.). Alexandria, VA: Association for Supervision and Curriculum Development.

Della Vedova, T. (2013). Teaching and leading in a "Facebook meets face-to-face" environment. *ASCD Express, 8*(12). Retrieved from www.ascd.org/ascd-express/vol8/812-vedova.aspx

Delors, J. (1999). *Learning: The treasure within.* Report to UNESCO of the International Commission on Education for the Twenty-First Century. UNESCO Publishing. Retrieved from http://unesdoc.unesco.org/images/0010/001095/109590eo.pdf

Dewey, J. (1910). *How we think.* Boston, MA: Heath. Retrieved from: http://archive.org/stream/howwethink000838mbp#page/n9/mode/2up

Dewey, J. (1938). *Experience in education.* New York, NY: Collier Books.

Dewey, J. (1966). *Democracy and education.* New York, NY: McMillan/

Free Press. (Originally published in 1916).

DeZure, D. (1999). Interdisciplinary teaching and learning: Essays on teaching excellence. *The Professional & Organizational Development Network in Higher Education*. Retrieved from www.podnetwork.org/ publications/teachingexcellence/98-99/ V10,%20N4%20DeZure.pdf

Doidge, N. (2007). *The brain that changes itself*. London, UK: Penguin Books.

Drake, S. (1993). *Planning integrated curriculum: The call to adventure*. Alexandria, VA: Association for Supervision and Curriculum.

Drake, S. (2007). *Creating standards-based integrated curriculum*. Thousand Oaks, CA: Corwin Press.

Drake, S. (2010). Enhancing Canadian teacher education using a story framework. *The Canadian Journal for the Scholarship of Teaching and Learning, 1*(2), Article 2. doi: http://dx.doi.org/10.5206/cjsotl-rcacea.2010.2.2. Retrieved from http://ir.lib.uwo.ca/cjsotl_rcacea/ vol1/iss2/2

Drake, S. (2012). *Creating standards-based integrated curriculum: The common core edition* (3rd ed.). Thousand Oaks, CA: Corwin.

Drake, S., & Reid, J. (2010). Integrated curriculum. What Works? *Research into Practice Monograph #28*. The Literacy and Numeracy Secretariat. Toronto, ON: Queen's Printer. Retrieved from www.edu.gov.on.ca/ eng/literacynumeracy/inspire/research/WW_Integrated_Curriculum.pdf

Drake, S., Reid, J., & Beckett, D. (2011, May). *Exploring best stories of assessment experiences*. Ministry of Ontario/Faculty of Education Conference, Toronto, ON.

Dufour, R., & Marzano, R. (2011). *Leaders of learning: How districts, schools and classroom leaders improve schools*. Bloomington, ID: Solution Tree Press.

Dunsiger, A. (2012, October 13). Linking curriculum and student interests. *Living Avivaloca* [Web log message]. Retrieved from http://adunsiger.com/ 2012/10/19/linking-curriculum-and-student-interests

Durlak, J., Weissberg, R., Dymnicki, A., Taylor, R., & Schellinger, K. (2011). The impact of enhancing students' social and emotional learning: A meta-analysis of school-based universal interventions. *Child Development, 82*(1), 405–432. doi: 10.1111/j.1467-8624.01564.x

Dweck, C. (2006). *Mindset: The new psychology of success*. New York, NY: Random House.

Earl, L. (2003). *Assessment as learning*. Thousand Oaks, CA: Corwin.

Earl, L., & Katz, S. (2006). *Rethinking classroom assessment with purpose in mind: Assessment for learning, assessment as learning, assessment of learning*. Western and Northern Canadian Protocol for Collaboration in Education. Retrieved from www.wncp.ca

Earl, L., Volante, L. & Katz, S. (2011). Unleashing the promise of assessment for learning. *Education Canada, 51*(3), 17–20.

EduGAINS. (2012). Adolescent literacy: Engaging research and teaching. Retrieved from www.edugains.ca/ resourcesLIT/AdolescentLiteracy/ AL_Resources/TalkingtoLearn ALERT_8X11.pdf

EduPress. (n.d.). *Questions for the revised Bloom's taxonomy*. EduPress Inc. EP 729. Retrieved from www. edupressinc.com

Egan, K. (2010) *A brief guide to learning in depth*. The Imagination Education Research Group. Retrieved from www.sfu.ca/~egan/A%20Brief%20 Guide%20to%20LiD.pdf

Eggen, P., & Kauchak, D. (2012). *Strategies and models for teachers: Teaching content and thinking skills*. Toronto, ON: Pearson.

Emerson, R. W. (1903). *The complete works (Vol. III)*. Boston, MA: Houghton Mifflin.

Erickson, L. (1995). *Stirring the head, heart and soul*. Thousand Oaks, CA: Corwin Press.

Erickson, L. (2005). *Concept-based curriculum and instruction*. Thousand Oaks, CA: Corwin Press.

Erikson, J. (2011). How grading reform changed our school. *Educational Leadership, 69*(3), 67–70.

Estes, T. H., Mintz, S. L., & Gunter, M. A. (2011). *Instruction: A models approach* (6th ed.). Upper Saddle River, NJ: Pearson.

Expeditionary Learning. (2013). *Academic achievement*. Retrieved from http://elschools.org/our-results/ academic-achievement

Field, E., & Kozak, S. (2011). Advancing integrated programs framework. *EASO Formal ED Committee Report*. Retrieved from www.esdcanada.ca/ files/IP%20steering%20Advancing% 20Integrated%20Programs%20 Framework.pdf

Fisher, D., Frey, N., & Pumpian, I. (2011). No penalties for practice. *Educational Leadership, 69*(3), 46–51.

Fleming, N., & Mills, C. (1992). Not another inventory, rather a catalyst for reflection. *To Improve the Academy, 11*, 137.

Fogarty, R. (1991). *The mindful school: How to integrate the curricula*. Palantine, IL: Skylight.

Friesen, S., & Jardine, D. (2009). *21st Century Learning and Learners*. Retrieved from http://education.alberta .ca/media/1087278/wncp%2021st% 20cent%20learning%20(2).pdf

Fullan, M. (2013). *Stratosphere*. Toronto, ON: Pearson.

Galileo Educational Network. (2000–2013). *Discipline-based inquiry rubric*. Retrieved from www.galileo. org/research/publications/rubric. pdf

Gardner, H. (1983). *Frames of mind: The theory of multiple intelligences*. New York, NY: Basic Books.

Gipps, C. (1999). Sociocultural aspects of assessment. *Review of Research in Education, 24*, 375–392.

Goodrich, H. (1996/1997). Understanding rubrics. *Educational Leadership, 54*(4), 14–17.

Guskey, T. (2003). How classroom assessments improve learning. *Educational Leadership, 60*(5), 6–11.

Hargreaves, A., & Fullan, M. (2012). *Professional capital: Transforming teaching in every school.* Toronto, ON: Ontario Principal's Council.

Harlen, W. (2005). Teachers' summative practices and assessment for learning—tensions and synergies. *The Curriculum Journal, 16*(2), 207–223.

Harris, L. & Brown, G. (2009). The complexity of teachers' conceptions of assessment: Tensions between the needs of schools and students. *Assessment in Education: Principles, Policy & Practice, 16*(3), 365–381.

Harrison, B. (2012a, October 14). Mathematizing mathematics. *The Open Office.* [Web log message]. Retrieved from http://brian-harrison.net/2012/10/14/mathematizing-mathematics

Harrison, A. (2012b, October 23). What can you see? *Expanding teaching, exploring technology* [Web log message]. Retrieved from http://techieang.edublogs.org/2012/10

Harvey, L., (2004–2009). *Analytic quality glossary.* Quality Research International. Retrieved from www.qualityresearchinternational.com/glossary

Hattie, J. (2009). *Visible learning: A synthesis of over 800 meta-analyses relating to achievement.* New York, NY: Routledge.

Hattie, J. (2012). *Visible learning for teachers: Maximizing impact on learning.* New York, NY: Routledge.

Hattie, J., & Timperley, H. (2007). The power of feedback. *Review of Educational Research, Academic Research Library, 77*(1), 81–112.

Helm, J., Beneke, S., & Steinheimer, K. (2007). *Windows on learning: Documenting young children's work* (2nd ed.). New York, NY: Teachers College Press.

Hlebowitsh, P. (2005). *Designing the school curriculum.* Upper Saddle River, NJ: Pearson.

Horn, M. (2013). *Disrupting class: How disruptive innovation will change how the world learns.* Presentation at

OERS (Ontario Education Research Symposium).

Huxley, A. (1970). *The perennial philosophy.* New York, NY: HarperCollins Publishers.

Inglis, L. & Miller, N. (2011). Problem-based instruction: Getting at the big ideas and developing learners. *Canadian Journal of Action Research, 12*(3), 6–12.

International Baccalaureate Organization. (2009). *Primary years programme: A basis for practice.* Wales: Cardiff House.

Jacobs, H. (Ed.). (1989). *Interdisciplinary curriculum: Design and implementation.* Alexandria, VA: Association for Supervision and Curriculum.

Jacobs, H. (Ed.) (2010). *Curriculum 21: Essential education for a changing world.* Alexandria VA: Association for Supervision and Curriculum Development.

Janks, H. Dixon, K., Ferreira, A., Granville, S., & Newfield, D. (2013). *Doing critical literacy: Texts and activities for students and teachers.* London, UK: Routledge.

Johnson, L., Smith, R., Smyth, J., & Varon, R. (2009). *Challenge-based learning: An approach for our time.* Austin, TX: The New Media Consortium.

Johnson, S. (2012). Day 47: Sarah Johnson, Teacher (Cougar Canyon Elementary): The global read aloud. *180 Days of Learning!* Retrieved from https://deltalearns.ca/180daysoflearning/2012/11/14/day-47-sarah-johnson-teacher-cougar-canyon-elementary

Joint Advisory Committee. (1993). *Principles for fair student assessment practices for education in Canada.* Centre for Research in Applied Measurement and Evaluation, University of Alberta, Edmonton, AB. Retrieved from http://www2.education.ualberta.ca/educ/psych/crame/files/eng_prin.pdf

Kanoid, T. (2011). *The five disciplines of PLC leaders.* Bloomington, IN: Solution Tree Press.

Kearns, L. (2011). High-stakes standardized testing and marginalized

youth: An examination of the impact on those who fail. *Canadian Journal of Education, 34*(2), 112–130.

Kilpatrick, W. (1918). The project method. *Teachers College Record, 19,* 319–335.

King, A. (1995). Inquiring minds really do want to know: Using questioning to teach critical thinking. *Teaching of Psychology, 22*(14).

Klein, J. (1990). *Interdisciplinarity: History, theory and practice.* Detroit, MI: Wayne State University Press.

Kohlberg, L. (1981). *The philosophy of moral development.* San Francisco, CA: Harper & Row.

Krathwohl, D. (2002). Revising Bloom's taxonomy. *Theory into Practice, 41*(4), 212–218.

Krebs, D. (2011, November 2). Genius Hour. *Dare to Care.* [Web log message]. Retrieved from http://mrsdkrebs.edublogs.org/2011/11/02/genius-hour

Kuhlthau, C., Maniotes, L., & Caspari, A. (2007). *Guided inquiry: Learning in the 21st century.* Westport, CT: Greenwood Publishing Group Inc.

Leighton, J. P., Gokiert, R., Cor, M. K., & Heffernan C. (2010). Teacher beliefs about the cognitive diagnostic information of classroom- versus large-scale tests: Implications for assessment literacy. *Assessment in Education: Principles, Policy & Practice, 17*(1), 7–21

Levine, M. (2012). *Teach Your Children Well: Why Values and Coping Skills Matter More than Grades, Trophies or "Fat Envelopes.* New York, NY: HarperCollins.

Lew, J., & Hardt, M. (2011). *Controlling complexity: An introduction to question structure.* Burnaby, BC: Skillplan B.C. Construction Industry Skills Improvement Council. Retrieved from www.skillplan.ca/tools-and-publications

Literacy GAINS. (2013). Alert! Make room for students to pose and pursue questions. Retrieved from www.edugains.ca/resourcesLIT/AdolescentLiteracy/AL_Resources/QuestioningALERT_11X17.pdf

Littky, D. (2004). *The big picture*. Alexandria, VA: Association for Supervision and Curriculum Development

Locke, J. (1693). *Some thoughts concerning education*. Retrieved from http://archive.org/details/13somethoughtscon00lockuoft

MacPhail, A., & Halbert, J. (2010). 'We had to do intelligent thinking during recent PE': Students' and teachers' experiences of assessment for learning in post-primary physical education. *Assessment in Education, 17*(1), 23–39.

Maiers, A. (2011, July). Guidelines of passion-based learning [Web log message]. Retrieved from www.angelamaiers.com/2011/07/guidelines-of-passion-based-learning.html

Maiers, A., & Sanvold, A. (2010) *The passion-driven classroom: A framework for teaching and learning*. Larchmount, NY: Eye on Education.

Manitoba Ministry of Education. (2006). *Grade 7 Social Studies: People and places in the world: A foundation for implementation*. Retrieved from www.edu.gov.mb.ca/k12/cur/socstud/foundation_gr7/index.html

Manitoba Ministry of Education. (2009). *Grades 9 to 12 mathematics: Manitoba curriculum framework for outcomes*. Retrieved from www.edu.gov.mb.ca/k12/cur/math/framework_9-12

Marsh, H. & Martin, A. (2011). Academic self-concept and academic achievement: Relations and causal ordering. *British Journal of Educational Psychology, 81*, 59–77. doi: 10.1348/000709910X503501

Martellacci, R. (2012, October 2). Canadian School Boards Association endorses the "Shifting minds: A 21st century vision of public education in Canada," document. *C21 Blog: Canadians for 21st Century Learning and Innovation*. Retrieved from www.c21canada.org/2012/10/02/canadian-school-boards-association-endorses-the-shifting-minds-a-21st-century-vision-of-public-education-in-canada-document

Martin, R. (2007). *The opposable mind: How successful leaders win through integrative thinking*. Boston, MA: Harvard Business School Press.

Marzano, R., & Heflebower, T. (2011). *Teaching and assessing 21st century skills*. Bloomington, IN: Marzano Research Laboratory.

Maslow, A. (1970). *Motivation and personality*. New York, NY: Harper & Row.

McDonald, H. (2012, July 9). One genius thing we did in our class this year. *Today is a great day for learning*. [Web log message]. Retrieved from http://hughtheteacher.wordpress.com/2012/07/09/1-genius-thing-we-did-in-our-class-this-year

McKenzie, J. (2005). *Learning to question to wonder to learn*. The FNO Press Bookstore. Retrieved from http://fno.org/qwl/qwl.html

McLaren, P. (1989). *Life in schools: An introduction to critical pedagogy in the foundations of education*. New York, NY: Longman.

McMillan, J. H., Hellsten, L., & Klinger, D. (2010). *Classroom assessment principles and practice for effective standards-based instruction*. Toronto, ON: Pearson.

McMurtry, A. (2011). The complexities of interdisciplinarity: Integrating two different perspectives on interdisciplinary research and education. *Complicity: An International Journal of Complexity and Education, 8*, 19–35.

Miller, L. (2005, June). Professional learning communities: Model for collaborative teaching or the latest bandwagon? *Professionally Speaking*. Retrieved from http://professionallyspeaking.oct.ca/june_2005/plc.asp

Miller, J. (2007). *The holistic curriculum* (2nd ed.). Toronto, ON: University of Toronto Press Scholarly Publishing.

Milligan, A., & Wood, B. (2010). Conceptual understanding as transition points: Making sense in a complex world. *Journal of Curriculum Studies, 42*(4) 487–501. doi: 10.1080/00220270903494287

MISA. (2012). Assessment and evaluation: Understanding learning skills and work habits videos. Retrieved from http://misalondon.ca/ae_01.html

Mishra, P., & Koehler, M. (2006). Technological pedagogical content knowledge: A new framework for teacher knowledge. *Teachers College Record, 108*(6), 1017–1054.

Naidu, S. (2008). Enabling time, pace, and place independence. In J. M. Spector, M. D. Merrill, J. J. G. Van Merriënboer, & M. P. Driscoll (Eds.), *Handbook of research on educational communications and technology* (3rd ed.) (pp. 259–268). New York, NY: Lawrence Erlbaum Associates.

Neal, M., (2012). Appreciative assessment: inquire! *Education Canada, 52*(5). Retrieved from http://www.cea-ace.ca/education-anada/article/appreciative-assessment-inquire

Nobori, M. (2012) A step-by-step guide to the best projects. *Edutopia*. Retrieved from www.edutopia.org/stw-project-based-learning-best-practices-guide

Nolen, S. B. (2011). The role of educational systems in the link between formative assessment and motivation: Theory into practice. *The College of Education and Human Ecology, Ohio State University, 50*, 319–326. doi: 19.1080/00405841.2011.60739

O'Brien, C. (2011, November/December). Sustainable happiness for teachers and students. *Canadian Teacher Magazine*, 18–19. Retrieved from www.sustainablehappiness.ca/wp-content/uploads/2011/11/CTM-NovDec11-sustainable.pdf

O'Connor, K. (2011). *A repair kit for grading: 15 fixes for broken grades* (2nd ed.). Boston, MA: Pearson.

OECD (Organisation for Economic Co-operation and Development). (2011). *Education at a Glance 2011: OECD Indicators*. Retrieved from www.oecd.org/education/school/educationataglance2011oecdindicators.htm

Ontario Ministry of Education. (2000). *The Ontario curriculum, Grades 11 and 12: Social sciences and humanities*. Retrieved from www.edu.gov.on.ca/eng/curriculum/secondary/sstudies1112curr.pdf

Ontario Ministry of Education. (2002). *The Ontario curriculum, Grades 11 and 12: Interdisciplinary studies.* Retrieved from www.edu.gov.on.ca/eng/curriculum/secondary/interdisciplinary1112curr.pdf

Ontario Ministry of Education. (2004). *The Ontario curriculum: Social studies Grades 1–6; History and geography Grades 7 and 8.* Retrieved from www.edu.gov.on.ca/eng/curriculum/elementary/sstudies18curr.pdf

Ontario Ministry of Education. (2005a). *The Ontario curriculum, Grades 9 and 10: Canadian and world studies.* Retrieved from www.edu.gov.on.ca/eng/curriculum/secondary/canworld910curr.pdf

Ontario Ministry of Education. (2005b). *The Ontario curriculum, Grades 11 and 12: Canadian and world studies.* Retrieved from www.edu.gov.on.ca/eng/curriculum/secondary/canworld1112curr.pdf

Ontario Ministry of Education. (2007). Student self-assessment. *The Literacy and Numeracy Secretariat Capacity Building Series.* Retrieved from www.edu.gov.on.ca/eng/literacynumeracy/inspire/research/StudentSelfAssessment.pdf

Ontario Ministry of Education. (2008a) *The Ontario curriculum: Grades 9 and 10: Science.* Retrieved from www.edu.gov.on.ca/eng/curriculum/secondary/science910_2008.pdf

Ontario Ministry of Education. (2008b) *The Ontario curriculum: Grades 11 and 12: Science.* Retrieved from www.edu.gov.on.ca/eng/curriculum/secondary/2009science11_12.pdf

Ontario Ministry of Education. (2010a). *Student success differentiated instruction educator's package.* Toronto, ON: Queen's Printer for Ontario. Retrieved from www.edugains.ca/resourcesDI/EducatorsPackages/DIEducatorsPackage2010/2010EducatorsGuide.pdf

Ontario Ministry of Education. (2010b). *Growing success: Assessment, evaluation and reporting, improving student learning.* Toronto, ON: Queen's Printer for Ontario. Retrieved from www.edu.gov.on.ca/eng/policyfunding/growSuccess.pdf

Ontario Ministry of Education. (2010c). *The Ontario curriculum: The arts.* Toronto, ON: Queen's Printer of Ontario.

Ontario Ministry of Education. (2010d). *Learning goals and success criteria: Assessment for learning video series viewing guide.* Retrieved from www.edugains.ca/resourcesAER/VideoLibrary/LearningGoalsSuccessCriteria/LearningGoalsSuccessCriteriaViewingGuide2011.pdf

Ontario Ministry of Education. (2011). *Learning for all: A guide to effective assessment and instruction for all students, kindergarten to Grade 12.* Retrieved from www.edu.gov.on.ca/eng/general/elemsec/speced/learningforall2011.pdf

Ontario Ministry of Education. (2013). *The Ontario curriculum: Social Studies, Grades 1 to 6; History and Geography, Grades 7 and 8.* Retrieved from www.edu.gov.on.ca/eng/curriculum/elementary/sshg18curr2013.pdf

Piaget, J. (1963). *The origins of intelligence in children.* New York, NY: Norton.

Pink, D. (2005). *A whole new mind.* New York, NY: Penguin.

Pink, D. (2009). *Drive: The surprising truth about what motivates us.* New York, NY: Riverhead Books.

Pink, D. (2011, July 18). The Genius Hour: How 60 minutes a week can electrify your job. *Daniel H. Pink* [Web log message]. Retrieved from www.danpink.com//2011/07/the-genius-hour-how-60-minutes-a-week-can-electrify-your-job

Pope, N., Green, S., Johnson, R., & Mitchell, M. (2009). Examining teacher ethical dilemmas in classroom assessment. *Teaching and Teacher Education, 25,* 778–782.

Popham, W. (1997). What's wrong—and what's right—with rubrics. *Educational Leadership, 55*(2), 72–75.

Popham, W. J. (2008). *Classroom assessment: What teachers need to know* (5th ed.). Boston, MA: Pearson.

Prensky, M. (2001). Digital natives, digital immigrants. *On the Horizon, 9*(5) Retrieved from www.albertomattiacci.it/docs/did/Digital_Natives_Digital_Immigrants.pdf

Prensky, M. (2013). Our brains extended. *Educational Leadership, 70*(6), 22–27.

Pulfrey, C., Buchs, C., & Butera, F. (2011). Why grades engender performance-avoidance goals: The mediating role of autonomous motivation. *Journal of Educational Psychology, 103*(3), 683–700.

Quebec Ministry of Education. (2003). *Policy on the evaluation of learning.* Quebec: Government of Quebec. Retrieved from www.mels.gouv.qc.ca/lancement/pea/13-4602A.pdf

Quebec Ministry of Education. (2007). Integrative project. *Québec education program.* Retrieved from www.mels.gouv.qc.ca/sections/programmeFormation/secondaire2/medias/en/08-00749_IntegrativeProgram.pdf

Ravitz, J. (2009). Introduction: Summarizing Findings and looking ahead to a new generation of PBL research. *Interdisciplinary Journal of Problem-Based Learning, 3*(1), Article 2.

Reeves, D. (2011). From differentiated instruction to differentiated assessment. *ASCD Express, 6*(20).

Rennie, L., Venville, G., & Wallace, J. (2012). *Knowledge that counts in a global community: Exploring the contribution of integrated curriculum.* London, UK: Routledge.

Reynolds, A. (2009). Why every student needs critical friends. *Educational Leadership, 67*(3), 54–57.

Reynolds, C. (2012, October 31). Why are schools brainwashing our children? *Maclean's.* Retrieved from http://www2.macleans.ca/2012/10/31/why-are-schools-brainwashing-our-children

Rogers, C. (1969). *Freedom to learn.* Columbus, OH: Charles Merrill.

Rolheiser, C., Bower, B., & Stevahn, L. (2000). *The portfolio organizer:*

Succeeding with portfolios in your classroom. Alexandria VA: Association for Supervision and Curriculum.

Saskatchewan Ministry of Education. (2010). *Renewed curricula: Understanding outcomes.* Regina, SK: Author. Retrieved from www.education.gov.sk.ca

Schleicher, A. (2010, September). *Is the sky the limit to educational improvement?* Presented at the Education Summit, Toronto, ON.

Schön, D. (1983). *The reflective practitioner: How professionals think in action.* London, UK: Temple Smith.

Schwab, J. (1983). The practical 4: Something for curriculum professors to do. *Curriculum Inquiry, 13*(3), 239–265.

Schwartz, J. E. (2007). *Elementary mathematics pedagogical content knowledge: Powerful ideas for teachers,* Boston, MA: Allyn & Bacon.

Sewell, K. W. (2005). Constructivist trauma psychotherapy: A framework for healing. In D. Winter & L. Viney (Eds.), *Personal Construct Psychotherapy: Advances in Theory, Practice, and Research* (pp. 165–176). London, UK: Whurr.

Shepard, L. (2000). The role of assessment in a learning culture. *American Educational Research Association, 19*(7), 4–14.

Siwak, H. (2011, January 23). My students need me after all. *21 Century classroom: The Amaryllis.* [Web log message]. Retrieved from http://www.heidisiwak.com/2011/01/my-students-need-me-afterall.html

Skinner, B. F. (1954). The science of learning and the art of teaching. *Harvard Educational Review, 24,* 86–97.

Skinner, B. F. (1968). *The technology of teaching.* East Norwalk, CT: Appleton-Century-Crofts.

Small, G., & Vorgan, G. (2008). *iBrain: Surviving the technological alteration of the modern mind.* New York, NY: HarperCollins.

Smith, T. (2012). Take one sheet and really get to know your pupils. *Teacher Network: Resources, jobs and professional development for teachers.* [The Guardian Web log message]. Retrieved from www.guardian.co.uk/teacher-network/teacher-blog/2012/nov/28/school-personalised-learning-system-one-page-profile

Smith, E., & Tyler, R. (1942). *Appraising and recording student progress.* New York, NY: Harper & Brothers.

Sobel, D. (2004). *Place-based education: Connecting classrooms and communities.* Great Barrington, MA: Orion Society.

Sousa, D. A. (1998). The ramifications of brain research. *School Administrator, 55*(1), 22.

Southwick, S., & Charney, D. (2012). *Resilience: The science of mastering life's greatest challenges.* New York, NY: Cambridge University Press.

Steinberg, C. (2008). Assessment as an emotional practice. *English Teaching: Practice and Critique, 7*(3), 42–64.

Stephan, Y., Caudroit, J., Boiché, J., & Sarrazin, P. (2011). Predictors of situational disengagement in the academic setting: The contribution of grades, perceived competence, and academic motivation. *British Journal of Educational Psychology, 81,* 441–455. doi: 10.1348/000709910X522285

Sternberg, R. (1988). *The triarchic mind: A theory of human intelligence.* New York, NY: Viking.

Sternberg, R. (1997). *Thinking styles.* New York, NY: Cambridge University Press.

Taba, H. (1962). *Curriculum development: Theory and practice.* New York, NY: Harcourt Brace Jovanovich.

Tanner D. & Tanner, L. (1995). *Curriculum development* (3rd ed.). New York, NY: Macmillan.

Taylor, F. (1911). *The principles of scientific management.* Project Gutenberg eBook. Retrieved from www.gutenberg.org/catalog/world/readfile?pageno=1&fk_files=2268784

Thomas, D., & Seeley Brown, J. (2011). *A new culture of learning: Cultivating the imagination for a world of constant change.* CreateSpace.

Thorndike, E. L. (1911). *Education.* New York, NY: MacMillan.

Tierney, R., & Simon, M. (2004). What's still wrong with rubrics: Focusing on the consistency of performance criteria across scale levels. *Practical Assessment, Research & Evaluation, 9*(2).

Tierney, R., Simon, M., & Charland, J. (2011). Being fair: Teachers' interpretations of principles for standards-based grading. *The Educational Forum, 75*(3), 210–227.

Tomlinson, C. (2001). *How to differentiate instruction in mixed-ability classrooms.* Alexandra, VA: Association for Supervision and Curriculum.

Tomlinson, C., & Imbeau, M. (2010). *Leading and managing a differentiated classroom.* Alexandria, VA: Association for Supervision and Curriculum.

Tomlinson, C., Kaplan, S., Renzulli, J., Leppien, J., Purcell, J., Burns, D., Strickland, C., & Imbeau, M. (2009) *The parallel curriculum* (2nd ed.). Thousand Oaks, CA: Corwin Press.

Toronto District School Board. (n.d.). Equinox Holistic Alternative School. Retrieved from www.tdsb.on.ca/schools/index.asp?schno=5903

Tough, P. (2012) *How kids succeed: Grit, curiosity and the hidden power of character.* New York, NY: Hougton, Mifflin and Harcourt.

Truss, D. (2013, March 25). How do you teach digital literacy? *EDTECH: Focus on K–12.* Retrieved from www.edtechmagazine.com/k12/article/2013/03/how-do-you-teach-digital-literacy

21st Century Fluency Project. (2013). 21st Century Fluencies. Retrieved from http://fluency21.com/fluencies.html

Upitis, R. (2011). *Arts Education for the development of the whole child.* Prepared for the Elementary Teachers' Federation of Ontario, Canada. Retrieved from www.etfo.ca/Resources/ForTeachers/Documents/Arts%20Education%20for%20the%20Development%20of%20the%20Whole%20Child.pdf

Van Zoost, S. (2012). realfriends: A student social action project. *Education Canada, 52*(1), 25–27.

Vars, G. (2001). On research, high stakes testing and core philosophy. *Core Teacher, 50*(1), 3.

Vega, V. (2012a). A research-based approach to arts integration. *Edutopia.* Retrieved from www.edutopia.org/stw-arts-integration-research

Vega, V. (2012b). Research-supported PBL practices that work. *Edutopia.* Retrieved from www.edutopia.org/stw-project-based-learning-best-practices-new-tech-research#graph

Vega, V. (2012c). Social and emotional learning research: Annotated bibliography. *Edutopia.* Retrieved from www.edutopia.org/sel-research-annotated-bibliography

Vega, V., & Terada, Y. (2012). Research supports global curriculum. *Edutopia.* Retrieved from www.edutopia.org/stw-global-competence-research

Vickers, B. (Ed.). (2002). *Francis Bacon: The major works.* Oxford, UK: Oxford University Press.

Vygotsky, L. (1978). *Mind in society: The development of higher mental processes.* Cambridge, MA: Harvard University Press.

Walker, E., McFadden, L., Tabone, C., & Finkelstein, M. (2011). Contribution of drama-based strategies. *Youth Theatre Journal, 25*(1), 3–15.

Walsh K. (2012, August 19). Tailoring the classroom of the future with the fabric of the past. *Emerging EdTech* [Web log message]. Retrieved from www.emergingedtech.com/2012/08/tailoring-the-classroom-of-the-future-with-the-fabric-of-the-past

Washburn, K. (2010). *The architecture of learning: Designing instruction for the learning brain.* Pelham, AL: Clerestory Press.

Washburn, K. (2012, November 21). Inscribe upon my wrist: Emphasizing effort to empower learning. *Smart Blog on Education* [Web log message]. Retrieved from http://smartblogs.com/education/2012/11/21/inscribed-upon-my-wrist-emphasizing-effort-empower-learning-kevin-washburn

Wesson, K. (2012, April). From STEM to ST²REAM: Reassembling our disaggregated curriculum. *Education Week.* Retrieved from www.edweek.org/ew/articles/2012/10/24/09wesson.h32.html

Whitehead, J. (2012) Educational research for social change with living educational theories. *Educational Research for Social Change (ERSC), 1*(1), 5–21.

Wiggins, G., McTighe, J. (2005). *Understanding by design.* Alexandria, VA: Association for Supervision and Curriculum Development.

Willingham, D. (2004). Reframing the mind: Howard Gardner and multiple intelligences. *Education Next.* Retrieved from http://educationnext.org/reframing-the-mind

Willis, J. (2006). *Research-based strategies to ignite student learning.* Alexandria, VA: Association for Supervision and Curriculum.

Willis, J. (2008). *How your child learns best.* Naperville, IL: Sourcebooks Inc.

Willis, J. (2011, June). Understanding how the brain thinks. *Edutopia.* Retrieved from www.edutopia.org/blog/understanding-how-the-brain-thinks-judy-willis-md

Willms, D., Friesen, S., & Milton, P. (2009) *What did you do in school today? Transforming classrooms through social, academic and intellectual engagement.* Toronto, ON: Canadian Education Association.

Willms, J., & Friesen, S. (2012). The relationship between instructional challenge and student engagement: What did you do in school today? *Research Series Report Number Two.* Toronto, ON: Canadian Education Association.

Winger, T. (2009). Grading what matters. *Educational Leadership, 67*(3), 73–75.

Wolpert-Gawron, H. (2012, April 26). Kids speak out on student engagement. *Edutopia.* Retrieved from www.edutopia.org/blog/student-engagement-stories-heather-wolpert-gawron

Worth, K., & Grollman, S. (2003). *Worms, shadows, and whirlpools: Science in the early childhood classroom.* Portsmouth, NH: Heinemann.

Wraga, W. (2009). Toward a connected core curriculum. *Educational Viewpoints, 51*(2), 11–31.

Wright, S. (2012, November 8). I used to think . . . *Powerful learning practice* [Web log message]. Retrieved from http://plpnetwork.com/2012/11/08/think

Wyatt-Smith, C., Klenowski, V., & Gunn, S. (2010). The centrality of teachers' judgment practice in assessment: A study of standards in moderation. *Assessment in Education: Principles, Policy & Practice, 17*(1), 59–75.

York Region District School Board. (n.d.). Character matters. Retrieved from www.yrdsb.edu.on.ca/page.cfm?id=ICM200203

Zvi, G. (2012). Genius Hour: Exploring your passion. *Innovative Learning Design.* [Web log message]. Retrieved from http://innovativelearningdesigns.ca/wordpress/?p=740by

Index